# The
# AFTERDEATH
# JOURNAL
## of an American
### Philosopher

OP

S
6L

## BOOKS BY JANE ROBERTS

How to Develop Your ESP Power • 1966
The Seth Material • 1970
Seth Speaks: The Eternal Validity of the Soul • 1972
The Education of Oversoul Seven • 1973
The Nature of Personal Reality (A SETH BOOK) • 1974
Adventures in Consciousness: An Introduction to Aspect
    Psychology • 1975
Dialogues of the Soul and Mortal Self in Time • 1975
Psychic Politics: An Aspect Psychology Book • 1976
The "Unknown" Reality (A SETH BOOK), Two
    Volumes • 1977–1979
The World View of Paul Cézanne: A Psychic
    Interpretation • 1977
The Afterdeath Journal of an American Philosopher: The
    World View of William James • 1978
The Further Education of Oversoul Seven • 1979
Emir's Education in the Proper Use of Magical Powers • 1979
The Nature of the Psyche: Its Human Expression (A SETH
    BOOK) • 1979
The Individual and the Nature of Mass Events (A SETH
    BOOK) • 1981
The God of Jane: A Psychic Manifesto • 1981
If We Live Again: Or, Public Magic and Private Love • 1982
Oversoul Seven and the Museum of Time • 1984
Dreams, "Evolution," and Value Fulfillment: Volume I (A SETH
    BOOK) • 1986

# JANE ROBERTS

# The AFTERDEATH JOURNAL of an American Philosopher

## The World View of William James

PRENTICE HALL PRESS • NEW YORK

Published in 1987 by Prentice Hall Press
A Division of Simon & Schuster, Inc.
Gulf + Western Building
One Gulf + Western Plaza
New York, NY 10023

Originally published by Prenctice-Hall, Inc.

PRENTICE HALL PRESS is a trademark of Simon & Schuster, Inc.

Library of Congress Cataloging-in-Publication Data
Roberts, Jane
   The afterdeath journal of an American philosopher.
   Includes index.
   1. Spirit writings.   I. James, William, 1842-
1910.   II. Title.
BF1311.J25R62        133.9′3        78-4040
ISBN 0-13-018564-7 pbk.

Manufactured in the United States of America

10  9  8  7  6  5  4  3  2  1

First Prentice Hall Press Edition

Dedicated to the historic William James
and his ever-expanding reality.

# CONTENTS ———————————

# Introduction

## 1. Front-Door People, Back-Door People, and World Views

I find myself with still another unconventional manuscript, left at the back door of my mind. The pages fluttered down into my awareness one by one, as if left by some invisible newspaper boy, day after day; the latest installments in a steady line of communications that seem to come from strange lands.

Without painting this analogy in too glowing colors, I'd like to point out my feeling that the conscious mind is like a house of awareness, with an elegant front door through which we receive usual callers and messages. ("Hello. How are you? State your name and business.") This front entrance is swept and well tended; to its doorstep come all official magazines and newspapers. The shrubs of our beliefs are trimmed and pruned, and the regular mailman, whistling cheerfully, leaves the mail at the proper, anticipated times. Neat curtained windows look out to the well-organized streets of the world, and we're told that all messages must come to us through that front door; the only entrance—or exit.

But no matter what we're told by all of the officials and authorities, we seem to remember a secret back door from the time of our childhood; a "magic" entrance that we discovered when we were left by ourselves, perhaps on rainy afternoons—a door that opened into other worlds. Vaguely we may recall finding and opening that door on innumerable, nearly forgotten occasions. We may have sensed messengers coming and going; once or twice we may even have found strange packages or papers on the back-door stoop, wet with rain as if they'd been waiting there for a long time. But the next time we look, the door is invisible. The wall of awareness is smooth, and we see only the whitewashed walls we've been taught to expect.

1

Some of us are just too stubborn and curious to ignore those unofficial events, so symbolically speaking at least, while I keep my front door well tended, I've learned to watch at the back door of my mind. Now and then I stand on the mind's back porch, and sometimes I take a few tentative steps down unofficial paths that lead to unexplored psychological lands that just might correlate with other realities than the one we know.

*The Afterdeath Journal of an American Philosopher* was automatically delivered, then, at that back mental doorstep; the installments appearing day after day, while I went about my business, winter turned to spring, and the regular magazines and papers brought by the postman kept me up-to-date on the official world.

*Those* periodicals are easy to read. They're written for the front-door people. But we're all both front-door people and back-door people, whether we know it or not. The trouble is that we know how to read the important news that comes to us through the exterior world, but often we just don't know what to do with the equally valid messages that come by the unofficial back route.

For one thing, the messages left by inspiration or the intuitions are highly personal, intimate; left at our back doorstep and no other, and they have to be read by the part of the mind that is peculiarly suited to their translation. They may deal with symbols, for example, instead of the good clear alphabets we're used to. Sometimes their messages may even seem to contradict the news that comes in the front door, and not only can't we confirm the data with our neighbors, but we have to restructure our own thinking before we can even accept it ourselves.

So at first I didn't know how to interpret this present manuscript either. Should it be taken literally or symbolically? I tried to put together my knowledge of reality as it comes to me through official *and* unofficial sources of information, and to use all of my intellectual and intuitive abilities to find the answer.

Our ordinary consciousness is tuned toward our front-door callers, and when our physical senses are stimulated, the front doorbell rings and we respond to whomever or whatever wants our attention. Usually we're so busy responding to those messages that if the back doorbell rings, we don't notice. I've learned to tune my consciousness toward the back of my mental house and always to keep a portion of my attention focused in that direction.

In a manner of speaking, I have my own messenger from those unknown psychological realms.

Like many people, my husband, Rob, and I have a small yard in the rear of our house; but beyond that, there are hills and forests. In my analogy these represent the unofficial areas of the psyche, down whose natural untended banks rush winds from other psychological skies, and messages tumbling like small speckled exotic stones.

My trance personality, Seth, comes into my consciousness from those other, inner, landscapes. Twice a week he comes through my mind's back door and takes an honored place in our living room. I go into trance and he begins to speak, while Rob takes notes. Seth writes his own books in this fashion, explaining the greater realms of consciousness that exist outside our cozy villages of mind.

It was in the middle of one such session (the 717th for November 4, 1974) that I first became "acquainted" with William James, the well-known American psychologist and philosopher who died in 1910. This is what happened: Mentally I saw a small paperback book, opened midway through, and I knew that it was titled *The Varieties of Religious States*. At first the book was in miniature, but it grew larger, so that I could read it clearly, sentence by sentence. At the same time I knew that somehow the book was written by William James. I was already familiar with James's name, since several years previously I'd partially skimmed his *Varieties of Religious Experience*—a book that Rob really enjoyed, though I didn't, particularly. James's reputation as a psychologist also came up in our reading matter now and then. I explained to Rob what was happening. Then, while he took notes, I read out loud the pages I saw.

We both took it for granted that the image of the book in my mind's eye was symbolic, but the message I read was quite literal—and literate. I found James more personally likable from these passages than I did from the real book of his I'd read. More than this, I felt that the copy itself also contained James's emotions and feelings, which were somehow "played back" when you read the words.

This wasn't all. As described in my own book *Psychic Politics*, during that same session other material also came through—supposedly from another dead psychologist, Carl Jung. I was intrigued by James's quaint, rather elegant prose, and rather taken aback by the uneven exuberance with which the Jung material showed itself. Mostly, my front-door mind was startled by the implications of the entire affair. So we just let the whole thing slide by.

Seth didn't. He instantly began a series of sessions on "world views." Briefly stated, Seth says that the feelings and experiences of each person continue to exist after death, and that these can be perceived under certain conditions. In other words, each of us has a unique version of reality that makes up our own private world view. This is not just a passive perception of multidimensional properties, but an active, volatile phenomenon that interacts at many levels with other world views, and combines with them.

People who read *The New York Times* must first have an interest in that particular paper, and must then take certain steps to buy it or have it delivered. They'll also probably have some interests and characteristics in common with other people who read the same paper. So, according to Seth, certain world views are perceived by people whose interests, desires, or characteristics somehow fall into the same general area as the particular world view involved.

Still, I found the entire matter of messages from the famous dead hard to take, world views or no. While Seth continued to dictate his book *The "Unknown" Reality*, I finished my own *Psychic Politics* and started a sequel to my novel, *The Education of Oversoul Seven*. Then, once again, the unexpected happened, and this time it was triggered by a domestic event. I asked Rob what he wanted for Christmas of 1975. He answered, "A book on Cézanne" (meaning Paul Cézanne, the French artist who died at the beginning of the century). Two mornings afterward, unable to sleep, I got up and went to my typewriter. To put it mildly, the signals started flying. Beginning that dawn, I "received" an entire manuscript, *The World View of Paul Cézanne*, which was published by Prentice-Hall in 1977.

In this case, my love for Rob and my desire to get him what he wanted merged with my knowledge of the mind's greater resources. I sent out my unconscious message and tuned into precisely what I wanted—yet I was never consciously aware of making any such efforts at all. What was delivered to my mind's back door was a view of the world as seen through an artist's eyes, and Cézanne, at least as he appears in the manuscript, didn't care for much beside painting. The book was devoted to the meaning of art, its greater implications and technique. "My" Cézanne didn't care what had happened to the world since his time. He said nothing about life after death. His focus was undeviating, unique, and carried the indelible stamp of his personality.

When Cézanne was finished, I got back to the matter at hand, my sequel to *Seven*. I'd put the James episode out of my mind. Then one afternoon in May 1976, thoughts of James suddenly began intruding as I worked on my own book. I found myself feeling some very definite emotional connections with James as if—God forbid—we were reincarnationally involved or had some background in common. I say "God forbid" because reincarnation is one of those subjects that I agree with in theory (with certain changes, such as the existence of simultaneous time) but have trouble with in practical terms. I shook my head, frowning at myself: the idea was too pat, too obvious, a psychic cliché; so I put my feelings aside and went back to my writing.

But again Seth didn't let me get away with it. That night at our regular session, instead of dictating his own book, Seth delivered some excellent material on the nature of consciousness—and Rob, knowing my attitude, grinned often as he watched me while Seth spoke about my relationship with William James.

The implications of that session are fascinating, though, and important to all of us as Seth traces the everchanging patterns of human consciousness and desire. It was a warm, humid evening; the house and neighborhood were still as Seth began to speak. As usual, Rob took notes. The following is a verbatim account of that previously unpublished session.

# Introduction

# 2. Seth on William James and the Affiliations of Consciousness

Session 775
May 10, 1976
9:36 P.M. Monday

*("I feel Seth around," Jane said at 9:33. She laughed. "On William James, unfortunately. I just got a glimpse of what Seth's going to say and I thought: 'Now how are you going to make sense of that?'"*

*(Jane's reaction came about because earlier this evening she'd caught herself thinking that she might be reincarnationally related to James—an idea that she'd rejected at once. Yet, there was her world-view material on James. Whereupon I suggested that she just forget about it and see what Seth had to say. Not that we hoped she would turn out to be connected to James—that idea was just too coincidental for our tastes—but it would be interesting to know why she'd found herself thinking along those lines to begin with.*

*(Seth always refers to Jane as Ruburt and to me as Joseph—our entity names.)*

Good evening.

*(Good evening, Seth.)*

Ruburt can attest to his own identity. In ordinary terms, he counts his identity as beginning at the time of his birth in 1929, and he sees it as reaching through to the present. In those terms he has a time history, with letters, mementos, snapshots, and so forth to prove it.

He met you at a certain point in space and time. You both agree upon this and upon the continuity of your two identities; so Ruburt can attest that he is himself.

The true story of consciousness has not been written, for it will always in essence escape such description. In our early sessions I spoke as simply as possible, and yet those sessions also contain in their own way the kernels of much that

6

appeared later, and that has not yet appeared. Early, I used the term "fragment personality" simply to give you this idea that identity was not a unit that could be easily defined.

Our later material led even further away from the concept of an easily defined self. All consciousness is interrelated. It flows together in currents, rises and falls, eddies and breaks, mixes and merges. In this great interplay, however, each identity, however brief in usual terms, is never annihilated. It is indeed inviolate. On the other hand, it can also form affiliations with other identities, for there are psychic formations as there are physical ones. The world has a physical structure that forms its contents. There is a bank of physical elements.

In greater terms, each person's experience—while privately his or hers—also becomes part of the psychic bank, belonging to the species as a whole, containing within it abilities, attitudes, purposes, and plans. These form a heritage from which each person can draw. This drawing takes place not only before birth, but also at any point during life. You can change in life far more than you suspect, while still retaining the identity that is your own.

*(9:54)* In some cases you change so much that people knowing you at different times would seem to know and describe entirely different people. The theory of reincarnation is an attempt to see the basic, inviolate, yet many-faceted self in terms that can be understood, and that are in keeping with popular concepts of time. As you yourself, Joseph, have realized on occasion, you are actually "reincarnated" many times in one lifetime.

You leap over your own identities, scarcely noticing, again and again. There are no boundaries or limitations to the self, except those you accept. The miracle of your transformations escapes your crude definitions. *(Louder and with amusement:)* I am not speaking of your crude definitions, but use the word generally.

*("I understand. Thank you.")*

There are often great challenges to which you respond. You pick these for your own reasons. In doing so, you often change affiliations. In conventional terms, Ruburt was not William James—but through Ruburt, certain challenges and purposes left unsatisfied by James have been picked up by

Ruburt; and to that extent a portion of William James's consciousness is merged with Ruburt's.

Again: Ruburt's identity is his own; but few have dared to look into the true components of identity. Those unanswered questions of James's happened to coincide with Ruburt's own questions at a certain time in Ruburt's current life—who at that time became attracted to that heritage bank—looking, so to speak, for someone with like interests, backed up by a lifetime of experience.

*(To me:)* You early recognized the possibilities of such a connection, being drawn to James far before Ruburt's interests.

Your drives, desires, plans, and purposes, while uniquely yours, also in their way belong to the species as a whole. They are handed down, so to speak, to those who are attuned to them. You pass them on. James, to some extent, now, sees his unanswered questions sifted through another unique consciousness, so that they are given a different slant. Consciousness, individual consciousness, is many-faceted, and in that respect a portion of James's consciousness is reflected through Ruburt's.

*(10:16)* Ruburt is then given James's knowledge concerning those questions, as source material, providing references he himself would not ordinarily possess. Consciousness forms and reforms, always in new combinations, yet in your terms nothing is lost that has gone before.

*(A one-minute pause.)* There is indeed an "archaeology" of the self, in which the consciousness of the past and present merge, but this is a far more democratic arrangement, for in your terms the future is also involved, so that in those terms future consciousness and identities are even now being formed from the heritage of your own purposes and desires.

Because you do not catch important transformations that occur in your own life, as retaining your identity you still leap—you will have to put this in quotes also—"from self to self," so you do not understand how the inner components of consciousness change their "shapes and forms," even as the natural elements of the earth form its everchanging face.

*(Long pause.)* Give us a moment... In a way, and using an analogy, the consciousness of any given nation has a shape and form as definite as the contours of the physical land upon which it resides. In those terms, during your lifetimes, a continent retains its form: though trees upon it rise and fall, rocks and stones are washed away into the oceans, generations are born and die, governments altered, still a man in his lifetime will find the continent generally familiar and intact. Now in your lifetime, you change in the same way that the continent does, while generally finding yourselves familiar and intact. Your identity, while your own, is still a gestalt of consciousnesses that in your terms have come before, or will come in the future. Those other identities, reflected through you, become unique and inviolate. So, however, is your consciousness and identity reflected in all others.

Take your break.

*(10:35-10:56)*

As usual, I caution you that these matters are most difficult to explain.

Consciousness forms patterns of identities. They move faster than the speed of light. They can be in more than one place at one time. They can operate in a freewheeling fashion, as identities in themselves, or as "psychological particles."

They can also operate in a wavelike fashion, flowing through other such particles. They can form together into endless, infinite combinations, forming psychological gestalts. Certain portions of these gestalts can then operate as psychological particles in time and space, while other portions operate in a wavelike manner outside of time or space.

These represent the unconscious elements of the psyche, which become "particleized" in physical existence.

*(Long pause.)* Your own purposes, intents, and desires attract to you, so to speak, those other "fragments" of consciousness that mix and match to form your psychological being as, for example, atoms and molecules mix and merge to form your physical being. Your body is yours, stamped with your own purposes and intents. You are

unaware of the molecular transformations involved as long as the overall pattern remains familiar and relatively intact.

In a like manner, as long as the contours of your consciousness remain relatively familiar, you do not question their composition. You are not aware of the changes that occur. In certain terms, then, your identity is a pattern of identification, your stamp set eternally upon the universe—a shape that you recognize, but one that is filled with multitudinous activity, alteration, and change—all of which generally goes on beneath your notice.

In those terms, chunks of your own consciousness have long since fallen away and been used by others, while you still retain your identity, even as rocks are swept away from a continent into the ocean, while still the continent retains its form. In earth's own time even the continent will change, falling off beneath the waters, or joining with another while still retaining some of its own characteristics, and in those terms carrying with it its previous coloration. So each of you alive changes in like manner, yet you carry the mark of your identity, and that is inviolate.

(11:18) Bits of your consciousnesses, Joseph and Ruburt, go out through these books. I am not speaking symbolically. These portions will mix with the consciousnesses of others. Portions of your intent and purpose become theirs.

My own psychological reality is not particleized. My identity includes the identities of many others. Each of them operates in his own fashion. In those terms, I am a wave formation. More specifically, however, and to a lesser degree, each physical person operates partially as a particleized being and partially in terms of a wave. But identity, being itself inviolate, is on the other hand everchanging—and there is, in the larger system of reality, no contradiction.

The great men and women, historically speaking, serve as psychic models, throwing into the physical realm explosive bursts of desires, purposes, abilities, plans, and intents that cannot be satisfied by any one person in any one lifetime, however heroic their performance.

These, then, serve as impetuses to others, but no desire and no intent exists by itself alone, only by virtue of the identity that holds it, so an identity explodes outward from itself in all directions, showering portions of itself which are used by others so attracted. Each identity is itself and no other; and yet it is composed of myriad fragments of other identities.

Take your break.

*(11:32-11:51)* Now: James's consciousness is to some extent, then, reflected through Ruburt's, shining with a different cast, and henceforth forming a new combination—one that is original and represents a new creative world view.

In this combination or gestalt, Ruburt's identity predominates, so that James provides Ruburt with one other focus through which to view reality. At other levels, James as himself predominates in another kind of existence. In your world, your quite conscious desires and intents attract the components of your consciousness. There is never, for example, any kind of invasion or possession in conventional terms. It is, in fact, impossible for one consciousness to possess another.

Each identity possesses an integrity that will not allow any affiliation of which it does not approve. Using an analogy, psychological antibodies are far more potent than physical ones. The self or identity quite literally closes its boundaries to any forces that do not follow its own purposes and intents. There are no exceptions.

This integrity allows the identity always to maintain its own pattern or mark, permitting within its peripheries only those affiliations that serve its unique purposes. In those terms, the self or identity cannot be defiled. Here I would like to add a brief side note having to do with cases of apparent "brainwashing," in times of war, for example.

You form your own reality. Those captured in such encounters, therefore, are captured because they are already operating in a system of beliefs that <u>does</u> suit their greater purposes. This subject is highly complicated. Perhaps someday we can pursue it. But in any case, the so-called brainwashing suits the purposes of those so treated. This does not mean that no sympathy should be granted them. A really close examination of their <u>conscious</u> beliefs and purposes, however, would show an acquiescence and acceptance of such experience, and a need for it to occur.

End of session. I bid you a fond good evening.

*("Thank you, Seth. The same to you." 12:10 A.M.)*

# Introduction

## 3. How This Book Happened and the Webs of Consciousness

Seth's session on James and consciousness was held in May 1976. Rob filed it along with other miscellaneous sessions that weren't part of Seth's books, and I nearly forgot it. For one thing, I had no intention of trying to tune into James's world view—and besides, the whole affair went into the psychological background as I worked on other manuscripts. I took time out to help Rob prepare Volume 1 of Seth's *The "Unknown" Reality* for publication; I was typing the completed Cézanne book; and Seth had begun dictating his next, *The Nature of the Psyche: Its Human Expression.*

Yet Seth must have known what was going to happen, in some fashion or other, because over six months later, in January 1977, I awakened one morning with the title of this present book in my mind. Just the title, nothing else. I didn't think too much about this; I've had titles and sometimes whole outlines of books suddenly come to me before—sometimes they "take," and sometimes they just end up as footnotes in other books.

After breakfast, though, I felt restless; and instead of working down at the big table in the living room, where I'd done my writing for months, I went out to the small studio off the kitchen. This was the same room, I remembered later, in which I had begun the Cézanne manuscript. At the time, I didn't make the connection.

Rob and I always read during meals. I was thinking vaguely of an article I'd read at breakfast, and sipping coffee, when in the next moment the entire first paragraph of *The Afterdeath Journal of an American Philosopher* suddenly filled my mind. I think I muttered something like, "Hey, what about that!" and started taking the words down as fast as I could on my typewriter. Although I knew instantly that the "American philosopher" of the title was William James, I hedged a little on this in the beginning. After all, I thought,

12

James's name wasn't mentioned in the title, and it didn't appear in the rest of the material that came as quickly as I could type for the rest of the morning.

And, as I wrote, the usual questions annoyed me like a swarm of buzzing bees. Was this manuscript supposed to originate with the historic William James? Was the material my creative version of the man instead, or was something else happening—some commingling of consciousness in which valid knowledge from unofficial levels of reality expressed itself in a form that I could understand? Though these questions went through one part of my mind, they in no way disturbed the flow of words that came in rapidly and smoothly. You can question what's happening on a TV screen while you watch it, and in the same way I could wonder about the events that were occurring on this other unofficial screen of my mind. In fact, I almost always do.

And I kept thinking: <u>Strange</u>. Nothing in our immediate lives had triggered this sudden new manuscript, and by the fact that the title had been given, and by the feel of the words, I could tell that somebody—James?—was definitely beginning something he meant to finish. I thought of the few pages of James's *Varieties of Religious States* that I'd seen in my mind a year and a half before, and felt some bewilderment. This wasn't *that* book. And rather quarrelsomely I thought that psychics.were always "getting" James. This last thought was the one that bothered me most, and had since I first saw James's small paperback book in my mental vision. I'd nearly forgotten Seth's statements about James; if I'd remembered them, I would have felt better.

From the first words of this present manuscript, though, something else bothered me: James obviously was commenting on our world in a way that Cézanne hadn't. This implied a responsive James, continuing his interest in our reality. Again, if I'd remembered that [775th] Seth session of last May, I'd have been better prepared for James's liveliness in this respect, and for the numerous interactions between us that happened as the manuscript continued.

The delivery of the manuscript developed its own set of conventions along the way. Most of it was written automatically, first and final draft directly on the typewriter (except of course for the publisher's copy, which had to be neater). Much of it came in a surprising way, though, when I was sketching and thought I was finished with the day's writing. As a result, my small sketchpads were filled with page upon page of scribbled James material that I took down with whatever colored pen I happened to be using at the moment for my ink sketches. Then I'd have to type up that material the following day, and often while I was doing *that*, James would begin again with new material. Finally, as spring approached and I went out on the front porch to sketch, I'd be prepared with two sketchbooks—one for James and one for me. But there was something quite pleasant, intimate, and almost cozy about getting James in longhand; and *I* think, at least, that he liked this procedure the best. On too many occasions to remember, dictation would suddenly begin while I was doing the dishes or other house chores— and several times during lunch.

I've added a few notes of my own through James's manuscript to show when I sensed any emotional interaction between James and myself, because that always surprised me. With Cézanne, I felt rather like a secretary, while James and I had a more personal working relationship. James, oddly enough, seemed aware of my sketching, and as you'll see, he commented at times. Cézanne, however, either couldn't have cared less about my amateur attempts or just considered them beneath his notice. I suspect that Cézanne wasn't aware of my reality to any strong degree; only of his own. James also entered my dreams several times, and I experienced two clear visions that explained certain portions of his text. These are also described in my notes, along with the date and time of day of each entry.

The manuscript came definitely as a book with its own title and structure. All I did was add chapter headings. James begins by discussing parapsychology, evolution, and religion in his time and ours, stressing areas in which he feels his vision was not daring enough. He traces the development of such ideas as they relate to democracy and to the growth of the United States, and stresses the connections between man's image of himself, God, and governments.

Then begins a fascinating discussion of his own experiences of life after death. Some passages in particular are full of humor and brilliance as James, the psychologist

and philosopher, finds himself in a "school for philosophers" where he is definitely a junior member. In any case,
here we see a definite personality, with his own interests and
characteristics, moving from one level of reality to another.
As, someday, all of us will.

I felt for James, and for myself, as I took down his
description of the doubts, hopes, and bouts of melancholy
that had characterized his life. It was impossible not to think
of all such people, caught between faith and doubt, inner
and outer experience—impossible not to identify with
James's own strongly conflicting ideas about humanity. Yet
it was James's "knowing light" and "atmospheric presence"
encountered after death that most captivated—and comforted—me; his "divine psychology" and his intent to share
his new knowledge, to teach as he learns.

*As he learns?* Did I suppose that a William James, a
discarnate person, was sitting at a celestial desk somewhere,
dictating through mentally sophisticated dictaphone equipment—namely me? No, no, no. There are places in the
manuscript where James describes his part in our rather
bizarre arrangement, and there were several instances where I
was so caught up in his emotions that for a moment his
purposes merged with mine, or mine with his, so that the
two of us spoke at once—synchronized, united, each from
our own positions in time and space.

This book doesn't involve any literary stance, but a
stance taken by consciousness itself; it's not a communication from William James in the conventionally understood
manner of mediums and spirits, but a situation in which one
consciousness takes the stance of another and views reality
from that standpoint.

There are definite differences in my experiences with
world views so far. When I'm inspired myself, emotional
excitement seizes me according to the impact of the ideas and
feelings I'm presented with. Except for the instances of
emotional involvement with James just mentioned, however,
with world views I'm not caught up in the writing myself. It
just...comes. I respond to it, but it isn't "mine." I realize
that on other levels I must be translating the other-
consciousness perception into my own vocabulary to a
certain extent, and that the material must be mixing with the

contents of my own mind; but I'm not aware of any of that.

I'm not in a trance as the word is currently understood, either. In a way, it's like having two mental or psychological focuses instead of one. I can be doing chores, quite busy with my own thoughts, for example, when new lines come to me from other sources. They're intrusive in that I recognize them as not mine. On the other hand, I can close them out at will if I want to, so there is never any compulsion involved.

And if the thoughts in this manuscript were mine, then why cast them in James's guise? Not for financial reasons, certainly; the mass market would prefer a good disaster novel. And not for creative reasons; I can write my own books, in that regard. I could have written James's thoughts as my own. Yet while I share most of his opinions and agree heartily with his opinions on Freudianism and Darwinism, some of his opinions (on age, for example) aren't mine at all. More than this, the manuscript reflects the ideas of a man; one perhaps too autocratic, for all his declarations of man's equality, perhaps too "elegant" for the democratic comradeship he espoused.

Both *The World View of Paul Cézanne* and *The Afterdeath Journal of an American Philosopher* were written while Seth was delivering his own book *The Nature of the Psyche: Its Human Expression*, and I don't believe any coincidence is involved. Instead, both world-view manuscripts illustrate the ways in which the individual psyche can reach beyond itself into other psychic and psychological realities.

Both manuscripts illustrate Seth's contention that our consciousness, while individual, can make many kinds of alliances; that its knowledge is not limited to physical information alone; and that its mobility and gifts far surpass our current psychologies. I explain the entire affair to myself as follows: the James reality still exists. It can be tuned in to. Because we're the kind of creatures that we are, when this happens the information *comes alive* through us, mixes with the contents of our minds and interacts with them so that a new reality is formed, a new creative synthesis.

In other words, when our kind of consciousness "tunes in" to the still-present consciousness of someone like James (who is dead in our terms), the combination automatically clicks together, forming a real personality combining the separate sets of traits—a viable transpersonality that stands for what we are and what the other reality is. The personality I sense as James is a construct, I believe; unconsciously formed as an automatic process when my consciousness tunes in to his reality—and it stands for or represents whatever James's reality "really is" now.

The difference is important, for several times I sensed a figure I thought was James walking up and down the living room floor; arms folded; deep in thought—and aware of me. I found it difficult to believe that a spiritualized James existed *in that particular fashion*, even though I did believe that James still existed. A moot point, perhaps. But I still think that when we make such assumptions, often we only project our own limited ideas about personality into an afterlife. At times, for example, I mentally heard James commenting on my sketches, and I think that in such situations we end up with the creation of a quite real personality, capable of originating action, responsive; in this case the "psychic offspring" of Jane/James; able to operate between his world and ours.

My own experience shows me that the boundaries of the self are of a stranger nature than supposed. They shift, opening up other areas of subjective thought and fancy; as if any one personality following a journey through his own reality would encounter other, quite-as-valid selves, each with its own existence, and ultimately find within that vast psychological structure the reflection, at least, of each other person alive on our planet in this or any other time.

I believe that each person's private reality, fully explored, would eventually bring him into contact with every other individual on a subjective level; that each person is reflected in every other; and that through the creative processes we can and often do open up doors leading to experiences that "are not our own"; writing from a viewpoint that is someone else's, living or dead, and viewing reality from a completely different standpoint.

Because of my own experiences, I wonder how many writers have doctored their material, rewritten it from their own focus, changed names and references in order to fit their work into the cultural, scientific, or religious context of their times. That kind of pretense is against my nature but it has its advantages, and I was tempted, at least, to present everything from *The Seth Material* on in such a manner. Such a disguised version would be accepted on its own, with no necessity for me to explain the status of the author or, more difficult, to explain that the author was a composite of my own consciousness and a consciousness at another level—or of my consciousness and the consciousness of "someone else" at another level.

The trouble is that our psychological theories are too small to contain our reality. They certainly don't explain the nature of our creativity or arts. So *The Afterdeath Journal of an American Philosopher* presented me with considerable questions and philosophical dilemmas. Again: I'd been suspicious of manuscripts supposed to originate with the well-known dead; and now I had two of them.

I could view Seth as a sort of superpsyche since he seemed tied to no one historical period. Cézanne, however, was a famous artist. I think that it was my desire to please Rob that let that manuscript come through, at least in large part—that, and my own curiosity, which is seemingly endless and more exuberant than my attempts to explain what it uncovers. And through the years, Rob has mentioned William James, though he's only read one of his books; there are many other authors both living and dead that he speaks of far more often. So why James? I really didn't "want" James from one standpoint anyway—because other automatic scripts are supposed to originate with his authorship.

Yet for all my qualms, from the first moment I saw that small book in my mental eyes, I was taken with James on a personal level; with his rather old-fashioned manner of thought and expression, and the tension he suffered between his emotional and intellectual beliefs during his lifetime. I think that I identified with that tension, for like James, I'm continually aware of the different conclusions often drawn by emotions and intellect. And most likely, as Seth states, that identification was the key.

I recognized that James's feelings reflected mine in certain areas, at least; and that this coincidence opened up the mental and psychological connections necessary between us. I, too, was distressed at the gaudy trappings of the psychic field; the uneasy mixture of pseudoscience and pseudo-spirituality. I, too, was scandalized by some muddy-thinking scientists with "psychic bents," by psychics who cast their spooky predictions in scientific garb, and by the generally poor quality of periodicals and journals dealing with psychic phenomena. In short, like James, I often disapproved.

Yet, again like James, I hoped—and continue to hope. Like James and like many of my readers, I'm caught between the idealistic picture of mankind and man's practical performance. But James has a different viewpoint from mine or yours. James can "look back" and put himself in our position and then, from his new reality, point out directions that each of us can follow to our advantage. His material on biological faith particularly intrigues and comforts me, and as he moves his discussion from his experiences in life to those afterward, he shares profound insights that offer an end to melancholy for those so inclined, and a philosophy that allows us to see the best in man while avoiding Pollyanna attitudes toward his sometimes reprehensible behavior.

More, however, James offers faith to those who feel they must also enjoy a certain independence from any specific religious beliefs; and he describes a divine psychology in a way that inspires the emotions and intellect alike.

Botanists collect exotic species of plants and flowers. Other people collect rocks. Scientists observe the strange properties of physical matter. I collect my own unusual subjective experiences, observe the classic meeting of the psyche with knowledge and data not its own, the opening of the psyche to seemingly alien subjective environments. Then I try to examine what I've found and place it in a context of creativity larger than the pat categories already prepared by our society, religions, or psychologies. So I guess I go on subjective field trips through the psyche and then bring back what I can to the laboratory of my own mind, asking, "What have we here?" and trying to discover how the seemingly exotic species of psychic events fits into the entire picture of reality.

Seth's conception of consciousness certainly corrob-orates my own experience, and I think that sometime or other each of us finds bits and pieces of "other consciousness" in our minds, lying there like odd shiny pebbles on the shores of our awareness. As children we may have reacted with delight and astonishment, turning such thoughts over and over in our mental hands, playing with them like toy balls that bounced against our own imaginings. But as adults, we're so worried about defending our own identities, so jealous for their boundaries, that we run away at the first glimpse of a feeling or thought that we can't categorize; any idea we consider uncharacteristic; any stray hope that might, eventually, let us down.

So we cut our psychological reality down to size, allowing "foreign films" to be played on the screens of our minds only in dreams, where we don't have to acknowledge them—or account for them. We ignore our fantasies, desperately worried about testing them against reality, because our definitions of reality might then have to change. We might discover that the fantasies provide a rich dimension to life that has been lacking, fenced out by "proven truth."

We may discover that dreams are more practical than facts in the long run, and what an awe-ful surprise that will be! We may discover that only the imagination can glimpse those greater dimensions of our being in which our lives are couched. We may die of boredom though our bellies are full of wholesome bread, and find that nutrition is, indeed, more than what we eat. We may find that fiction can be closer to truth than facts are, and that proven facts are merely the fictions we've authenticated—our official fiction, as it were.

Perhaps by demanding predictable experiments—that is, experiments that always produce the same results— science short-circuits itself and us; because we are not predictable, and no two of us are really alike.

So though my times and James's times are decades apart, and in our terms I am alive and he is dead, to some extent the two of us speak with one voice. For he had high hopes, James; for psychology and the sciences; and since his time they've fallen far short of their promises. So if James could speak with his own voice, this is what he would say.

# 1. A General Introduction to My Interests and Times

Tuesday morning
January 25, 1977

This book will consist of a series of "lectures" held in the theater of the imaginative mind, for it is in that larger dimension of experience in which I now have my being. No more will I address my colleagues in the hallowed academic halls, for there I will have lost the credentials that once brought me such respect, since the very conditions of my existence now would make me an outcast from such conventional gatherings.

In the world in which once I so gladly took my place, the dead have few rights for their existence goes unrecognized, and no psychologies prepare them for the transitions that occur as the soul moves into realms for which no earthly education *can* prepare it.

Being of melancholy mind, I anticipated my own death so often, however, and built such dire forebodings of dissolution and decay that the fact of death came as an intellectual and emotional revelation of unspeakable degree, whose brightness dimmed all other events of my life, so that by contrast my death became the crowning achievement of my life.

This need not have been the case, however, for had I understood and followed the natural contours of the mind, then I would have allowed the unconventional aspects of my heart and mind alike greater freedom; and I would have perceived amid the tumultuous details of my life, those other vaster shapes of emotion and natural force upon which our earthly existences unerringly ride.

My world was a lively one that saw the birth of psychology, not realizing that it was swaddled in the

21

placenta of old religious beliefs and still immersed in ancient prejudices. Mine was a time of techniques, when academicians and scientists and world leaders were all convinced that certain techniques—of government or psychology or religion—could bring about an age of enduring prosperity, peace, and contentment and subdue the natural world, which included men's natural inclinations and physical environment.

A spirit of high but false optimism often prevailed, as one by one new techniques were applied and failed, so that in my own private life I teetered between the loftiest sentiments of hope and faith, and the darkest depths of disillusionment and despair. Melancholy robbed my peace of mind. When I addressed colleagues or students on the larger aspects of the mind or soul, I constantly questioned my own speeches and criticized the results of my investigations; and when I spoke most resoundingly about the opportunities of democracy, I wondered most about the qualities of the individual upon which any democracy must basically rest.

I was at once overly credulous and overly critical, so that my emotions and intellect rarely met as friends on any common ground, but rather as adversaries geared for battle, each prepared with its own arguments and defense. My melancholy then denied me of even an animal's content with its days so that I grew querulous even to myself. Yet equally I sensed in myself and in others the highest potentials of enjoyment and achievement, and wondered what invisible psychological veil separated us from at least a partial realization of our fondest hopes.

Freed by death from the conventional frameworks of thought and belief that surrounded me, I have gained in death insights and comprehensions of the greatest consequence. Ironically, I wonder why these did not come to me in physical life, where certainly I could have put them to as good a use—particularly when it is obvious that they were as available in life as in death—and I am convinced that only certain beliefs and attitudes of mind made these insights psychologically invisible.

Those beliefs and attitudes of mind come equally from psychology and religion, which meet like a bride and groom at a shotgun wedding: unwillingly, and bringing to birth an offspring of which each parent is secretly ashamed. The groom, psychology, accepts the importance of emotions only so that they can be intellectually categorized and laid away in lifeless compartments, isolated from the faculties of the reasoning mind. Religion, on the other hand, steadfastly offers gifts of hope and intuition, exultation and creativity, while nervously shying away from any critical examination that might reveal flaws in emotional diamonds that are displayed, never used, but packed away like ancient wedding gifts.

These are perhaps unjust comments, but as one who dabbled in psychology and religion both, and attempted to form from each one unified philosophy, I feel in some regard responsible for those insights I might have added to such issues—yet did not. I find myself determined to lend what light I can upon such matters, particularly since my experience of time is now so luxurious as to provide unlimited access to thought's processes, unhampered by appointments or life's necessities. At the same time I am also hesitant, realizing that perhaps the dead *should* not have any rights in the world of the living, since the dead have had their time of action in that regard: the limelight was once theirs, and only a greedy actor and an exceedingly egotistical one returns to play a scene when his part has been cut out.

Nor can I, as myself, directly intrude, for that precise focusing of intent, mind, and vision is no longer mine and the psychic components of my personality now form a different cast, reflecting other experiences that by themselves preclude any tampering of note with your own world. So, instead, like an aged experienced actor, no longer taking part in tragedies, farces, or morality plays but possessing still a nostalgic love of life's stage, I speak lines from the vast theater in which life's plays have their setting, and point out what I have learned of life's props and plots.

Even so, I must take unconventional ways that allow me to speak between the lines; to utter my words between sentences spoken by others; to make my gestures between those official ones that are written into the script of the players' lives. I must, therefore, cast my thoughts through the mind of another, one now acting, flush in the middle of life; one willing to listen to promptings that seem to come from strange sources.

Strange sources indeed! I myself in life studied and

probed the odd unofficial elements of the mind or soul, trying to tread a careful line between the tenets of science and religion, and seeking out the distant corners hidden within the dogmas of each. I sought out the scientific laboratories and the séance rooms, the learned and the ignorant, the humble and the proud, in an effort to track down "strange sources" from which scientific inventions or religious conversions could, alike, emerge.

In almost all cases, either intellect or emotions were outraged. What emotionally elated me brought only intellectual embarrassment, not just from colleagues but from the judgments of my own overly wearied mind; and those theories that sent my intellect reeling with delight and excitement left my emotions afterwards dry and unwarmed, as if that intellectual fire burned with a flame that was cold and white—blinding, but not life-giving.

I find myself in that respect at least, more lively in death than I was before—somewhat a pity, for that bone-dry life of mine could have used such healthy, natural, kindling firewood as I have only lately discovered. I hope, then, that the insights I have to impart will add to the emotional richness of my readers' days, so that life is felt in all its natural warmth. A life in a castle of a soul is no blessing if that castle is dark, cold, damp, or filled with the musty beliefs of ancient histories; while a cottage of a soul, cozily lit, can be most pleasant and provide the self with a kindly roadside inn that makes even long journeys enjoyable and venturesome.

So I have turned from being an investigator of "strange sources" into a perfect instance of the kind of phenomena that in life I would have tracked down—filled with hopes and skepticisms and carrying my own bag of beliefs invisibly with me, as much a part of my psychological attire as my trousers and waistcoat were of my exterior wear. For in life you are always surrounded by a comedy of manners: social conventions that are sometimes easy to espy though more difficult to break and an interior set of psychological manners or psychic niceties that go unrecognized.

In so intruding upon your world and adopting such an unacademic method of expression, I am therefore dismissing as beneath my notice some very important psychological conventions."Children should be seen and not heard." The dead, it seems, are expected to remain unseen *and* unheard, polite enough not to intrude in the conversations of the living—who will only pretend not to hear, or at best try to find another "more logical" explanation. In this regard, I can be accused of having poor spiritual manners.

There are, on the other hand, those who will only too gladly hear any voice as a messenger from the dead, who will assign to the most innocent knocking of door or wall evidence of the power of the dead's forces, and who possess in their way a dogma and set of conventions as rigid as those of any "hard-headed scientist." Yet the tendencies and characteristics of those seemingly opposite groups represent the unresolved fractions of the human soul caught between faith and doubt, logic and intuition, and poised between the alternating dramas of daily life and dreams.

Certainly it seemed to me in life that the morning's dawn and the midnight were parted by a design that also echoed the mind and heart of man, in which the intuitions and the intellect reigned separated from each other, each ruling different worlds that dominated opposing fractions of the soul. Everywhere I was surrounded by the rousing daytime routs of industry, the galloping growth of governmental power with its shining emblems, the waking of archaeology with its blustery exploitation of the sleeping past. The great virile energy of the people swelled in energetic bursts of objective *doing,* and a brassy optimism swept before it so that it seemed that each secret of nature and of the human heart would soon lie bare.

For my last years were the last of the nation's innocence, before exuberance turned frantic, when it seemed that any problem could be solved if only the proper gusto were applied; the right techniques in the approved American style.

Yet that period was already darkened with psychological shadows that spread from Europe's past, and that age gave us both Freud and Myers.* The country followed Freud

*F.W.H. Myers was one of the founders of the Society for Psychical Research in London in 1882. He was the author of *Human Personality and Its Survival of Bodily Death* which became a classic in the field, and his work was known to William James.

and found the inner portions of the soul distasteful; containing relics of unbridled lusts and passions, primitive tribal impulses that would, if not ripped out by the roots, destroy the objective structure of the world. And those forces seemed passive, stubborn, "feminine"—and unconquerable. At best they could be evacuated, thrown out into the cheerful workaday air, poked fun at; so that the reek of nature could dissipate in the new smoke that rose from the thousands of factories born from technology's gusty triumph.

Wednesday morning
January 26, 1977

Yet, what a rambunctious nationalistic romp, and it was matched with almost missionary fervor by the psychologists, out to rout from man's soul all of those inconsistencies and passions that were buried there; and to leash these as well for the splendid pursuits of progress, industry, and the physical manipulation of nature for man's use.

So, energetically, we set out to probe the mind, the will—determined to mine all of our resources; and some of us, myself included, found hidden within man's more mundane abilities hints of powers that more than equaled technology's promise. We discovered the existence of clairvoyance, precognition, telepathy—like finer precious metals lying half obscured by the ordinary, grosser thinking processes of men's minds. More, we sensed within the commonest of men and women a sleeping motive energy that could at any time suddenly awaken, transforming the individual's life and bringing to the forefront abilities, faculties, and energies not there before.

Safely, from the respectable social and intellectual framework of my occupation, I "dabbled" rather seriously in these matters, using my intellect like a sturdy carpet to hold my feet above the mud, for these precious gems of abilities were often found in muddy mental ground indeed—and I began to sift and weigh those instances of seeming supernormal abilities that I found. A messy business often

enough, yet one in which there was always the possibility of
discovering a talent of great merit, a report that checked out
with scientific accuracy, a dream that came to life with such
similarity to the original that its precognitive nature *must* be
accepted as scientific fact.

We joined learned societies, left our academic halls, fully clothed, however, in our professorial attire; canes or um-
brellas tapping smartly upon the walks, hats correctly tilted,
gloves properly cuffed; and any afternoon or evening might
find us strolling grandly into a medium's lacy parlor, where
the sobs of the newly bereaved drowned out the cheerful,
businesslike twittering of sparrows in the busy air outside.

"Nearer My God to Thee" was a favorite of the many
hymns played, usually on a poorly tuned piano or sung by a
sad-eyed soprano, as the bereaved were told to concentrate
their thoughts upon the beloved, recently dead, presumably
absent member of the family—because that member might in
truth be present, though in a different form; aware, though
with another kind of perception; and it was the medium's
job to serve as the spark connecting the coiled realities of the
living and the dead. A sorry task at times, yet if the mind of
man could transform the face of the country, harness
physical energies of which we'd only dreamed before, might
it not survive death after all? Perhaps the scientist, innocent
of religion's darker superstitions, could discern the truth and
discover even in the shoddiest of séances that one indisputable proof that would release man from his ancient fear of
death and annihilation.

If the mediums strenuously objected to lights, insisting
that *their* conditions necessitated darkness, they could not,
we reasoned, shut out the light of the intellectual,
scientifically tuned mind; and that illumination we were
determined to use unremittingly. At the time, I considered
myself something of a bold explorer, often risking the dirtied
psychological environment of the ignorant and unlettered,
the superstitious and the unprincipled, treading unhealthy
psychological waters when necessary, in order to conquer the
inner continents of the mind as surely as men in other fields
and persuasions had conquered the land.

Wednesday afternoon
January 26, 1977

We took notes of any proceedings, however ludicrous, that
seemed to offer promise. We investigated, interviewed and
tested, and often we were scoffed at (gently and behind our
backs) by our colleagues—and sometimes openly, by the
mediums themselves. Yet on our parts I insist there was an
integrity of intent, and if we were bookish, easily fooled on
occasion, even blinded by our own lofty principles or taken
advantage of because of them, still we were not entirely lured
by the more shallow aspects of democracy and technology,
but determined to bring these to deeper, more mature
fruition by examining the mind or soul that gave them birth.
"The power of the mind," "the subliminal self"—these
phrases stirred us to the depths, for as doers we were positive
that a democracy could truly develop the individual, raise his
abilities to the nth degree, and harness them for the good of
God, man, and society.

Though seeking to map the dimensions of the soul, we
sought to align ourselves professionally with the intellect,
with an enlightened Protestantism and virile optimism that
could, we felt, best protect us from the mire of emotionalism,
fanaticism, and sheer idiocy that sometimes surrounded the
matter at hand. While giving lip service to such sentiments,
however, I myself suffered the darkest melancholy for much
of my life, and I was particularly struck by the fact that
religious conversions, for example, while releasing power
and energy in individual men, could exaggerate some of
their less favorable characteristics also, deepen their prejudices, and increase a paranoia that earlier had been only
latent.

To add to my concern, there seemed no *scientific* proof
for survival of the dead. Even indisputable instances of
apparitions of the departed could be explained in other
ways—as perceptive errors, hallucinations, or even as
interpretations of telepathic data then reconstructed imaginatively by the perceiver. I felt most strongly that an
investigation and exploration of the soul of man must
parallel his mechanistic development, however, and was
convinced that such studies must take place under the

respected banners of science and the academic community.

We sought out particularly the reports of staunch citizens, therefore, people innocent of duplicity, known in their communities; and we quickly discovered that precognition and telepathy—those unconventional quirks of mind— were experienced even by citizens who were otherwise unimaginative, devoted to their work and families, and in no way different from their fellows.

Yet the data depended often upon conversations of the past, or scribbled notes written on the back of envelopes; and the very nature of the dream state meant, of course, that few witnesses were present when and if a startled dreamer awakened to blurt out a clairvoyant dream vivid enough to jar him from sleep. With all of this, however, our evidence was enough to convince me that such unofficial elements of the mind existed, and that they ignored known laws of science.

It was impossible then not to muse about the future existence of a technology-of-mind, more splendid than industry or science's mechanical triumphs, a technology able to utilize perhaps stronger energies than those available otherwise, and it was unthinkable, at least to me, that the powers of the mind could really contradict the laws of science: they would simply point out new directions for science to follow, and help it avoid limitations caused by its own beliefs.

The experiments of the laboratory are predictable but, alas, the mind is the least predictable phenomenon in the world. The emotions, sweeping across the mind's broad expanse, often seemed to distort reliable data, and it seemed to me that my own emotions gave me more trouble than feelings give most men. For one thing, I was afraid lest my emotions contaminate my investigations, realizing that mediums were sometimes good psychologists, quite willing to assign to spirits the insights gained from the practiced, shrewd use of common sense. So I resolved not to wear my feelings upon my sleeve; to guard my utterances, even my facial expressions in such instances, and my bodily stance as well. And that reticence on my part was instantly interpreted by some mediums as a pompous bag of secrecy to be poked, probed, and prodded with exuberant glee.

Thursday morning
January 27, 1977

I *was* modest and secretive in my ways. I strove to be mannerly without overdoing protocol, and adventuresome without accusing others of undue timidity. With my colleagues and in the academic halls I could allow my creativity reign; that is, I dared to speak about issues like mysticism and cosmic consciousness. I gave *some* stirring speeches that aroused in my listeners those aspiring emotions of faith and hope; and speaking, I felt faith and hope. Yet I allowed myself such emotional luxury only because I was surrounded by an emotional economy and dryness that would automatically temper my enthusiasm. And always, speaking, my demeanor was reasonable, in that those feelings were not allowed to affect my actions in such a way as to cause embarrassment. My pronunciation was so correct, for example, that its very preciseness served to rein in any permissiveness that emotionally tinged words might otherwise—and quite normally—suggest.

Professionally I was regarded as avant-garde in my fashion because I did give voice to subjects avoided by others, and because I tried in however cautious a manner to introduce questions of the soul to scientific speculation.

In the séance room, my natural modesty was offended by the exuberant, sometimes rambunctious creativity I found there; the almost tawdry overindulgence in energetic power. At the same time, I was often in awe, as one is when faced with the sheer vitality displayed by the very young—undisciplined, unadult, unreasonable by usual standards, but hinting at such raw power that the adult wonders at the forgotten energy of his own youth.

It's quite possible that my own disciplined manner elicited such response on the part of mediums, in particular, for I had a reputation of scientific objectivity to uphold. No sleight of hand or emotional ploy could be allowed to dull my wits; no religious setting or sentimental tears of piety make me forget the sometimes sly duplicity with which some of the most sincere-seeming mediums could deceive the psychic investigator.

Some such mediums were simply psychic frauds, plying

their trade; and yet performing a service in their way, for to these humble living rooms, furnished with religious emblems, pictures of Christ and the saints, came the poor and disturbed—the shopgirls, poor matrons, wives of icemen and factory workers. These people were aliens to the world of psychology. They never visited the psychologist's study, nor were they ever welcomed in Europe to Freud's couch. The theoretical psychologist wanted nothing to do with this segment of society. Often the very existence of such people seemed to present a sharp slap to the face of democracy and psychology alike. For these were the league of democracy's unsatisfied, interested in the results that democracy promised but could not produce wholesale. And for *all* that, in that time, it was the wholesale production of happiness that gave democracy its lure.

The goal is not one that any government can provide. Safety can legitimately be expected from good government, and the free opportunity for the development of individual abilities, the creative use of resources, and the existence of worthy employment. But happiness itself is more elusive and comes from sources that cannot be legislated.

Many ladies of all ages and stations earned pittances as mediums, tawdry queens of sorry neighborhoods, offering needed counsel and advice, some of it quite sage, to those who were—because of poverty, lack of education, or personal inadequacies—outcasts from the mainstream of American life. These people embarrassed the religions, government, and psychologists alike.

The front face of Protestantism was pragmatic. God helped those who helped themselves. All negativism was to be routed out. If man had a soul—well, let the spiritualists produce it, and without a lot of teary nonsense. Let the spirits of the dead make good sense and prove their case, not go skulking about in ghostly gowns in Mrs. Chowder's back parlor.

Thursday afternoon
January 27, 1977

Yet it was precisely to such Mrs. Chowders' back parlors that

I was often led, hat hesitantly in hand, skeptical eyes politely lowered, as initially I spied out the lay of the land—for it was difficult to see how miracles of the spirit could emerge from such grubby settings: chipped wainscoting, dirty doorsteps, entire rooms saturated with the intermixed odors of incense, candle wax, boiling onions, potatoes or beef of the poorest persuasion, garlic, cough potions, and other spices or oils of musty but otherwise mysterious properties.

Could the recipe for the soul's comfort be mixed in such kitchens? Better to keep on your muffler, wind it about your nose to keep out the noxious odors, sit down, and get to business, leaving such questions and mutterings for a more comfortable moment. For our work was more intimately concerned with homey paraphernalia than our scientific documents might show, and also connected in most devious ways with the passing of the seasons.

For example, our investigations were twice as complicated in the winter, for rather amusing reasons not at first apparent; particularly in Boston, where the dampness had a bone-chilling effect that even the sunny-minded felt most acutely. Ladies, therefore, went about fully decked, even in their households, with layers upon layers of wool and muslins beneath their skirts, to say nothing of the shawls, sweaters, capes and aprons that they wore atop. Winter, then, provided legitimate excuse for bulky underclothing that was often used not so much for warmth as for the concealment of magnets (to make tables move), nuts (cracked together to make "rappings"), and scribbled messages on pieces of paper that later materialized as if freshly written on by the dead (a like piece of blank paper being first, obviously, placed on the table, and later quickly replaced with the concealed one).

It took the greatest of courage, the most delicate coughing, the most gentle yet demanding of glances for an investigator under such circumstances to suggest that the good woman's clothing might be concealing more than ample hips or bosom, and those men brave enough—in certain situations—to request permission to search the lady's underpinnings were accused of having more than scientific interests on their minds.

In that chill northeastern climate, however, and in the evening when many séances were held, there was a certain

charm; perhaps—who knows?—an innocent-enough hope
that against the deeper winter of the soul, here such homey
ingredients might spark those necessary elements of the heart
that must, if any do, unite the living and the dead. The
scientist well knew that he lacked whatever emotional
impetus might be needed, so bemoan the circumstances as he
might, he also felt himself to be an outsider, a watcher,
seeing what spark the emotions of the others might provide,
that he could use.

Alas, we were often deceived—and yet as I shall explain
later, not deceived but taught deeper lessons than we knew. I
was acquainted with the rudiments of hypnosis, as were
many of my colleagues; and while we spoke about
suggestion from our side, it never *really* occurred to us that
many of these unlettered women were far better hypnotists
than we; that they learned techniques more effective,
quicker, and often more pleasant than our own; or that
indeed they understood better than we the dictates, needs,
and yearnings of the human heart.

The lessons usually escaped us. I recall how often I
fussed and fumed, stomped angrily from a dark front porch
out into the waiting carriage; deriding in low but fierce tones
the transparent trickeries of some woman I had caught in
fraud. I had indeed perceived deceptions—"ectoplasm" made
of cotton, the entire roll once dragged out in the middle of a
séance by the family cat—but the sitters who should have
been angriest turned their ire on me rather than upon the
perpetrator of the deception.

"Poor ignorant people," I would think, shaking my
head, missing an important point entirely: the medium's
excellent use of hypnosis was such that even in the face of
disclosure, her sitters literally heard her voice only, her
arguments; and she had convinced them, *all evidence to the
contrary*, that they had been visited by the dead. In a fashion,
this was as much an extraordinary performance as a
legitimate visitation of the deceased, for the sitters believed
what they saw under the medium's suggestions even when
the props were shown to be deceptive—the ghost turns out to
be the medium's young sister, parading through the
darkened room in slippers; or the plaintive moan, "Mama,"
proves to be the neighbor's child, hidden behind the drapery,

paid a penny for each "Mama" cried on cue.

Friday morning
January 28, 1977

One of our errors was in regarding the intellect alone as
capable of judgments, and as the final arbiter of events.
Feelings and sentiments can be used, should be used also, for
the emotions make their own judgments of reality and it is
against those more volatile opinions that we ultimately
assess our acts. That is, the emotions also provide a
legitimate though different framework with which to test the
results of any event, paranormal or otherwise, and the
emotions' truth may respond to an inner objective reality
that has its own rules and values that are not mysterious or
hidden, but perceivable *if* you use the proper measuring tool.
  Such a proposition is most difficult to defend intellectually, yet there are some analogies to be found. A novel can
be true in the deepest sense, for example, though the details
within it are quite "false" in scientific terms, if the places
and people mentioned therein do not exist "in fact." The
scientist, judging such a work by the rules of his own
discipline alone, might indeed entirely miss the dimensions
of the artistic, creative world, or dismiss such works as
beneath serious adult consideration. The fictional events of
the novel are symbolic statements about inner emotional
realities that have deep validity. There is a definite
correspondence between such imaginative events and the
objective world.
  The trouble is, of course, that this correspondence is not
measurable in usual terms. To dismiss it for that reason,
however, would be to rob the world of its invaluable artistic
heritage and accomplishment. While I became, in life, more
and more disillusioned with the results of paranormal
investigations, therefore, I became in time more and more
convinced that the "fictionalized" events of many séance
rooms—those spooky dramas formed of desperate hopes,
emotional frenzies, creative fabrications and subconscious
dramatizations; those morality plays in miniature, occurring
in neighborhood after neighborhood—stood for inner

realities. They symbolized inner facts, if you prefer, even when they were fraudulent, and held the same correspondence to events after death as conventional novels or plays did to daily life.

We could compare the works of art to the events they symbolized, but the reality of the afterlife presents us in life with no ready yardstick with which to measure what truths or inner facts reside in the séance, or other such psychological events. The séance is, however, a social event in that there are participants, an audience oftentimes, and we are faced by the same problems that witnesses provide whenever they are expected to state clearly the bare facts of their experience.

Such are the powers of the creative imagination that such participants may *in fact*—that is, physically—perceive the fictionalized events; may actually see the apparition under the suggestion of the medium in a psychological drama in which the medium herself is convinced of the apparition's appearance—because, like the scientist perhaps, she trusts the evidence of her senses. And those senses might indeed show *her* the shadowy image of a person—the deceased, clearly positioned. She may hear words which she repeats for the sitter. Taking it for granted that no fraud exists in such a hypothetical case, what are we to say? We must say that we do not understand perception itself. So I told myself.

More of this later. But if we look at the séance as a creative dramatic psychological event, we can at least compare it to other more conventional dramas, such as religious or artistic productions and ceremonies. We have, for example, a set of conventions and a loose cast of characters—the Indian guides, doctors, philosophers, poets, and other personae—the denizens of the dead, in other words, who serve as "controls" or mediators between the medium and the deceased.

Perhaps these *are* artificial productions; fictionalized characters coming to life so to speak through the medium's gestures, voice and actions, instead of simply appearing on the printed page as the main characters of a novelist's art. Or perhaps this also represents a kind of creative synthesis with which we're usually unfamiliar, a psychological reorientation that allows the medium to tune in to a different perceptive environment, which is then interpreted in terms that we *do* understand. Again, so I told myself.

I wondered: if the theater productions of the actor's world stand for an objective reality, then what is behind the séance's creative drama? Is the medium's experience a symbolic role-playing, I asked, that tries to depict through personification a definite alteration of consciousness that does, in fact, occur after death?

I must profess that those séances I attended in life were far from quality artistic productions, however; and those performances that came under the guise of art—such as automatic writing—gave little evidence of creative merit. I found primitive art charming, but such primitive gropings with the written word embarrassed me to the core. At least, such was my own reaction to those manuscripts that came to my attention.

There were also, however, more cultivated ladies, from sheltered environments, who held their séances in the tasteful parlors of the well-to-do, amid rich wall hangings, with maids serving tea and cakes; parlors visited by quite educated men of letters—women whose honesty and sincerity were beyond doubt. Here the setting was more proper, the rapport between medium and investigator far more comfortable. Current news and gossip might be discussed before the curtains were drawn—but in their anxiousness to prove their cases, such ladies often produced only a more stately version of events with which the investigators were already familiar; a more cultivated package, perhaps, but with no more content.

These more respectable ladies regulated their own emotional tones, perhaps automatically, in response to the investigator's distrust of sentiment, trying to be even more reasonable, more logical, so that the results of their intuitive experiments would be favorably received. This was a pity, for such attempts worked counter to whatever abilities the ladies possessed.

Paranormal events, however, had been labeled in such a way, often by psychologists themselves, that the incidence of them carried the tinge of unrespectability at best—and at the worst implied the most dangerous kinds of hysteria. Experiments by psychologists in hypnosis deepened these connections by producing, through suggestion acting upon hypnotist and subject alike, those results that were expected. So-called split personalities were psychologically manufactured by such dallyings, tailored to fit the hypnotist's preconceptions. A good hypnotist automatically hypnotizes himself before he begins to work his suggestions upon the mind of another—a fact not in the least understood then or now.

Nor did the true scientist dare allow himself to experience paranormal events, generally speaking, for to do so would put him into the same kettle; bringing into question those qualities of objectivity, intellectual discrimination, and emotional balance that he *believed* separated him from those he studied. The more such a man tried to dismiss his emotions, to retain an objective stance, the more his emotional needs strained at the academic leash; and the more he became fascinated by the emotional elements under investigation, the greater his risks of losing his psychic virginity.

Friday afternoon
January 28, 1977

Exploring the frontiers of the mind was more than a metaphor: the optimistic, aggressive, democratic march was to extend not only across the continent but to the very soul of the country. Unfortunately, the techniques that fostered industry and emerging technologies were not those that best encouraged the research into man's mind. For one thing, the mind was to be harnessed, directed, focused in order to help man in his battle against nature, and against what he saw as the unreasonable, savage impulses of his own nature.

At the same time, the highest ideals of democracy were often pursued with brawling indifference to the needs of others; with a disregard for sentiment except when it met national or patriotic needs. Those needs were largely understood in terms of Protestantism, interpreted according to American interests: Godliness meant social works, but in a no-dallying manner, and God helped those who helped themselves.

To that end, the psychologist tried to retain a crisp manner, a clear-cut optimism, a scientific stance that all in all stood for no nonsense—except, of course, that perpetuated in psychology's name. In this general atmosphere it seemed safest to me to concentrate my efforts in theory rather than practice; and to serve as a messenger of sorts between men working in the field so to speak, and their colleagues in the universities. I also settled upon certain other refinements, dictated certainly by the characteristics of my own temperament.

That temperament, while attracted by the hurly-burly, the rambunctiousness of its time, by the democratic spirit in action, was also aristocratic, withdrawn, one might say queasy at the overrich diet of democratic comradeship—and also tinged by an almost constant melancholy. For a scientist I was overly aware of my own states of mind, overly preoccupied with my moods, yet I was too critically attuned, too skeptical of the emotions to give *them* sway, and so lacked the emotional energy of the artists. No coincidence then, that I settled upon a critical analysis of states of mind; the intellectual investigation of religious inspirations; the sometimes gloomy pursuit of man's triumphant spirit in death, since in life that triumph eluded me so steadily.

Had I tied these two characteristics of mine together, I could have ridden emotion's power into the highest states of creativity—at least to the best of my ability—and at the same time given my intellect a creative freedom; forming a synthesis that I know now should be the natural state of man's psyche. In an understanding of man's creative forces and of the tension between intellect and emotions, can be found those thus-far elusive clues to the powers of the psyche that *do* indeed allow it to continue its existence after death, though in an altered state of consciousness, and in an environment that bears the same relationship to physical life as physical life does to the theater production—while combining the most creative elements of each.

. . .

(After my writing for that day was finished, I decided to do some sketching for a change of pace. Suddenly I found myself involved in a new kind of experience—the first of many—in which the James of my subjective experience reached out beyond his manuscript in one way or another.

(This particular incident happened quite unexpectedly. I was sitting at the living room table and had just opened my sketch pad. In the next moment, in my mind's eye, I saw a man seated in a study. I was sure that this was William James, but I wasn't sure whether I was seeing a portrait of James or an actual image of him in a chair. In any case, I drew what I saw, though not too expertly. I'm quite poor at perspective and in handling the proportions of the human figure.

(Instantly, as soon as I was done, I saw three framed oil paintings—two landscapes and a seascape—and I felt that these had once hung in James's study. The images were fairly steady; I knew I was supposed to duplicate them. I don't work in oils much at all, so I grabbed my acrylics and tried to reproduce the paintings. They were entirely different from anything I'd done before in just about every way—color choice, mood, and composition. I was quite exhilarated, yet frustrated. It's really difficult to translate inspiration into a medium in which you aren't proficient.

(When I was done, I kept staring at my amateur work, comparing the paintings with those I saw in my mind. The mental ones were heavily painted and reminded me of old paintings I'd seen years ago in an art gallery—American landscapes of the nineteenth century—moody, featuring great trees blowing in the wind, skies lashed by storm clouds; and beneath, virgin romantic forests.

(Did my attempts represent paintings that had once hung in James's study? I'll probably never know. But I won't forget that evening when I painted so frantically, and felt so close to James's surroundings in life.

(Did the "portrait" bear any resemblance to James? I didn't know that either; it showed a man with dark hair and beard, facing the foreground. I just sighed and put the sketches away. I was somewhat bewildered, though, by the connection between James and my painting since as I've mentioned, I felt no such interaction when I was doing the Paul Cezanne script.

(Several months later, however, in a national magazine I read that James was an amateur artist. That was news to me, and certainly implies that James was interested in art, and may have had original paintings on his walls. Perhaps his amateur status made him sympathetic to my own painting efforts. Our interest in art may have served as another link between us, though our primary one is obviously verbal.)

# 2. Depression, Precognition, and the Dynamics of Creativity

(Monday morning as the snow fell, our new kitten raced through the living room, and my husband, Rob, painted in his studio, I sat down at the typewriter and started up again. With the first words, I knew that James was beginning a new chapter. He never gave any chapter headings, though, so I titled them myself when they were done.)

Monday morning
January 31, 1977

In life the dynamics of creativity are hidden from us in a way that logical thought processes are not. A splendid natural scene, a strain of music, or the contemplation of a great painting often stirs the emotions in a seemingly miraculous fashion, so that suddenly an individual's overall personality is altered: faith replaces doubt, vibrant health retones the body, intellectual faculties before strained by anxiety are quickened, sharpened—and yet filled out with a new power, attaining an additional substance or thickness of content.

Such experiences appear in small or grand manner in each lifetime; sometimes so seemingly insignificant that they nearly go unnoticed, perhaps not even changing our plans for the day though altering the cast of those events in the gentlest, kindest way; or occurring as revelations that completely rewrite the script of a lifetime's future actions.

We cannot account for such experiences, intellectually, for the same scene that so inexplicably fires our emotions and rouses our awe may be one that we have passed, unaffected, countless times: the painting may have earlier struck us as quite mundane; and we may have heard that particular strain of music so often in the past that we automatically ceased hearing it for all practical purposes.

The opposite can also occur, when an innocuous scene strikes us with sudden, sharp desolation; the sight of a masterpiece plunges us into deep depression; or the strains of a familiar piece of music unaccountably touch off a melancholy all the more desperate because it seems so out of proportion to the triggering event.

I used to think that the somber New England landscape accounted for my own melancholy to some extent, for the feeling of my consciousness at times mirrored perfectly the cold, gray bleakness of the world outside my cozy study. The ships, coming to port, sounded a mournful note as if the sorrowful dead, particularly at twilight, made a ring, arms entwined, gazing toward the land with nostalgic despair, filling the air with the sound of their dirge—a sound that merged with the ocean's roar, the ships' foghorns, and the whistlings and rattlings of the cold waves.

Romantic, sentimental, floppy fancies! My intellect held me up to scorn for them, and I would confess them to no one. Staunchly reminding myself of the harbor's lusty bustle, I would imagine the lights, commotion and shouts of the sailors. I would try to smell the odor of the day's catch, to hear the thumping of returning feet on the slippery wooden docks, and to see the barrels of cold water thrown over the glistening nets of fish—for all of this I had experienced often, on long walks, and I always found the entire affair quite refreshing. Yet when that particular fantasy overcame me, I was mentally struck instead by the sight of blind fish eyes staring upward, slimy weathered rocks, the hearty yet now distasteful indifference of the fishermen for the wiggling catch beneath their booted feet.

Was it for this sense-cluttered desolation, this gluttonous denial of life for other creatures that the dead yearned? I wondered in such moods what about life could possibly attract the dead, who were cleansed of such petty violences, who were absolved from a clamor of conflicting desires in which victory for one was despair for another. For while I yearned toward comradeship and found conversation the liveliest and most civilized of social pursuits, I was also on other occasions sickened by the same kind of discourse and the same companions that, at other times, gave me the deepest satisfaction.

So why my fantasy of the wailing dead? During such attacks of desolation, I felt too fastidious for life, even outraged by its conditions, drawn toward a life of solitary contemplation—yet such contemplation I reasoned, would only deepen my distress. And quite in line with my feelings (rather than with my intellectual attitude toward them), out of nowhere there would emerge a barrage of dire images, gathered together in lightning swiftness from my entire experience—tragic events of my life or from novels I had read or dramas I had seen, images instantly brought to somber yet brilliant life that only moments before had been buried in my memory.

My feelings had literally conjured these images into fresh existence, searched through all of the important and trivial data with which I'd ever been concerned from birth and presented these to me with a priceless organization that consciously would have been quite beyond my means, if I were asked to draw up such a list of associations. The extent of such images seemed endless, providing a steady procession of tragic mini-dramas, each deepening my morass until finally I simply refused to entertain them any longer and forcibly turned my attention elsewhere.

What unwanted guests of the unconscious, what unbidden demonic company! So I told myself, admitting no responsibility at all for their arrival and insisting instead that I was put upon by the dictates of a melancholy temperament that was mine, but not me.

I was unduly fascinated also with the progression of the generations in their twofold fashion; for each generation followed the previous one into life and into death, like some strange mermaids and mermen lifting above the surface of the waves but without ever losing the fins of their true specieshood; and falling back into the ocean's depths after but a glimpse of the land. For surely, I reasoned, we were dead for longer than we lived, and how could life's brief iridescent light shed any real illumination into that vast darkness that surrounded life on all sides?

And how strange, I thought, that life's concentrated focus was so full of conflicts, tumults, divisions, and questions that seemed by their nature to have, in life, no possibility of resolve. Did one life possess enough stimuli to satisfy the dead for untold centuries? Did the dead mull upon their life's experience, gnaw mentally upon the bones of their own contention? Was life like some unspeakable complicated problem in emotional mathematics, each soul given one, and then sent back into the realms of nonbeing where concentration was expanded in some equally inexplicable way? But to what point?

So all of these thoughts assailed me as I heard the ships come into port—in direct contradiction to my conscious experience of the docks, and in spite of my cheerful appreciation of the fishermen's gusty diligence when I actually visited there. And if the dead did possess any secrets, if their mental mulling of their life's events gave them any solutions, none certainly appeared in the séances I attended, nor did any of my investigations of such affairs bring me comfort.

The existence of clairvoyant and telepathic dreams was another matter, and though no real objective evidence could be ascertained, in my opinion there was no doubt that man's mind could and did peer into the mind of another; and could also at times perceive the intent of the future. It struck me furthermore from the dream reports we collected, that the dream events came together or were conjured up in the same way that my own dark waking fantasies were.

Where my images were confined to events from the past or present of my own experience, however, such dream images reached into future events and often involved experiences that were not personal. In this respect the dreamer's mind sought from an interpersonal field of relationships those images that formed the dream, but organized them according to some inner hidden intent. The dream events seemed to just fall together, as did my fantasies, organized with an inner facility beyond normal conscious means and utilizing a far vaster field of information than is normally at hand.

It occurred to me that dreams were notorious mood-changers and this whether or not the dream events proved "true." That is, the dream effects were often undeniable, and led to definite behavior changes, even though the dream events themselves were not precognitive.

I reasoned, then, that those who were, like me, of melancholy temperament—but also more gifted—might dream their desperate fantasies only with an extra far more creative twist, so that the details unconsciously chosen came not from private past or present experience, but were the result of a far more extensive ferreting in which the future also served. The private sense of disaster, I believed, could be of such intensity, the anticipation of danger so acute, that some individuals in an accelerated sleeping state of creativity sought out those data from the future, involving others not themselves; collected predictive elements; and dreamed events that were about to happen in the objective world.

But to what purpose? For surely precognitive dreams of disasters must lead to feelings of helplessness and confusion. How to warn the unknown passengers of a train that on the tracks ahead lies a certain collision? Into what depths of suspense must the dreamer of such a tragedy be plunged; caught wondering and waiting to see whether or not the disaster will in fact occur? Imagine such a man or woman, worriedly scanning newspapers for such reports, questioning if the dream could in any way be responsible for the ensuing events if they do occur? So what psychological value could such dreams provide?

I found some answers, late in life, through examining my own dire fantasies, though they were waking ones and not precognitive. Some of us more than others, it seems, are struck by a sense of life's vulnerability, and though we may learn to display the hearty, everyday manner of our more blustery neighbors, we quail, cringe, and protest against characteristics of life that others quite take for granted. A bird with a broken wing; a caught fish, dumb mouth open; the household kitten trailing the dead mouse, blood-spattered, yet protected from crime by his innocence; and the bouts of illness with which children are often afflicted—these injustices forever capture our notice. How we envy the bustling mother who reacts in a practical manner, certain that tomorrow the child will be outdoors at play—while we see the funeral in our mind's eye and imagine the crying relatives. In any case, there are those of us who in life expect the worst turn of events; whose very blood would seem to have a dull gray cast; whose freshest thoughts are tinged by regrets and overconscientiousness.

Such is the certainty of disaster that in a given day if

none be found, the pressure grows, for from what hidden avenue might life's retribution come? Any excuse at all to hang such a feeling upon is better than none. Fantasies will serve. If the melancholy person hides that anxiety from himself, promptly with moral rectitude dismissing such sentiments as unworthy, then perhaps in sleep that need triggers creativity to such an extent that the dreamer reaches into the future for an event to pin his anxieties upon—and hence, to express them.

If the foreseen event involves others, not himself, what a sense of relief—disaster, yes, yet: the dreamer was right, and his feelings of anxiety were justified, while he himself is saved. The foreseen catastrophe also provides a continuing drama as the anticipated events are nervously awaited, so that the melancholic feelings of which the individual is ashamed can find a carrier to hold their content.

The artistically gifted might instead paint a dark landscape of swirling storm clouds, or disaster at sea, or some other painting whose deep shadows and stern visage suggest the despairing passions. The poet might write a somber verse—a dirge, or ode to death. But the hidden creative powers lie beneath all of these achievements, despite their content, method, or final form. And behind the creative powers lie the majestic energies of the emotions; those same emotions that I envied in others during my life, while I treated them like psychological stepchildren in myself, unless they paraded in their best Sunday clothes.

It was only after death that I understood life's full achievement; appreciated the fine focus of consciousness tuned so precisely and triumphantly to one place and time; and felt the power of earth-dimensioned life as in life I had never known it. As a result I came to terms with my own spirit, and gave it its freedom while in life I overtended it, believing that it was ill served by mortality's experience.

It is to comment upon that earthly experience that I now once again shape the components of my consciousness into that general cast they once possessed, and adopt to some extent the characteristic bent of thought by which my works were known. To do so will at least hint of those creative aspects of personality that lie beneath each life and allow it to reach into dimensions other than its own, out of the strength and power of its own intent.

In life I was of course aware of those with cheerful temperament, whose natural feelings, left alone, were optimistic; those who seemed genuinely content; and I envied them even while suspecting that they were of shallow mind, given to easy emotions while blind to the passions—or I romanticized them on other occasions as Natural Man, human, but as innocent of moral challenge as the kitten or tiger.

The idea of the life force intrigued me and I could envision it in Man or Woman or Child or in The Individual, but had the greatest difficulty in perceiving its existence in any given person; and while I theorized about its force, I felt within myself only the probing need to feel that power I imagined any simple animal possessed.

I looked therefore for its evidence in others and in the experience of paranormal events as they were reported to me, and largely ignored the thrusting drive of my own emotional life, which struck me then as an impediment of sentiment against which I must exert all the energy of my will and intellect.

I wanted to examine the emotions without feeling them; study the nature of creativity while holding myself aloof from its full sway; explore the force of life by standing apart in lofty isolation; promote the brotherhood of democratic man while confining my personal relationships to the scholarly; and most of all, to find scientific evidence for the belief in God by assiduously maintaining an objective stance against any emotional belief that might jeopardize the framework of disbelief that made the search itself respectable.

Some of this intellectual posturing was in response to the times; yet to however weak an extent, I molded the times in turn, marking them with a stamp of temperament and belief, even as my contemporaries each did. And also to some extent those characteristics uneasily mirrored the generation that came before, that believed in faith, good works, the hand of God's destiny—and yet in the face of tumultuous growing industrial events, dared not criticize the daily national experience their faith had wrought.

If God was in his heaven and all was right in the world, and if democracy was the favored form of government, divinely protecting men's rights and freedoms; if free employment and competition were the answers to poverty and the class systems of European heritage, then what about child labor and the notorious conditions in factories and sweathouses? So we were often torn between faith and doubt, fascination with technology and an alternating romanticization of nature, uneasy between the overly sentimental and the overly critical stance.

In my study, isolated, with books my trusted companions, I theorized most easily and readily about the brotherhood of man; while personal encounters often left me annoyed and despairing, and led me to question those moral principles that I followed in my mind but found so difficult to experience when I met face to face with my fellow men.

Wednesday morning
February 2, 1977

(I awakened groggily this morning at 2:50 A.M., realizing that I was getting James—lovely long sentences. I sat on the side of the bed and took down two segments. After the first two paragraphs, I lay back down and snuggled beneath the covers; then the material started up again.

(In the morning, as I typed up what I had written down in bed, I kept getting new interconnecting material. Obviously I'd missed some fragments and paragraphs, and as I typed, they were filled in. I underlined them—just to preserve the distinction.)

. . .

I tried to prove in fact the sweet products of my intuitions as they appeared to my creative imagination, for such "intimations of immortality" did, indeed, carry me above my intellect's dry grounds <u>by providing soaring concepts and emotions that freed me momentarily from my own habitual patterns of sentiment and thought.</u> But once I tried to prove these inner intimations by evidence and deduction, once I tried to bring them into the realm of science, I began an often thankless task, for neither intuitions nor intellect were really ever satisfied.

I became critical of emotional comprehensions or rousing flights of fancy that I knew could not be objectively proven, where earlier I gave my imagination full sweep with no thought that such immortal urgings could have a base in fact, but kept such religious sentiments aloft from the kind of scrutiny I gave other more mundane subjects. Therefore, my poetical inner knowledge held its validity when I judged it in its own framework, but once I cast it in the light of science, the conflicts began. No longer then could I accept my intuition's comfort, for a religious or spiritual belief became only a premise in its intellectual translation, and the soul's rich drama fell apart when reassembled into the geometry of mind. For that geometry required a definite series of steps and methods before it would give its QED to hypotheses for which the intuitions needed no such graded synthesis.

Indeed, the inner structures of such intuitive securities, however strongly felt, seemed to dissolve in toto whenever they were tampered with intellectually, as if they were composed of the finest yet flimsiest materials—or else of ingredients solid enough in their native realms, that could not however be transferred to the physical world.

One part of me thought: "Of course, faith cannot stand the light of reason. The scientist must keep his beliefs separate from his world of facts and not seek to prove, in the laboratory or otherwise, those unprovable promptings of the soul. Let them be delegated to art or religion or philosophy—disciplines which do not have to set their theories to such rigors."

On the other hand, I felt compelled to check faith's comprehensions and to bring all hidden aspects of consciousness into the democratic light of day, into the new world of progress and technology, where I hoped the spirit's proven knowledge might then be used as an extra impetus in man's objective search for the answers to reality—and also serve to temper the unscrupulous use of knowledge itself for selfish gain.

For if we could mine the earth's resources, dig deep into the planet's core and bring forth ores and minerals, why should we not also mine the resources of the soul in like manner, bringing to the surface of men's minds those precious gems of faith and hope that lay, I thought, beneath the surface of the mind?

So I began to search for such intuitive knowings and spiritual intimations wherever they could be found—in the churches or séance rooms, the reports of dreamers—seeking out the stories of respectable and eccentric alike. Yet the integrity of my own emotional comprehensions suffered, nor could I take comfort any longer from them. Moreover, my intuitions were scandalized to discover their knowledge judged by the often tawdry activities of many séance rooms— faith reduced to magicians' tricks and husky whispered promptings as apparitions paraded in gauzy gowns.

How could man's grave and loftiest spiritual proposals come to such a fate that their validity would be considered dependent upon such maudlin sentimentality and bab- blings? How could those sparkling prisms of faith be turned into cheap baubles under the investigation of logic and the disciplines of control?


Wednesday afternoon
February 2, 1977

The poet could rejoice in his intuitive revelations and give them enduring (and protective) clothing in his verse; intuitions and intellect in this case wedded, joined in symbolic sacrament; wordless intimations fleshed out in cadenced verse—so that the poet, like a spiritual banqueter, could have his poetic cake and eat it too. No one asks him for the recipe or ingredients. But cast the same intuitive data into the terms of usual reasoning and the cake melts, the frosting is a gooey mess, and the impatient guest gets a mouthful of disappointment.

Was faith then such a tenuous concoction that it fell at the slightest touch? Open the door to the unconscious, where the delicious loaves of inner sustenance bake—and lo and behold, we have only the cheapest of breads, soggy and unappetizing? Often I felt such to be the case, and so my melancholy grew as I examined the products said to come from that creative fire.

Not until after my death did I really realize that such unconscious servings took the shape of the psyche in which they were baked; that however the ingredients were stirred or however fresh they were originally, they flowed into the contours of each individual psyche—and though like bread they might rise, so must they level out to fit the mind's container.

And that container was far from pure or uncontaminated but held also the invisible residue of all the mind's more prosaic meals; messy concoctions in which even the finest spices would be lost and overpowered. The analogy is not too far off the mark with its connotations of taste and tastelessness, for even an excellent painting gaudily framed is the worse off. It is, perhaps, miraculous in itself that the products of the intuitions continue to manifest themselves in spite of the shoddy containers that men provide for their storage or display.

I told myself that the search for extraordinary merit or revelation or evidence of man's greater validity was, in its way, undemocratic, and cast aspersions on "the common man," since nowhere in my fellows could I really perceive even a glimpse of such enduring quality; nor when I was in such a mood, did the objective condition of the world serve to reassure me. Was I alone, then, blind to a spirituality and superior caliber constantly spoken about so glibly by others, and to which I myself gave lip service? As inconceivable as this seemed, I gave the matter considerable thought.

In the world at large, in social conditions and private experience, I *did* recognize great energy and tried to take pleasure in the idea that I was too discriminating and disapproving; believing perhaps that the innocence of others was distorted in the light of my own melancholy, and taking comfort in the thought that excellence of mind and spirit existed though my own temperament hid it from my eyes.

So I sought to perceive even in the shoddiest of performances that glimpse of high-mindedness and creative virtue that must be contained within. Yet all the while I went dissatisfied, not realizing that only the proper blend of

intuitions and intellect can provide true vision or understanding, or hope to act as a lens through which man can
reflect the inner fires that provide the continuing life of the
world.

The creative abilities, as I know now, give the most
reliable and highest evidence of those qualities that absolve
man from his own shortcomings and intrinsically lift him
above even his own experience of himself into a spiritual
validity that outlives his life and death alike.

Such faculties represent the mental equivalent of the
animals' prime innocence, and at the same time are cast in
the light of God's most treasured characteristic—His
creativity—from which all worlds emerge. The term "God"
is the simplest one to use here, though it is interchangeable
with many others, all referring to a point in our thinking
where comprehension stops: we can no longer even mentally
verbalize what we feel. The word, then, suggests that source
out of which intuitions and intellect each spring; and in
which they are so invisibly, securely, and intimately couched
that they and their source are separate and united at once.

These creative abilities, in their finest performances,
defy time and space, lift man out of the limited context of
intellect or emotion alone, and forge both into a higher
faculty in which experience *is* more evidential than any
demonstrable fact; and in which facts themselves are seen to
be like wobbly weeds stuck only momentarily in evershifting
sands on the shores of eternity.

Thursday morning
February 3, 1977

(The following material came to me just as I lay down to
take a nap Wednesday afternoon. I scribbled it down at once,
and typed it Thursday morning.)

· · ·

I would also consider certain acts of valor and daring as

creative in the highest sense, in that during such moments man transcends—first of all, imaginatively—ideas of basic limitations and goes beyond his usual experience of reality. In so doing, he actually for that moment creates that superior world with its observable conditions. I am referring to events where in crisis situations the body performs in ways that, momentarily at least, contradict known individual or mass beliefs about its limits and possible achievements; when it outdoes itself and hence through its performance breaks old records that were earlier held up as representing the ultimate possible in bodily achievement.

Such acts take place first in the imagination, in bursts of corporeal insight that can strike with the same force as any revelation; and under that sudden impetus of mind, the body miraculously responds—and brings to the physical arena a new idea of what is practical or possible.

It is the tension between the search for fulfillment or perfection and the actual performance possible in the physical world that promotes creative acts as they are understood. For true creativity always destroys limitations and increases the mental, spiritual, psychic or physical areas of expression open to man.

The Greek conception of the fit mind in the fit body is important in this context; yet that ideal finally disintegrated into a futile search for a dreary, stereotyped mental and physical perfection whose modeled edges blurred the vitality of any individual variances. I see, however, how these principles can in an altered fashion be applied to a modern democratic society, while retaining their original insistence upon high aspiration *and* individual fulfillment.

· · ·

(I typed this material, then got up, heated water for instant coffee, and washed the dishes while I waited. As I stood at the sink doing these chores, suddenly a whole burst of James material came into my mind, in a circular fashion, difficult to describe, so I rushed back to the typewriter to record the following):

• • •

In some dreams, inspirations and revelations, in the performance of artistic pursuits and some athletic achievements as well, man then displays abilities that are record-breaking; that set new standards and destroy past limitations either of mind or body, and therefore bring into conscious awareness new areas of action, contemplation, and creativity. Dreams or flashes of telepathic insight can also momentarily destroy the usual barriers that separate one mind from another, and make mockery of science's concepts concerning space, time, and the nature of the species.

Such incidents suggest the immortal existence of at least some portion of man's consciousness by displaying those characteristics and abilities that show his knowledge not to be bound by the laws that before had seemed to restrict him. I prefer to list all such activities, paranormal or not, under the heading of high creative acts; for each one is creative in that it opens new areas of action or thought, and expands man's capacity to think or behave in new fashions.

Beginning in my time and continuing in yours, however, certain misconceptions on the part of psychology have grossly diminished man's opportunities for expression and creativity by handing down average standards that supposedly govern individual behavior, beyond which the normal person is not to venture. Hence in my time, the birth of parapsychology came as a new artificial division to include activities not of a normal nature; a container for all of those experiences that did not fit into the original cramped tenets adopted as the sum of man's psychological reality.

Freud's European background and America's experiment with democracy were each partially responsible for these misconceptions and their unfortunate results. In a democracy, without a rigid authoritative government; in a political structure in which the individual is given greater free play, inner authoritative measures are taken to protect the society against what it considers the very dangers of individual action that its Constitution says it wants to promote.

Psychology was initiated when the new society was

trying its wings; and its father, Freud, with his authoritative heritage, symbolized for America its own position: it must maintain clear conscious lines of action, while trying to give vent to all the unconscious "primitive" drives in such a way that they were released—but not allowed to damage normal life. The individual must be taught that his deepest drives were suspect, so that self-discipline could replace authoritative government. Certain feelings, actions, and attitudes were considered normal and others not. The individual was given a book of rules to follow from birth to the grave, in which the unconscious replaced both the devil and harsh government, forcing obedience through fear of the natural self.

Such standardization was then promptly applied to the democracy's unlike, unhomogeneous citizens. The Italians, English, Irish, Spanish, Dutch—men and women of all racial heritages—were therefore expected to follow individual norms that would allow the person a political and social freedom that he would be psychologically unable to misuse.

In this hodgepodge, inner restraints would serve to replace a paternal government. Adventuresomeness, creativity, and energy would all be directed toward the collective goals of society—toward physical triumph over the land, and industrial achievement. All was an attempt to use and yet curb the fantastic energy of a people who came from every conceivable background and national heritage.

The inner life of the American individual became standardized, however, stripped of religion's old rich symbolisms, yet given no new ones, constructively speaking. Freud translated religion's demons into the instinctive impulses, retaining these while throwing aside the grander symbols of a heroic (and authoritative) God. Precisely because of his own experience, Freud then sometimes felt unendurable upswings of intuition and telepathic data; surges of creativity and the deepest, undisciplined emotional conditions. These only intensified his certainty that the inner life of man was dangerous, and that he was doomed by his own early heritage.

Freud perceived and experienced the creative force as primarily sexual in nature—in a broader way than usually supposed—but also in a Germanic sense of the word: a sexuality that was deeply and darkly passionate, with overtones of surrender or triumph, and with further implications of conflict and warfare.

His psychology standardized and explained the feelings of men and women in a way that left them no individual interpretations of their own that mattered. Psychoanalysis could come up with individual personal episodes of the most intimate nature, but these were in response to an explanation already given, in which individual feelings existed on a standardized basis.

Again, creative acts are nonstandard. They break records. They are not predictable. Creativity, then, became suspect. Freud tried to tie it to man's most frightening fears; to chain it to repressions rather than to aspirations or fulfillment. Those characteristics promoting creativity were suspect, nonstandard, the very ones to be exorcised. Intuitional insights were then assigned to hysterical behavior—but hysterical by whose standards? The devotion to contemplation or solitary thought or to the arts, particularly for a male, became most suspect of all; and those who did not channel their creative drives toward the democratic society's safe materialistic goals felt that society's wrath.

Against this background, do-it-yourself séances sprang up throughout the country, along with religious societies and various pseudoreligions. Christian Science in particular tried to right the balance, by applying positive thinking with as heavy a hand as Freud had applied repression. The people felt that it was safest not to explore the subconscious described by Freud, and indeed, the common man could not afford to do so. He was effectively left with a psychological hell instead of a theological one, minus a compensating heaven, and made afraid of the very creative abilities that would have been able to release him—and the society. There were some countertendencies, as with Transcendentalism, but these were not the meat of the common man, but of the intellectuals.

The creative abilities are common in mankind, but uncommon in their individual expression, bringing out distinctions and patterns that extend the capacities of individual action and achievement. When an individual acts most like himself, most individualistically and least like others, he displays creative behavior and points out to others possibilities of achievement earlier not perceived—throwing these out as new aspirations for the individual and society. I hope to show that these abilities must be encouraged by any democratic nation that wishes to survive as such.

First, an examination of the creative faculties is in order; and again, I refer to a creative act as including telepathic and clairvoyant performance, which I see as an extension of normal creativity—considered paranormal only because of the standardization applied within psychology itself. What characteristics or conditions promote creativity? And how does creative action contribute to the vitality of social order?

# 3. Freud, Jung, and Protestantism

Saturday morning
February 5, 1977

I amused myself after death wondering what different kind of vision Jung might have presented if Freud had not been his teacher, or if he, rather than Freud, had been the elder. Freud's emotionalism gave me concern for I considered him somewhat of a religious fanatic, operating outside of religion's conventional context. In many ways he was a shaman, born in the "wrong" country, twice as jealous of his own "masculine characteristics" because he sensed within himself the "perverse" intuitive rushes and psychic leanings that he feared and believed could undermine the personal authority of the ego and the mass authority of the state.

In many ways also Freud's theories represented the darker aspects of Protestantism, cut free from the conventional belief in an omnipotent God, released from optimistic ascensions into heaven—a psychological hell replacing the earlier theological one, and demons turned into the primitive impulses which were stamped upon the psyche in its infancy. In such a manner, the most pessimistic elements of Protestantism were given a new scientific face and sophisticated justification—just at a time when organized Protestantism was embarked on a new venture in America, stressing the active, aggressive, hopeful aspects of personality that would test the individual's capacities to rule his own society with a government based not upon fear, but upon freely accepted restraints adapted to the service of the highest aspirations of man.

So Protestantism became schizophrenic; its bleaker side expressed in disguised form through Freud's theories, its drive for salvation allied with democracy's conventional churches. That drive toward salvation, nationally expressed, was translated as salvation through triumph over poverty, over the class systems of Europe, and over the land itself, with the help of growing technology. Nothing was to stand in the way. The democracy's deepest fears and hesitations, and its unspoken suspicions that its ideals might be too high, were expressed in Freud's hypnotic reminders that the natural self could not be trusted. Freud's unconscious represented the individual's past; and for Americans it also represented the new democracy's roots in convoluted European heritage.

Freud actually gave Puritanism a new basis, since he provided a scientific framework in which man's nature was seen as basically untrustworthy, in need of constant scrutiny in which even the seemingly highest acts of man could have the darkest motives. Psychoanalysis replaced the Catholic confessional. The psychologist became the new priest, in a maneuver of deepest significance by which Freud returned to Protestantism the elements dismissed by Luther, and reinstated a go-between separating God and man—only this time, that go-between was the psychologist, who stood between the conscious and subconscious elements of man.

The individual no longer needed a priest to interpret God's words or the Bible, but instead required an interpreter to understand the unconscious (and unsavory) aspects of his own psychological identity—for *there*, he had lost his authority. Had this maneuver been accomplished through the policies of a clearly stated religious movement, a new Luther would have arisen, acclaiming once again the individual's right to interpret his own religious reality: Or had Freud been less convinced of the malevolent nature of the subconscious, his own shamanistic qualities would have burst forth in a greater vision of salvation, providing a truly meaningful version of psychological redemption rather than the restrictive techniques of psychoanalysis that, in fact, resulted.

Attempts of that kind did arise in Freud's behavior with Jung; by then, however, Freud's life had been largely spent in constructing theories that reflected his own psychic organizations and frameworks. To change these theories would involve far more than making minor or even major adjustments to a life's work, but would necessitate the birth of a new inner man. To Freud, Jung represented that man—literally, in psychological terms, a messiah, springing out of the experience of the father (Freud)—and it was in that light Freud saw himself in regard to Jung.

With admiration, jealousy, and the strongest sense of fascination, Freud watched Jung outgrow him; and no matter what Freud said or did, he knew that the interactions between himself and Jung provided exactly the kind of tension that added to Jung's growth. When Jung's theories *did* mature, it was in the new field of psychology: he was psychology's Luther. In a way, of course, psychology's Luther was religion's loss, for Protestantism remained schizophrenic, and even in your time it has not again realistically come to terms with the good and evil aspects of man in relation to God or nature. That failure led directly to the birth of parapsychology, which tried to address the elements of the soul that religion refused to examine.

There were, naturally, overlappings in these processes. Earlier, for example, Myers was a much more beneficial example of a man immersed in questions of the soul and personality, with religious and scientific bents merged advantageously; yet he did not give voice or expression to those submerged darker elements (that were more apparent after Victorian closed curtains opened), those tendencies that democracy needed to understand and use, but instead conventionally denied.*

As a result of these issues, American séances beautifully and sometimes hilariously portrayed the idiosyncrasies of religion and science both in the adaptation of Freudian principles to religious experience or mystical behavior.

While democracy sprouted patriotic slogans about the ability of the individual to join in a self-governing society, then, Freudianism let the soul slip away, stripped of its powers, which were delegated to a mechanical reaction of instinctive drives that could be numbered and diagramed in a sort of muddy emotional shorthand. The soul disappeared, becoming instead a psychological chamber of horrors requiring the most expert of guides, for inside there were

*See my footnote on F.W.H. Myers early in Chapter One.

distorted mirrors that could show the unwary in a flash the grotesque basis for the greatest achievements and the sorriest failures.

Monday morning
February 7, 1977

It seemed sheer idiocy to look there for any of man's redeeming characteristics, for altruism and greed alike were seen as the result of mechanical, repetitive psychological processes that caused men to act in a given way. Predestination was given new biological and scientific clothes. In such a framework, men could not take credit for their achievements or be held responsible for their blunders, and self-determination was sorely undermined. Such ideas clashed with all of democracy's stated ideals, yet were held equally with them.

Many of these issues largely escaped me in life, yet I should have sensed their shape more clearly. Had I been more adventuresome, I might have helped tip the balance, or at least I might have pointed out the contradictions between these two opposing areas of thought and philosophy. To this end, I now speak my piece, for the attitudes that finally emerged in the mainstream of American life strongly affected the ways in which individuals viewed themselves and their creativity.

Not only was man robbed of true satisfaction with creative work, but he was led to preserve his own doubts and torments, since they were seen as responsible for art's achievement: artistic production was tied to a neurotic birth, and the artist in whatever field began to hoard conflicts, imagining that they were the source of his productivity.

• • •

(After getting the previous material Monday morning, I took a break, did some house chores, then Rob and I had lunch. I was in the middle of our gourmet feast of soup and peanut-buttered crackers when suddenly the James material started

up again, very quickly. I kept putting down my soup spoon
to take notes; I dropped my cracker in the pea soup. Finally
we just cut lunch short, and I went back to my typewriter. It
was a damp day, in the twenties, but James was energetic, to
say the least. I felt as if both of us were taking a walk on a
brisk bright autumn day somewhere, with him passionately
discoursing.)

• • •

Death has its own pleasures, allowing you to comment in
leisure upon your own time, seeing what came before and
what after, and judging how many of those future
developments you saw or understood in their embryonic
form.

If in the past, genius and madness were considered
allied, both were seen in a heroic light in their connections
one to the other, and if genius was sometimes tinged with
madness, so was insanity tinged with genius. The heights
and depths of man's soul were each seen by Freud, however,
as the result of infantile behavior patterns that rigidly
controlled man for his lifetime—the grandest dimensions of
experience reduced to a psychological determinism from
which only the deepest self-examination could bring
redemption; a psychological journey that no one could safely
take alone, and one in which the individual was most likely
to misread the direction of his own bents, having been taught
to scrutinize precisely those spontaneous learnings meant to
serve as psychological directional signals.

Creativity became no more than enlightened insanity;
and insanity a distorted creativity. Both were seen as the
inevitable results of conditioning and neurotic cravings, over
which the individual had little control.

Protestantism was based upon man's right to interpret
truth for himself on an individual basis, thus directly
challenging the authority of the Roman Catholic Church as
the only agency capable of such discrimination; and upon an
attempt to put the individual in a one-to-one relationship
with God and the universe. In ways, this was a "paganistic"
adventure, reviving ancient characteristics of religion that
had been buried but not lost when, for example, shamanistic

genius was used for the community or tribal good. Freud, however, took that Protestant right away: the individual was seen as incapable of knowing his own motives, much less able to interpret his own relationship with nature or the soul. Freudianism was, then, based upon the less fortunate of Protestantism's concepts, while stripping it of its heroic qualities.

Nowhere was the search for truth considered a natural component of personality. The penis replaced the cross; thus, one-half of the species—the more intuitively inclined— was denied redemption. And if the cross was itself in many ways a maligned religious symbol, it offered salvation to man and woman alike; beneath it the sinner still retained his dignity as an individual capable of free action, who had but chosen poorly. Freudianism replaced the saint and the sinner alike with a mechanical psychological man, programmed from childhood to fail or succeed; and tied man's grandest symbols to their least beneficial manifestation.

If religion as embodied in Protestantism had failed in large measure, its many denominations did allow for various interpretations: salvation through good thoughts, prayer or good works, through private contemplation or public achievement, personal revelation or strict Biblical reference. The educated and illiterate could each find a place; so too the virgin, mother, prostitute, scholar, workingman, the child, and the adult. The fit of the individual into the framework was perhaps a poor one at times, but there was psychic mobility, and the sinner could become the saint.

Granted, a shallowness ruled. The good person wore decent clothes and modeled a cheerful countenance, but the democracy hoped to provide those opportunities by which the poverty-stricken could discover employment. In Freudianism, however, the poor could not help being poor, due to neurotic conditioning in infancy, their drives forever frozen, immobilized so that they were robbed, in theory at least, of the self-determination allowed to others—as women were; for all of *their* drives were assigned to a sexual envy of the male that they could not escape.

The effect of all of this was to reduce the importance of individual creativity, but also to place it in a more suspect light than earlier; and worse, to encourage the artist to keep whatever spiritual or psychic discomfort he had—to forsake understanding—lest, along with his torments, he lose his creativity. Since the creative powers always seek fulfillment, and are innately curious about the self and all aspects of its reality, the artist was put into a position where he tried to use his creativity and not use it at the same time, lest his insights lead him to his creativity's source in infantile dependency and then disintegrate in understanding's light.

Tuesday morning
February 8, 1977

Since no one could be trusted to know the motives for his own actions, and since the democracy was setting the individual free of strong governmental authority to a new degree, psychology set its own standards, providing the "norm," flattening the peaks of experience while offering society the safety of more or less predictable behavior. In that framework, exuberance, energy, and creativity were acceptable when channeled into the competitive arena of national interests. The rich, for example, were absolved from "normal behavior" and allowed artistic or eccentric activity because their financial interests were considered such a practical investment in national life.

Yet the social and business arenas themselves were unpredictable. A poor immigrant might be tomorrow's millionaire; and in such a psychological environment, the old rules of social protocol based upon European class systems could not be counted upon as smooth bridges of communication. The *theory* of the independent individual ruled; and precisely because of the country's freedom and unpredictable social and economic climate, the countering theories of psychology's norms took pragmatic hold.

Parents were to blame for offsprings' deficiencies of character, even as any of America's problems were seen as resulting from Europe's dark parental heritage; yet the democracy still envied the Old World's rich creative past, so it latched upon Freudian theories connecting creativity and neurosis, and projected all of its own current tumults into a source in European decadence.

The American saw himself as "blazing ahead." His

immediate ancestors had opened up the continent. Now the new frontier was technology or business, the management of the country's resources and the acquisition of wealth—and as little government control as possible. Robber barons rose in the guise of the good Protestant burgher. No longer did religion's fear of God's retribution hold sway over men's minds—at least not strongly enough to urge caution; and psychology removed guilt or justified its sting. Guilt had little to do with basic values, therefore justifying crimes committed in the name of competition, since man was considered a confused mixture of primitive drives and needs; yet those drives had to be leashed and directed toward society's goals.

In all of this, contemplation of the soul had little place. Myers's theories concerning the subliminal self, after making early inroads, vanished from the mainstream of academic and philosophic life. That concept, stressing the inter-dependence of individual minds and the availability of superior inner knowledge, could have been used to augment democracy's basic principles to far greater advantage; stressing individuality while bolstering its responsibility and power of achievement, and emphasizing its relationship with interweaving natural and social arenas of activity.

Some of Myers's thought was incorporated into the positive-thinking schools and cults. These and Freudianism —mutually contradictory theories—showed the opposing polls of American sentiment; and each had roots reaching into Europe's past. Myers began with the hypothesis that man possessed an inner self of extraordinary creativity and organization—psychology's nearest corollary to the soul. Its directions could be misread; its language was symbolic; but it was of good intent.

The Freudian concept of the self lacked any good intent; that is, it was stripped of altruism in any trustworthy or purposeful form. It was the only kind of a self that could logically survive the theories of Darwin as popularly understood, the end result of an organism that survived by triumphing over other life forms in an endless battle for life. That self's one "virtue" was that it *did* survive, and if it lost its intuitive feel for nature in the process—well, that was nature's fault.

Altruism, displays of valor, philosophy itself, or creativity in terms of the arts—these were only possible because of their self-serving qualities, and beneath their gentle guise lay the infant's savage determination to exist, and the male's drive to slay his father in order to supersede him in life's battle. Such theories stripped human personality of any majesty and denied the possibility of heroic action that was not tied to the meanest inner motives.

For all of academia's separate precious journals, each specialized, fields of knowledge overlap. These concepts splashed over into archaeology, history, biology, and tinged the arts and sciences alike. Nor did the past escape: great artists of previous centuries became isolated eccentrics, their genius produced by hormonal malfunction or sexual deficiency, and history was rewritten to fit. Evolution's dogmas became Freudianism's justification. If the animal's struggle for dominance resulted in the "survival of the fittest," then surely man as the most powerful victor of that saga must emerge as the carrier of basic drives best suited to ensure the species' continuance. The young democracy could thusly justify the unfortunate circumstances of a sometimes ruthless competition—it was each man for himself.

Yet in such a world there would be no order at all, an issue that even the most competitive were quick to see; so the Freudian reasoning, simply put, read this way: We are basically amoral, primitive, and self-serving. These qualities ensure our survival, yet they must be artificially forced into a morality that will protect us against ourselves, and hence further our survival in a social and governmental context.

–The results of all of this were mixed. Freud painted such a dire picture of man's subconscious, and limited "salvation" to such a small number of people, that spontaneity was not fostered but instead diminished and constricted to competitive fields, where it was condoned. The spontaneous self, the impulsive portion of man's nature, became most suspect, for in his spontaneous acts man could unwittingly reveal not a basic goodness, but the hidden shoddiness of his motives.

The search for virtue itself became the grossest kind of moral posturing—an emotional hypocrisy. The robber baron at least was honest in his dishonesty, or so the feeling went. Compassion and sympathy not only went out of style, their expression was considered evidence of duplicity and a sanguine denial of man's nature. One species could not climb over another while feeling sympathy for its predecessor, nor could the members of any species afford pity for their less vigorous fellows.

Wednesday evening
February 9, 1977

Yet the American soul was cautiously idealistic even beneath the conflicting theories, and it was in its way innocent. If, as the psychologists stated, man was amoral at best—the end result of a deadly biological evolution; a surly scrambler to the top of the heap—here at least, in the new democracy, if he pushed and shoved hard enough a man could get enough to eat. He *could* even get his own business. His children *could* get an education. Here the new social ladder was still forming. A man could leap from one business branch to another, higher one, in economic treetops where brains and hard work took the place of the European family trees that had, in the past, given protection and shade to chosen generations.

Here the ordinary man could be equal under the law, even if the tyranny of his nature dictated a basic amorality that pitted each man against his neighbor. He could, through willpower alone, even achieve a kind of moral victory through using some restraint. Hence the suggestion "Every day in every way, I'm getting better and better" was hopefully set against Freudianism's determinism. Some of the more ambitious, of course, used such suggestions to implement their struggle in the realm of competition (the evolutionary battle transferred to the area of economics). Better and better often meant: "I'm getting smarter and more wily than my competitors."

Business became the most creative element in American society then, with the technological sciences catching up swiftly. Finally the two were so allied that the edges blurred, until in your time this became quite obvious as business and technology progressed together, bloated and overly confident, dizzy in an overstimulation that culminated in American war experiences of the twentieth century.

Encouraged by Freudian beliefs, and still operating under evolution's misconceptions, Western civilization found itself faced with a thematic situation in which no individua' was considered trustworthy but was biologically geared to undertake any course to ensure survival. The same applied to any nation. In your Second World War, the Japanese were depicted as caricatures of human beings, obviously from "lower down the evolutionary scale" and therefore not fit to survive. Wars were justified by many otherwise intelligent men as the human version of nature's unconscious evolutionary processes, and the old dictum "might is right" attained new power.

Psychology and science were simply taking up where the old conventional religions left off—providing a newer, more modern justification for policies of government long held in Europe. I glimpsed some of these shapes of the future—with some loathing and fascination, I might add—in that I foresaw the possibility that together all of the sciences—psychology, biology, archaeology, paleontology—might form a force that went unrecognized as a religion and yet provide an overall unity and philosophic structure as strong as that of the Roman Catholic Church in the Middle Ages.

I did not think that this was a strong possibility, since I vastly underestimated the alliance of business, technology, and science; and it seemed to me in my time that science lacked the economic glue that had held the Roman church together. The sciences, however, *did* form just such a structure, and the philosophy it held unified the arts, and the business and social organizations. The general views of Freudianism and evolution merged, flowed like a dark, threatening stream through all of the sciences and arts, business and social structures; so that all other aspects of life, past, present and future, were seen in what amounted to the murky but hypnotizing light of a new dogma.

The universities, foundations, and the family itself—all of these elements of American life altered their viewpoints drastically. Though the changes were beginning in my period and will come to an end in yours, not for many years hence will it be seen that the twentieth-century Western world was as united in basic scientific philosophy as the Europe of the Middle Ages was in religious rigidity.

Freudianism, evolutionism, and technology became the new inspiration for the arts, and the American government sponsored those foundations that fostered those beliefs. Science fiction also was often the projection of evolutionary theories out into space—the human animal spreading his superior genes with the use of technology.

Other philosophic theories were held, but they did not flourish or rush into the mainstream of American life. People were not generally jailed for holding opposing beliefs, though some were. America's freedom of speech was at least adhered to in the main, but the definitions of normality thrust upon the ordinary person were those that upheld the theories just described.

These were, at best, limiting. At their worst, they served to alienate men from their private source of energy and strength, and to rob them of the very self-reliance that the democracy idealistically fostered. For the country did not give up its ideals. The common man held to them with desperate determination and glossy hope; with an optimism and application to hard work that saw millions of tattered children turn into tired, bewildered, but well-dressed citizens—who *then* looked to the religions, arts, and so-called finer things of life, searching for an answer to the unspoken question: what did we give up to get where we are?

Along the way, the religions joined largely with the business interests, settling for good works and ignoring such issues as the existence of the soul; for where could that nonscientific, unprovable phenomenon fit in with the seeming facts of evolution, particularly with the popularly understood version of man springing from a monkey? To counter science's laboratory demonstrations, what did religion have?

Religion had a good case of social embarrassment and spiritual constipation. Many of its ancient doctrines were no longer believed—with good reason—by anyone with sense. Religion had not cleared up its own house, and science huffed and puffed and nearly blew away the whole straw structure.

Any religion is a devotional umbrella of beliefs, attitudes, and habits, collected from many sources that together form a protective and thematic framework. Some of the various elements that compose it would not, alone or taken separately, seem to fall within religion's domain at all. Religions often collect bits of history, science, psychology, take them out of context and use them to strengthen other, older beliefs that have seen their day—beliefs that have left thematic holes which might weaken the structure enough to permit a raining deluge of opposing beliefs.

A given religion might have as its center post reliance upon history, the Bible, a given prophet, or a basic philosophy not originally religious in conventional terms. Its center post might be science or pseudoscience, predestination, salvation, or any of an endless number of other hypotheses. From this center, there will be revolving spokes, each connected to the center post, and each in some way dependent upon it.

While the new democracy professed to have no official religion, its main post was Christianity, with Protestantism as the handle. Democracy and Protestantism both expressed beliefs in the rights and abilities of the individual. Self-reliance, spiritual and social betterment, the importance of good works—these were all supporting ribs in a sturdy thematic framework that was large enough to include many variations.

Americans, whatever their formal religious persuasions, held to the center post firmly, espousing the rights and abilities of the individual citizen. Freudianism weakened this center post by undermining the basic integrity of the private person, upon which the entire framework hung. Religion could have quickly reinforced itself by· reviving the importance of the soul; by stressing its own subjective base; and by trying to re-examine and redefine the soul in the light of new knowledge. It could have dropped its ancient insistence upon blind faith unsupported by any kind of reason; stood its ground against Freudianism while accepting from psychology the invitation to explore the nature of man with an open mind.

Instead, the umbrella split. The intellectuals decided to risk the storm without religion's protection. Science and

religion became like two soaking pedestrians, out on the
street in a rain storm, each with half an umbrella and each
pretending to be entirely dry.

Fundamental religions were left with a shaggy half—
the spokes of the soul, stuck through the weakened dogmatic
fabric—wobbling in a base of blind faith that had lost its
center post. For both sides dispensed with the basic belief in
man's innate goodness or in the potential for heroic action of
a moral nature. Each believed that controls must be applied,
and neither the fundamentalists' sinning self nor the
Freudianists' savage instinctive self could be allowed
freedom. Yet to achieve that freedom was a national goal, an
idealistic crusade to which the country was committed before
the world.

The dilemma was basic, and the solution was to transfer
salvation from a religious to an economic and social arena—
where at least the results of grace could be judged—and to
depend upon technology to instill fear in men's hearts, since
fear of God no longer offered any protection. In a way, your
arms race and destructive nuclear devices became necessary
once man believed that he belonged to a species that killed to
survive; for in that context, no person or country could be
trusted to comply with civilization's niceties without the
initiative of fear.

It is to religion's shame that it earlier allowed the
concept of the sinful self to supersede that of the heroic soul,
for in the past religion at least provided psychological
devices by which the common man *could* ally himself with
his own good intents, but Freudianism, with its savage
unconscious, never provided an adequate hope of personal
salvation. There was no hope: God was abandoned. Man had
outgrown him. He was at best a symbol of the only-too-
fallible human father. And how could the common man rely
upon a self whose very instincts now lacked the natural grace
of the animals, while retaining an overly exaggerated
beastliness, projected as man's own?

The natural world was also seen in a new light.
Religion had insisted upon man's superiority over the
animals, but even then it professed to put man in the
position of gentle guardian to them. When evolutionary and
Freudian concepts ganged up on the natural world, however,

then the environment and all of its living details became fair game; and this at a time when technology was turning man away from his natural and practical relationship with animals and the land.

The early naturalism (and romanticism) of my century quickly began to vanish. Yet the very soul of the land lingered and would not die. Its virgin nature broodingly was reflected in the paintings of artists, both American and visiting Europeans, and that resplendent beauty reproached literate and illiterate alike; as if its stubborn presence remained to contradict that dark and curious, cunning mixture of European psychology and Protestantism that had sprouted so threateningly upon American soil.

Friday morning
February 11, 1977

Yet those who came here came because of a determination and a hope—a faith if not in God or man, at least in circumstances—a belief in a land of historic innocence, where one city was not built upon a counterpart whose past reached back to the time of Rome; a land not already peopled with ghosts. Those who came here, despite their mistakes and despite the ghosts they brought with them, worked heroically with what they had and formed a society that has never fulfilled its ideals because its dreams were so daring in the face of beliefs and theories that undermined the very self-reliance they hoped so to foster.

In any relatively open society where resourcefulness and vigor are prerequisites, women emerge as men's equal partners, yet Freudian concepts weakened the independence won by American pioneer women by reinforcing the male's privileged position, a position justified by Protestantism as well. The qualities that helped win the West—self-reliance, resourcefulness, courage—were in retrospect seen as masculine. Their very presence in a woman now cast an aspersion upon her femininity.

To make matters worse, the qualities that *had* been long admired in women were now held up in scorn. Those characteristics, generally in the intuitive areas of sympathy and sentiment at which women had excelled because no other avenues of expression were open to them—these were now looked upon as inferior hysteric tendencies.

Freudianism could not tolerate the intuitive abilities for they could not be relied upon, crusted over in its eyes as they were by libidinal lusts. And in America, such qualities had no place in the factories where they would prove only disorderly and disruptive.

I considered myself a man of science—an *American* scientist—yet I wanted to probe into the mind of man, into the experience and behavior of the individual, in order to find evidence of the elusive soul; not only to lessen man's fear of death, but to discover within the ordinary person those heroic abilities that *could* make democracy work. I strove to uncover in the common man those uncommon characteristics, those dynamics of the soul, that would demonstrate the individual's ability to rule himself by a divine right granted to each citizen, rather than to a crown prince or dictator. In a way, I suppose that I tried to substitute the kingliness of the individual for the royalty of European governments. In that, of course, I was overly romantic.

Hence my difficulties, which in *their* way mirrored the psychic situations of other men of intelligent pretensions beside myself. We kept leaning toward peculiarly innocent American thinkers, Emerson and Whitman for example, for their works contained American aspirations and no other. Yet we were also led back to the "realities of the day"—the misuse of industry, the galloping economics, and the disillusionment with the nature of man himself. More and more we encountered the pessimistic and fatalistic theories that were beginning, more strongly, to emerge.

It has been said that Freud at least opened the subject of the inner self to scientific inquiry, banished religion's overly stern and dogmatic insistence upon guilt by placing it in the personal subconscious (the child's distorted understanding of libidinal events), and pointed out the disastrous effects of early conditioning. Indeed, I have no quarrel with the man. His triumph was that he perceived his own nature and, to some extent, that of his Germanic contemporaries—and that required the utmost daring.

But theoretically at least, had he gone further Freud

would have begun to perceive those fountainheads of creativity that his own obsessions hid from him so well; and he might have understood that his own theories were intuitive constructs, not intellectual deductions, and that they were meant to lead him elsewhere had he not stifled the process, formalizing what was only the beginning of a long search. Jung, it is true, followed through to some extent, yet he was also tinged by Freudian concepts to such a degree— and so dominated by the man, Freud, and the ensuing relationship—that even at the last he could not free himself sufficiently to make the leaps required.

At a time when men were indeed trying to shake off the shackles of religion's meanest beliefs, Freud in the name of science gave them a new and dangerous foundation. Many intellectuals threw aside the idea of the soul along with the wishy-washy Christian heaven and Dantean hell. In return they found themselves bound by a self capable of the cruelest savagery, but incapable of the slightest deeds of heroic behavior; denied access to the soul through whose dictates man might right himself—and equipped instead with instinctive passions and self-deceptions that no man alone could hope to understand.

How could such a creature be self-governing, or dare to experiment with a society in which no autocratic class ruled and maintained order, out of a self-interest that at least maintained stability? The ingenious answer was the attempt to turn each man into a landowner, or at least a house owner, so that his own greed would be controlled, his needs satisfied, the animal savagery within him lulled. That was the shouted ideal. It became obvious that even with equal opportunity, men were unequal in certain quite practical respects. Some would fight their way to the top, true to their "evolutionary destiny," and others would fall by the wayside. So how was man equal? Equal to what? And how were the rights of the individual to be protected in the struggle for survival in which only the "superior" would be victors?

The answers were not available. Adjustments were made and remade but no solutions to the basic problem were found, though they did indeed exist, lying latent in Myers's work—and perhaps even in my own, though in my own works the answers were so obscured that even I only glimpsed them when I read between my own lines.

For each person is equal to every other only when we recognize within each person the presence of an inviolate, eminently precious force of identity and meaning that possesses its own innate dignity. This dignity exists beyond our ideas of superiority or inferiority at any time in history, and the spirit within the individual is equal in all degrees to the spirit within each other person. A sane and benevolent society is one that will give that inner potential equal opportunity to fulfill itself according to its own directions and intent. That inner spirit must be understood, therefore, to be of good intent. The individual may not always act in a beneficial manner but the intent of the basic self must be perceived as good, rather than evil or neutral. Freudianism even more drastically than many religions, robbed man of the self's good intent.

Some of us, embarrassed but concerned, continued our work in the face of growing disillusionment: to seek for the good intent in man, to search for the qualities of the soul, to bring the soul into scientific respectability by seeking proof for its existence through using science's own tools of objectivism, and to isolate predictably those characteristics that might show even to the most skeptical the correctness of our hypothesis.

We were careful to point out that we considered such a soul as hypothetical, not labeling it as a belief, and we particularly sought proof for extrasensory perception that would place consciousness in a context that lifted it above the instinctive impulses alone. If the inner self could transcend the rules of reality hailed so proudly by the scientific community, then surely, we reasoned, scientists must be impressed with the powers of the self and would have to grant within the mechanism of man some greater mechanism, some spiritual machinery that would lure them out of their isolationism.

In this search we received little help from the established churches or the sciences and so, rather uncomfortably, we found ourselves trying to maintain our professionalism, our scientific credentials, while at the same time exploring avenues of unconventional thought that we feared might turn us further away from the mainstream of American life. I, at least, persevered in that regard, forcing upon my colleagues dissertations whether they wished to hear them or not, stiffening my professional attitude to its sena-torial limits, and becoming almost as stuffy in my demeanor as I hoped I was free and open in my thoughts. But in such a way I guaranteed that my thoughts were heard.

Yet the country endured. American optimism managed to make giant leaps over even the darkest of theories. The new country would triumph over man's unsavory nature itself, win out over the species' twisted roots, and if domination over the suspicious areas of the self was impossible, domination over the land was not. The country was physically rich. It could be mined. It could support a population. Each man could have enough for his wants, and therefore have little reason to rob his neighbor.

Ideals always have to be considered in the light of their practicality. Freudianism and the bleaker aspects of Puri-tanism merged to give Americans a true inferiority complex on the one hand and, on the other, a compensating determination to succeed as a nation.

• • •

(The subject material of this chapter surprised me quite a bit in the beginning, since I've had no particular interest in nineteenth-century American thought, particularly as it applies to democracy. James's discussion of the soul in reference to the American democracy was brilliant, I thought, and it made me think of the private person's concept of the self in relationship to the community; something I'd never explored before.

(Besides that, I have to admit that I found these nationalistic attitudes rather amusing. If there's anything like an American soul [as opposed to a French or Chinese one, for example] then James has one. Yet as he continues with other discussions of science and religion from an American standpoint, and "says his piece," James moves into realms of thought so vast that all ideas of nationality disappear in visions of "another world" in which all earthly experiences have their source.

(I haven't wanted to intrude in James's manuscript except to add notes I felt were really pertinent, because the book has its own flow. Now and then, though, check the dates of entries and you'll catch sight of that inner rhythm with which the material itself was delivered.)

# 4.What Does Truth Mean?
## Science and Religion

Wednesday morning
February 16, 1977

The animals do not have governments, possibly because they do not have possessions as men do, or tools to defend them with. In nature the animal is his own possession, and his body is at once his life and his tool for protecting it. Men consider possessions to be extensions of themselves, so that no possession is neutral but a symbol of its owner, and so strongly has this principle been embraced that property is often treated according to law as being of equal value to life itself.

Governments are based upon man's attitudes toward three main issues: his concept of the individual, the value of his life, and the value of his property. While official religion can be separated from the seat of government, man's ideas and beliefs about his mind and soul cannot. Physically a country is the "joint property" of its people, at least in legal and political terms.

Dictums such as "the survival of the fittest" or "might is right" emphasize the most obvious instances of seeming inequality among men, justify the fiercest competition in all areas of private and public life and between nations, and visualize government as the natural human extension of nature's own "cruel" weeding-out processes as perceived through evolutionary dogma. Signs of animal cooperation and biological graciousness are ignored or minimized; yet whenever man downgrades the animals or the gods, he minimizes the dimensions of his own consciousness, since his existence lies so obviously between the thematic structure of those seeming opposites.

78

In past centuries, man's relationship with the animals involved him in a practical give-and-take with other species. Man and animals worked the land together, and the daily life of man was intimately connected with that of other creatures. Now, in your time, such a rift has developed that to the urban populations in industrial areas of the world, animals become absent, almost theoretical species; as removed from the land and daily life as the hypothetical existence of the gods. Other species lose their practical immediacy, then, and become subjects of hypothetical and theoretical discussions. They become "less real" to man. Their existence may be scientifically investigated, their habits explored and their haunts exposed, but this kind of objective investigation itself destroys the sense of basic interrelationship among the species.

Such an approach results in the gaining of information but the loss of knowledge, the accumulation of particular details and the diminution of the overall living picture in which the specific conditions exist. If man does not relate emotionally to the natural world and its creatures, then his information concerning them becomes anti-information in that while it provides facts, it also evolves a framework in which those facts become ultimately valueless. It is no coincidence that the theories of evolution emerged to full flower just as man began to lose his emotional rapport with other species and began replacing it with the objective accumulation of facts; when, in other words, he began to examine animals as if they were primarily objects.

I was a great proponent of scientific investigation, and advocated the freeing of man's imagination and curiosity from the old religious and superstitious dictates of the past. I thought that science could explore mind and matter, soul and body, emotions and intellect. Instead it chose to deny what it could not explain, dismissing mind, soul, and the emotions not only as subjects of inquiry, but as realities in themselves. They were considered as inexplicable by-products in the struggle for survival, or as imaginative posturings or mental pretensions; yet those same subjective phenomena are what distinguish man as a species, and therefore should have been science's concern.

Wednesday afternoon
February 16, 1977

Freudian psychology and evolutionism were not sciences as
such, for that matter, with the possibility of provable results
in a series of experiments, but a group of hypotheses that
basically could not be proven. Nor did Freud's psychoanalysis produce a body of case histories in which cures could be
definitely shown to result from Freudian techniques. Neither
can man prove the nonexistence of the soul, yet science
treated the soul *as if* it had been proven to be nonexistent.

I hoped to prove the opposite, by looking into man's
experience for hints of an overriding ability not dependent
upon the senses or other physical mechanisms alone; or for
an overperception that operated in spite of the sense's
seeming confinement to the immediate environment. I was
personally convinced that such a hypothesis came closest to
the truth about man's position. Again, as a scientist,
however, I was careful to distinguish between belief and
hypothesis, though many of my colleagues on the opposite
side of the fence were not so scrupulous.

Even now, having been a scientist to the best of my
ability, I hesitate to offer my own subjective continuing
reality after death as any kind of objective proof of survival,
in your world's terms. Indeed, I shall not do so, but will rely
instead upon those arguments, persuasions, and methods
with which you are familiar—only honed to such a degree
that their vigor alone, I hope, will express the soul's valor
and give evidence of its heroic nature.

That is, I hope to show the heroic and extradimensional
characteristics of human creativity; to demonstrate that
evidence of these is available in physical life; and to suggest
that it is at least possible to project these as existing apart
from the physical organism. Moreover, perhaps in an excess
of enthusiasm on my part and an overestimation of my
reader's concern, I hope at least to state the case for an
alternate hypothesis for science to follow.

It is not new and has been held to one extent or another
throughout the ages, though clothed in superstition and
misunderstandings and held static by bonds of dissension. It
is a hypothesis based on the existence of a nonphysical soul

or entity that provides inner direction, that emerges into time and space and exits; and on the projection of this soul or entity as being within all species to whatever extent, directing the overlife of the planet; and with cooperation rather than competition as the basic dictum.

To me it seems now obvious that the newness ever entering the world is proof of an inner source existing beyond all known biological mechanisms or organic organizations, and that the orderliness of organisms' intricate forms makes their accidental creation a logical contradiction. Yet in life, out of a misguided sense of duty to science, I seriously considered the possibility of a chance creation, thus wasting a good deal of effort on an absurdity.

Yet that very absurdity speaks of the creative abilities of the men who conceived it, and it is through those abilities that I believe a kind of evidence can be presented for the survival of man's consciousness beyond death. Those creative abilities must be exercised, however, and Freudian and evolutionary theories have to some extent blinded men to their own capabilities and limited the extent to which the living consciousness itself can perceive the greater reality in which it exists. That vaster reality does not simply spring into being at death. It is the medium in which life happens: living momentarily supersedes it, even while subsisting in its source.

The everyday world is the one in which living men have their experiences, and of course it is science's province to explore that world, make it more comprehensible and predictable. Yet the thoughts scientists hold about physical reality are themselves nonphysical. They cannot be piled like stones on a laboratory table, and even to the scientist his thoughts must appear transparent and lacking all of those qualities of solidarity that otherwise exist in the phenomenal world.

The same, of course, applies to the scientist's dreams. No matter how vividly in sleep he perceives the images of friend, lover, dog, ocean, or mountain, these images nowhere exist as solid either in his head, or in the bedroom in which he rests, or in any of the classified realms covered by his waking investigations. Yet the scientist, like any man, responds, and if he is honest with himself he recognizes how subtly yet surely these dream images affect his waking life.

Physical creature or not, man is everywhere in his subjective experience reminded of a nonphysical reality that ever impinges into the most intimate portions of his physically oriented life. The objects of his perception *should* be categorized, arranged in predictable patterns when possible—a worthy pursuit on science's part—yet those objects cannot be honestly considered without an equal investigation into the nonphysical properties of mind that give the objects their appearance of solidity.

For while the physical world is operationally predictable (and then, only generally speaking), that predictability is operative only when inner components of the mind act upon physical properties in a certain very precise fashion. The physical world must be "turned on." Only then does it appear with its predictable elements. Only then do objects have reality, flowers grow, seas turn with their tides, and the splendid sun's heat warms the land.

So far, science has only examined results. By its insistence upon the priority and superiority of matter's dominance, it ties its own hands. The very focus of its beliefs leads it toward an endless categorizing in which it follows minute particles into a deepening invisibility. The hypothetical discovery of each new minuscule particle exerts an ever-deepening hypnotic effect, leading the scientist down a road that is self-defeating if he hopes to delve into those phenomena that exist beneath the world's operating reality.

The mind, so entranced by these matters, so led astray, itself possesses the abilities to perceive the inner structure of life, but in a different fashion. The old methods of measurement do not apply to a nonphysical reality; yet the mind has its own values, its own methods and measurements, and the mind's very existence is its own evidence. To that evidence, science remains blind.

The scientist often says impatiently, "I deal with the true or false world. A phenomenon exists or it doesn't. An object is, or isn't. I deal with provable facts." This attitude alone shuts out from science's province the very unpredictability, the very creativity from which the predictable world emerges.

Modern science rightly rebelled against the excesses,

exaggerations, and superstitions of religion and against a rigid system of beliefs that encouraged man to interpret the natural world only in the light of its own dogmas. Yet science went overboard to prove itself, adopting many of those authoritative characteristics and denying the existence of any phenomenon that is not observable according to its own set of limited measurements, or that does not agree with its basic theories.

In whatever erroneous a fashion, however, religion did attempt to categorize inner realities, for it numbered its "species" with as much vigor and self-righteousness and determination as any scientist pinpointing the number and kinds of rocks, birds, gases, or particles. The demons, minor gods, mythological creatures, hells and heavens were all in their way the results of this same kind of specification, misapplied; for in the inner reality, such methods are ludicrous.

Both religion and science seek "truth," but the literal interpretation of physical reality is as limiting as the literal interpretation of the Bible. There are fundamentalist scientists quibbling over whether the universe is forever expanding, or is endlessly expanding and contracting—and that is as much an exercise in futility as medievals debating how many angels can sit on the top of a pin. The attitudes of mind, the childish literal interpretations are the same; equally absurd, if the greater issue of truth is to be involved.

The very definitions of truth are at fault.

Science and psychology owe their birth to religion's failure in conducting that search [for truth]. They are split-offs from religion, each with their own methods, yet they have to a large extent converged. For all of psychology's stated interest in man's subjective nature—held while still maintaining its basic objective stance—psychology is depending more and more upon technology and scientific instruments to measure the mind's products and behavior; a new futility also perpetuated because of limited concepts and misunderstandings concerning the pursuit of truth itself.

For what does truth mean? In scientific terms, it means a provable fact such as "Today is Wednesday" or "An apple is a fruit." These facts are operational; one categorizes time, and the other, an object. Neither tells us anything about time or objects, however. In *fact*, the belief that today, Wednesday, is followed by Thursday, while operationally true, also leads to drastic misconceptions about the nature of time itself, couching it in the consecutive terms of everyday experience. This discrepancy goes quite unnoticed when you meet a friend for a Wednesday appointment, and the convenient use of time is to be maintained in any orderly physical world.

Scientists know, however, that time is relative, and if the dictum "Time is relative" is a fact or truth, then is the fact of consecutive time true or false? If false, then no day is Wednesday, whether the statement is operationally true or not. For that matter, Wednesday does not exist in the same way that our apple does. In that regard, the statement that an apple is a fruit is the "truer" of the two statements. But even the apple's fruitness tells us nothing of the origin of fruits, or explains how the apple has fruit rather than animal characteristics; and no matter how far you go with this kind of truth finding, you will ultimately be led to a point where one fact contradicts another, or another framework of facts, or where you simply run into ignorance—a point of no answers.

The reason is astonishingly simple. The overemphasis upon categorization leads to an infinitely larger and ever-increasing number of facts, each considered true; and with this multiplication, the discrepancies collected along the way also multiply. You end up with various disciplines, each with their fact-truths, and under examination the facts of one discipline too often do not apply to those of another field—a "fact" that those in all disciplines often conveniently overlook.

Within any one school of knowledge these discrepancies are invisible, and overall people operate in a fairly predictable environment regardless, eating delicious apples and secure in the knowledge that each Wednesday is followed by a Thursday. It would serve no purpose, either, to say that apples are not fruits; a statement that is false if you accept the apple's fruitness. But the truth or falsehood of such statements are beside the point of basic truth, which should deal with the innate nature of time or with the innate nature of objects rather than with their specifics. Under what conditions is an apple a fruit or a chair a chair? Under what conditions do we experience time as Wednesday, or as a series of consecutive moments, and under what conditions might time behave elsewise? Do any of these phenomena exist independently of our perception of them?

How is it that dream objects mock physical objects so well, even satisfying all of our senses during the experience, while nowhere appearing in time or space? We may be involved in the most ecstatic or horrifying dream experience, our bodies thrashing in our bedclothes or immersed in the sweetest relaxation; we may be responding to perceived snakes or angels, or even participating in battle. Yet in life we assign more reality to the bedside clock than we do to the dream experiences that seize our emotions, excite us to a frenzy, or fill us with profound peace or dismay.

In waking life the same applies. Scientists assign reality to the objects of their experiments and to the technological tools they use, yet none to the mind with its thoughts—the same mind that assembled the tools from realms of the imagination that nowhere appeared in given fact terms. It is for this reason that the inner dimensions of events appear so obscure. The psychological thickness invested by the mind in phenomena is completely ignored, for in science's realm only the brain is granted reality.


Thursday afternoon
February 17, 1977

Religion finally failed as an organized belief system by which to judge and structure practical experience. Let science beware of falling into the same trap. Science is twice vulnerable, in that some of its less fortunate results threaten men with a physical destruction far more immediate than religion's threat of an afterlife hell. Moreover, a possible holocaust in which the entire world is destroyed by the hand of God is one thing to the common man: the same destruction brought down unnecessarily upon man's head by the misuse of science is quite another. The common man will undermine science in the most insidious ways before he will permit it to destroy the world it is supposed to be exploring.

Science is uneasy with the human personality and ignorant of basic motivations. While science produces, the common man will sit back for the expenditure of almost endless funds for scientific purposes. But let him decide that science has served *its* purposes, let him be convinced that science serves only science and is willing to sacrifice even planetary life to satisfy bloated, neurotic appetites, and the common man will close off funds, foundations, and grants with unbelievable rapidity; and science will survive as religion has—splintered, robbed of its fury, thunder, and effectiveness.

The fallibility of science, as practiced, becomes increasingly obvious and does immeasurable disservice to science, which should investigate all expressions of life and consciousness equally and open-mindedly, including men's values, ascertaining which of them add to the quality of life and which do not. Science cannot afford to invent weapons of incalculable degree while divorcing itself from the study of moral values or the rights of consciousness.

Friday morning
February 18, 1977

(Actually, I got the following material Thursday night, while watching television. Suddenly the sentences just began to come, very quickly, so I scribbled them down and typed them on Friday morning.)

Faith does not fall within the realm of science. Yet faith in God or man or nature is imperative, or all of the facts of science are meaningless, collected paraphernalia; the categorizing of chaotic chaffs of chance, without dignity; a kind of obsessive blind numbering of events within a universe in which events themselves—men and animals alike—are playthings of a mechanical process, without intent.

Man can suffer even tragedy better, believing in the malevolent intent of a capricious fate, than he can bear happiness in a universe without meaning, stripped of all of the heroic elements that are a part of his psychological heritage. He can at least grit his teeth and show contempt for fate if he believes that it controls his life; but a meaningless

universe leaves him no retort. Those systems of belief that
nourish such nonsense find themselves in an impossible
dilemma and ultimately defeat themselves, for those who
follow such hypotheses find no reason to continue living.
Inertia overcomes them. The theories are not life-giving.
They lack strength and so die out.

It is more than possible, however, that the "meaning of
the universe" cannot appear within the measurements of
logic alone, and that the very mental techniques used in
logical thought—the categorizing, the precision and separating, the searching for cause and effect—may themselves
break up an overlying unity in which that meaning might
otherwise make itself known.

You can study the techniques used in any painting,
musical composition, poem, or other creative work, understand perfectly how certain strokes or vowels or notes add up
to specific effects, and yet be ignorant of the "meaning"
within the entire work of art itself. The artist in any field
uses the <u>techniques</u> of art, yet puts them together in a
completely different fashion than a technician, say, combines the components of an electronic tube.

The preciseness and predictability that work for
technology and the productions of practical industry are the
results of a remarkable specialization: the analytical powers
of the mind honed and tuned toward "results that work." I
do not mean to diminish the importance of such attitudes or
methods in any way. Those same methods, however, do not
give results, say, in terms of art, but produce only the dreary
renderings of robots or finger paintings.

For in art, the elements of surprise and unpredictability
reign—within a certain framework, however. Techniques
are used, mediums and supplies, but they are used in a
completely different mental and emotional context, in which
art's meaning is often nowhere specifically apparent but felt
and emotionally perceived. Indeed, the senses are appealed to
in a different fashion. This is a highly important point, so
here I would like to briefly compare the universe to a model
of a multidimensional work of art, rather than, say, to a
mechanical machine whose components, examined, will
inevitably yield an understanding of its parts and overall
purpose.

If we use this analogy, however—comparing the universe to a work of art—we must also say that it is a work of art in progress, for changes occur in it constantly. We must further ascribe to this art a multisense appeal, granting it an aesthetic plan beyond any utilized by a human artist. The composition includes all the elements of reality as we know them. The grasses are not just described in words as they might be in literature; or painted; or evoked through musical notes; but they combine the techniques of all the arts and go beyond them. The grasses appeal to all of our senses; their color is not just painted on but ever rushing into their tender tips; ever changing hue and value while staying within color of a certain order. While alive, we are within this creative production ourselves, of course, and all of the categorizing in the world will not reveal its meaning.

• • •

(I finished typing the above material from my notes of the evening before, and then decided to do the dishes. I'd no sooner turned on the water when the following material came, so quickly that I was quite startled. I was staring out of the kitchen window at the trees, which were bare and gray, my mind on nothing in particular, one hand beneath the faucet, testing the water's heat. The material came almost swirling, in circular patterns, as the Seth material sometimes does. I rushed back to the typewriter, forgetting the dishes, and typed the following. Not until I read it later did I see that the way the material came illustrated just what James was talking about. I could feel his "different framework" just beyond the usual constructions of my mind.)

• • •

A different framework of thought itself is required, [one] that is similar to the creative processes. For there are different kinds of "logic." If building a radio component is your goal, then objective thought is scientific and produces results. If creating a poem or a sonata is your intent, then this other kind of intuitive thinking is equally valid and equally scientific, leading to results just as surely. Here, unpredictability can almost be considered a predictable working method.

The "meaning of the universe" may exist in this other framework, remaining invisible to the usual kind of scrutiny and actually becoming less apparent the more it is examined in a conventionally scientific, objective manner.

The same applies to the individual person within that universe. No information, however extensive, pertaining to the body or the brain, will result in an answer to the question, "What is the meaning of a person?" Not only that, but the methods of investigation—the naming and counting of separate components and the tracing of circuits—may make the information itself so misleading as to turn it into anti-information, as defined earlier: data yielding results that diminish knowledge.

I am not implying that such understanding is beyond man's comprehension, only that it is beyond the methods mistakenly used to achieve it; and I am suggesting that there are at least two contexts in which perception and knowledge happen.


Friday afternoon
February 18, 1977

Thinking of man or the universe as a machine and using this as a model presupposes certain hypotheses, regardless of how far we extend the machine's abilities. But most of all, we do not instill the powers of true spontaneity, basic creativity, or unpredictability into such a model. We do not see, using straight objective thought, *how* a creative intuition can come seemingly from nowhere; so we can hardly understand a universe springing out of nowhere, in "each moment," at each "point" of its reality.

Instead, we limit our model to one familiar to objective thought and also limit our hopes of comprehension, because such a model is in its way the result of schizophrenic behavior: it is a model produced by only one half of the brain, a one-sided model, as much limited as vision is when only one eye is used. We lose a depth perception that makes all the difference. In a manner of speaking, religion uses the other eye or side of the brain more than science does. In its determination to relate to the everyday world, however, religion made the same fatal mistake in its realm that science makes: it tried to turn creative truth into literal fact.

Again, its endless catalogues of demons, fallen angels, levels of spiritual worlds, gods and lords of the universe are often ludicrous attempts to enforce a particular kind of order over inner realities so as to correlate them with the world of facts. Hence fundamentalist religion's insistence upon literal interpretation of the Biblical creation of the world—and so a battle between science and religion on a matter in which both eventually will be losers.

The literal interpretation of the Bible's rendition of events, and science's insistence upon Darwinian facts are alike beside the point. Darwin's considerable achievement in perceiving the interrelationship of creature, species, and environment was entirely misinterpreted. His cataloguing of effects led him to perceive only competitiveness, and made him blind to the basic cooperative ventures existing between species, and between creatures and their environment. The same set of "facts" could have been read quite differently.

Darwin himself felt the conflicts: he believed in them, projected them upon his own work, and was tortured by a misconception about his own contribution. He personified the various species with the most regrettable of human characteristics, seeing murder and conflict instead of the inner balances worked out by the various species themselves. For other kinds of consciousness may well be as individually tuned as ours, but also able to leapfrog their own apparent death in a series of biological computations that completely escape us, particularly when we behold nature through the one part of our minds that is least intuitive, least willing to leave the ideological home of objectivity.

Darwin's work took for granted a certain hypothesis about consciousness that, scientifically, we have no right to take as fact. While denying animals a dignified consciousness of any variety at all, he still projected upon them man's worst tendencies. It was man's sense of the survival of the fittest that was projected upon the natural world, and not the other way around.

There is no reason why the existence of the soul cannot be a scientific hypothesis, but science itself must learn how ridiculous it is for the scientist to ignore his own nature—his emotional and subjective reality—through whose framework he perceives the natural world. Ideally, each scientist should become involved with an art; and each artist, with a science. In that way the intuitive and objective qualities would be merged, their separate abilities deepened, each one developing through its alliance with the other.

Friday evening
February 18, 1977

If science does not enlarge its thematic and theoretical frameworks, young scientists will drop out, as in your time, priests are [doing], and for the same reason: they sense that their training is dangerously lopsided. Taught to over-objectify, however, these scientists, often overcompensate and become antiscience and antitechnology in their attitudes, advocating instead an equally exaggerated overemphasis upon "faith without reason."

They are tired of academic competition and weary of protecting the ego against the onslaughts of Freud's subconscious instinctive drives. They want nothing so much as peace of mind, and so, often they fall prey to theologies or systems that dismiss individualism and desire, offering a distorted concept of cosmic consciousness instead. All such a person must do is let go the emblems of his specieshood—the emotions, intellect, and the illusion of individuality.

Such psychological policies contradict, of course, the basic concepts of political democracy. To many such people, not only is competition wrong, but work itself loses its value. Thusly, one exaggerated hypothesis leads to its opposite.

There are, however, two main ways of relating to the phenomenal world; each quite natural to man, spiritually and biologically. One has generally been dominant since the birth of history: we react to events and to the environment using logical thought to interpret a reality that is understood to exist "out there" regardless of our perception of it. Thusly, an apple is an apple whether or not we see it or eat it. A road is a road whether or not we ever walk or drive upon it.

The other approach, never to my knowledge *fully* followed, involves an identification with nature and events. Here we have the belief that thoughts and emotions not only have a direct effect upon matter, but direct events in some invisible or automatic fashion—a fashion that can be deduced, however, through trial and error. Using this method, man spies out and explores nature's inner workings by projecting his consciousness into it, not by examining it from the outside.

This second method, I believe, is closely allied with natural creative functioning as it is displayed through the constant creation of cells in the body; and mentally apparent in the thought processes themselves and in the formation of the arts. This method is also active and involves the creative formation of events through a focusing of natural forces, with an intent or specific purpose in mind. The follower of such beliefs takes it for granted that these forces act spontaneously in ways that escape his knowing, as the writer takes it for granted that his conscious intent will evoke the creative processes which operate beneath his conscious knowledge, and thus result in a creative product.

Since certain events are more probable than others in the phenomenal world, it is possible that such mental identification and focusing of intent is responsible for the experience of one specific event rather than another probable one. This mental and emotional force in man and nature, meeting, may represent the hidden "depth perception" science lacks in its own investigations.

In my time, however, Darwinian and Freudian theories began to predominate, yet the nation held with almost equal vigor those rousing concepts of individual liberty, those hopes of man's good intent, that faith in God, man, and country that was expressed, though often simplistically, in each corner of the land. An almost athletic optimism resulted, at least for a while, and the belief that the human will could prevail against all odds. The more prevalent the

Darwinian concepts became, the more they insinuated themselves into national thought; and the more insistent the nation's simple optimism became as it tried to counter the pessimistic trend.

When Freudian psychology merged with Darwinian ideology, but more importantly, when psychology allied itself with Freud rather than Myers, then the balance fell sharply away from optimism. None of the "Every day in every way, I'm getting better and better" schools could effectively counter the darker theories that swiftly seized all of the academies of both medicine and science.

Earlier, Protestantism and optimism merged with some uneasiness, but "God's in His heaven and all is right with the world" affirmations could not fit into the Darwinian survival theory. Briefly the citizen could combine the two. If he was fairly prosperous and healthy, then he could see himself as Darwin's pride of the species and Protestantism's man of good works—proof that God helps those who help themselves.

But this alliance could not hold, for the Darwinian man could not have a soul; his murderous instincts left no room for honest good works; and Freudian man had no effective will, only the instinctive subconscious that reached backward through Darwinian time to the animal's "savage" nature. Most unfortunately, psychology followed that path, taking science and medicine with it.

• • •

(As I was working on this chapter, more and more James material started to come while I was sketching and thought myself finished with writing for the day. Often also, I'd be typing up such material and have to stop because I'd begin getting new passages. I didn't want to interrupt James's script to note all such instances, or the many times that I'd suddenly "get James" while I was doing other things like house chores or reading.

(James also influenced my dreams in this period, oddly enough in connection with my ink sketches. Sometimes it was as if James preferred to have me take down his material on my small sketchpads, and at least in one instance he used a dream to connect one of my sketches to the material he'd given during the day. At the end of this book I'll discuss briefly what I think about such dream instances.

(On Sunday night, February 19, for instance, I dreamed that I was just finishing an ink sketch and was ready to brush it with water, as is my practice. I realized that I was dreaming, in bed, and that besides, there wasn't any water on the bedside table. So, cleverly, I decided to save the drawing until I awakened when the water would be available to finish it. Still in the dream state, I came to the disappointing conclusion that I couldn't do *that* either, and that drawings done while dreaming wouldn't be solid in the morning. As all of this went on in my dream mind, I was aware of James's presence: a kindly amusement and his appreciation of the dream sketch itself.

(The following night I again dreamed that I was doing an ink sketch, this time struggling to get it "just right." In the dream, behind me somewhere, James was commenting on the connections between sketching, creativity, and his model of the universe as a creative rather than mechanistic process. Again, he approved of my dream sketch.

(As I mentioned earlier, James's interest in my artwork surprised me, since there were no such instances as I received *The World View of Paul Cézanne*. During this same weekend another small but rather startling event happened involving my artwork. A fan sent me a bouquet of roses, and that Sunday I did an acrylic painting of it. When it was finished, I wasn't satisfied and sat staring at it dis-approvingly. Without any notice, mentally I "heard" James say, rather indulgently, "It's all *right*," with the emphasis on the last word, and again felt a kindly appreciation.

(It was during this period also that I finally located the Seth session included in my introduction to this book, and wondered if or how Seth knew about the James material months before the manuscript began.

(Mostly, James's "different framework" intrigued me, in which connections occur that escape our logical thought processes. That was the material I started to get as I stood by the sink ready to do the dishes, as noted earlier in this chapter. That moment captured my imagination so much

that I wrote the following poem, which in its own way
illustrates what James was talking about.)


I felt up to my elbows
in the work of the universe,
all without knowing
what I was doing,
as if fulfilling some purpose
beyond my own intent,
so that my most
unconscious act
fitted smoothly
into some universal event;
was part
of some giant gesture
in which the slightest motion
of my mind or heart
took unwitting part.

Isolation slid
off my shoulders.
My private breath
was such a public
portion of the universe,
that I felt it fill out sails
in ships skimming
the Mediterranean,
while I stood
continents away,
Alone and small
by my kitchen door.

# 5. Mind and Medicine

**Thursday morning**
**February 24, 1977**

No one can doubt that the body's mechanisms are practical; they work, yet the very treatment of the body as if it were a machine effectively separates the individual from his own body, his physical well-being from his own value judgments, and the body's workings from his own desires and intents. Man then seems to be the victim of diseases that sweep upon him for no reason. But no pill will cure the soul's melancholy, and to whatever extent the medical profession separates man from identification with and responsibility for his body, it deepens that melancholy, and the patient sinks down into philosophical chasms in which all hope seems lost.

In my time, at least, medicine had a one-to-one relationship with the patient who came, perhaps shaken and certainly anxious, to the physician's office. That office was often set aside only by a few closed doors from the physician's living quarters. Outside the lace-curtained windows, the family wash fluttered on the clothesline. The doctor's children, more often than not, could be heard giggling or running in the drafty hall between the office and living spaces, where they had been banished by their mother from the kitchen. The patient could relate to the doctor as another family man, whose own supper was even then cooking on the stove, the odors mixing with medicinal potions and sometimes superseding them in potency. The doctor's study, with its leather-bound volumes, solid desk, velvet hangings and footstools, was after all not that different from a burgher's or a professor's study, except in its particulars.

And in my time those particulars were relatively few: a stethoscope, thermometer, blood-pressure-testing device, some phenobarbital in liquid or pill form, bandages, iodine, cloves for dental problems, chloroform—but mostly, a listening ear and attentive manner, with more sophisticated instruments belonging to the surgeon, who was, indeed, the only specialist.

Croup and tuberculosis were the main complaints, the one caused by an infant's reaction to "parental distempers" and the other by a melancholy that affected the breathing mechanisms themselves. Simplistic diagnosis perhaps, yet the physician gave soothing potions for the one, along with stern lectures to the parents; and prescribed rest or a visit to the mountains for the other; and these "remedies" worked as well, if not better, than the more sophisticated techniques that later were adapted.

Maladies change with the tempers and beliefs of the times. Darwinian and Freudian theories altered the previous philosophies of medicine and changed patient's beliefs about themselves in relationship to disease; and in my time the contradictory schools of optimism and pessimism showed in the behavior of physician and patient alike. Man as the surviving animal was to be treated in a no-nonsense fashion: it was better to be portly than thin and spindly, which meant being overly sensitive to the world—tubercular—and to possess characteristics ascribed to women, artists, and other "temperamental folk" who could not cope as well in the world as others. As a result, parents stuffed their children with food, those parents lucky enough to have suitable means or employment. Chubby children were proof of one's own survival economically and the poor became a reproof to the democratic processes, examples of those who fell by the way in the battle of competitiveness, the weaker members of the species who could not quite keep up.

Unfortunately, the school I've termed the optimistic one didn't have time to mature before it was superseded, yet there were signs of maturity and development not followed, in which I myself took the highest interest. Psychic research was doubtlessly naïve in many respects, perhaps too studiously high-minded, yet had science and psychology used it as a meeting point, both would have prospered and prevented the philosophic rigidity that developed in both fields subsequently.

For while science and psychology each seemed to be moving ahead after my time, and while science particularly produced spectacular technological achievements, the philosophical motion was very limited. Nor did these fields use any logic in choosing those beliefs they decided to accept or reject. Science, of course, was forced to admit Einsteinian principles, but psychology acted as if Einstein's concepts had no relation to the greater environment in which each person has his being.

Myers's "subliminal self," for example, fits in quite well with Einsteinian physics, while the Freudian self is far too local a phenomenon, and the existence of precognition could also ride rather nicely along with Einstein's relative time. Psychology, however, ignored these very scientific theories that might have given a theoretical basis for the exploration of the soul, and settled instead upon the quite prosaic and deadening duty of fitting a Freudian ego with a Darwinian subconscious into an industrial society. In my time at least some scientifically oriented men were willing to investigate the existence of a soul, a task which even then took considerable daring. But afterward such attempts were discontinued, for who needs to investigate the reality of a fiction?

Except for the churches, then, the soul was not officially recognized, and the religions themselves, while giving the soul lip service, steadfastly refused to investigate its reality and labeled as heretics or demented anyone determined to do so. At least in my time, the telepath and clairvoyant, the medium and the dreamer were encouraged to speak up to the scientists; now they were silenced, their abilities seen as examples of the worst kind of emotional indulgence; the result of hysteria. The words "subconscious fraud" became labels of the sorriest duplicity, because the individual to whom they were applied was branded a liar by subconscious disposition, unable to see through his or her own fantasies.

More pertinent, however, nature was seen no longer as working for man or with him and his body, but as actively working against him. The individual was pitted in an unending battle for survival in the exterior world—against the land and his own fellows—and pitted in an even more horrendous battle against an instinctive subconscious that seemingly condemned him to act in certain contrary fashions because of psychological imprinting executed in childhood.

Diseases, now named and labeled more thoroughly than ever before, assumed their own aspects of minute demon-hood: the viruses and other elements in nature that seemed to exist for no other reason than to attack man's body; and the predisposition to illness itself resulting from events long buried by the mind, each triggering an unconscious response to which the individual was instantly vulnerable.

And the effects of self-predictive behavior made themselves known, for the habits of diseases changed to fit the theories. With the development of medical technology and with the treatment of the body as if it were a machine, man lost his sense of identification with his nature and his sense of having any control over his own health.

The medical sciences might pride themselves on the routing out of superstition, for illness was no longer seen as the punishment of an angered God upon a sinner. The sinner at least had the option of repentance and ultimate salvation, however, while the enlightened citizen was surrounded by a hostile natural environment and an alien inner physical one as well—a body swimming with malignant viruses that could at any time and with no reason rise up to attack his entire system, and a consciousness that followed the unknown, capricious dictates of a repressed subconscious run amok.

In the face of such new facts of life, such modern enlightened concepts, how naïve the idea of a well-intentioned subliminal self seemed, or even the idea of a body naturally equipped to promote health and possessing its own healing processes. For though the latter belief still lingered philosophically, it was effectively neutered, and certainly no one was going to rely upon it—not the physician, who related to his instruments more than he did to his patients, and not the patients, who learned to be more frightened of their own bodies than they were of the doctors.

Preventive medicine often has at its roots the pessimistic belief that the body will doubtlessly get any given disease unless it is inoculated against it, tricked into accepting a small rather than a critical bout of illness. Medicinal research is also done on the diseased. No one questions those who remain healthy, who do not visit the hospitals. No one looks for the secrets of the healthy or seeks to promote ways of making these generally known.

No one more than the physician is directly faced with life's incongruities. His training involves him in studies of the anatomy, in which cadavers must necessarily be used. His experience makes him an intimate of birth and death alike. Who else more closely sees life's contrasts: the bringing-to-life process of birth amid pain and agony; the body in all of its aspects, with its exquisite capacities for pain and pleasure alike; the final gasping of the last breath as the patient escapes all earthly ministrations?

Who is more familiar with man's estate, powers, and vulnerabilities? Or with man's lack of knowledge? For it is clichéd to speak of those patients who die despite excellent treatment and favorable prognosis, while others far more desperate live against all the rules of medical knowledge. Yet the doctor is a man of practicality most of all, one who is faced with the alarming examples of man's failure to understand himself or his body.

The healthy man has no need of the physician's services, so it is natural enough that the doctor is often of pessimistic temperament. He sees men at their worst, and so it seems to him that illness is and must be a constant in man's life.

Indeed, it seems almost foolhardy and dangerous to suggest otherwise, for who knows what disease might be incubating now even in the most healthy of persons? The idea of health becomes almost as fictional a quality as the existence of the soul; hardly any coincidence, for I believe that the same creative abilities that would give evidence of the soul are also those that would promote at least reasonable health throughout man's lifetime.

Lest this be regarded as the most Pollyannaish of statements, let me add a few embellishments. First, no statistics have been gathered in your time or mine on the numbers of the healthy, nor have any studies been conducted correlating the habits or beliefs of the healthy. Hospital and medical records, as mentioned earlier, necessarily deal with ill persons. Psychiatric studies are likewise formulated and carried out in the same prejudiced fashion.

The very suggestions meant by preventive medicine to

foster health promote fears, nervousness, and stress—
conditions that in themselves lead to disease. Teaching the
individual to look *for* symptoms utilizes suggestion in a way
that leads to the anticipation of illness. Yet the anticipation
of health seems unrealistic, dangerously optimistic, and
misleading.

Even in my time, however, the study of hypnosis clearly
showed the importance of suggestion, and emphasized the
intimate connections between suggestion, behavior, and
health. Medicine, never officially utilizing hypnosis, uses it
well—and often in the most negative manner. Such phrases
as "the importance and mystery of magnetism" were spoken
often in my generation, turning many otherwise open-
minded men away from solid research in the field. Granted,
the proponents and early practitioners of hypnosis often
overdramatized their cases, claiming not only cures but
miracles, yet the substantial work done by respected men
proved beyond a doubt two main points:

1. The existence of a power within man, latent but
appreciable, to better his own condition, right his course,
heal his body, accelerate learning and insight, and

2. the susceptibility of this power to suggestion.

This power or energy, then, can be awakened and
harnessed through suggestion, either through structured
hypnosis or sometimes by the person himself through a kind
of spontaneous self-suggestion. Hypnosis can be induced
through relaxation techniques or through the use of
startling sudden stimulation. Hence, no doubt, the confusion of early practitioners, the reliance upon theatrical
gestures, bizarre techniques, and the resulting comedy of
errors in which this natural power was supposed to reside in
the hypnotist alone, rather than in his subjects as well.

So it is hardly surprising that such forerunners in the
field were themselves dramatically inclined, full of energy
and vitality and given to eccentricities of manner. Yet,
perhaps in a democracy most of all, it is the eccentrics who
often point out in theatrical fashion the road to creative
inventions and frameworks of thought that other, less bold
men will use studiously for years to come.

The great men and women are not necessarily the most
well-balanced. They will not fit into psychology's norms,
and in life I seriously questioned the advantages of the well-

balanced schools of thought. For no individual is like any other, and it is precisely in those peculiarities of expression or original casts of mind that our individuality is most apparent. The democracy should be large enough to contain and foster such differences, where the nation can benefit from a pool of individual, eccentric, unalike talents and abilities that together add variety and power to all fields of national life.

Freudian psychology cast those differences in the most unfavorable of lights, taught the individual to mistrust his own impulses and to turn away from the inner voice of intuition. The Freudian concepts were basically in direct opposition to Myers's subliminal self. Myers did not deny the confusions, distortions, fears, and guilts that could arise in human experience—the subjective terrors—but he did not regard these as the most basic badge of humanity. He saw them instead as regrettable instances of human ignorance that served to hide from man the existence of his subliminal power, that source of being from which each individual life springs.

As the medical profession became more technically oriented and treated patients with more and more impersonality, the patients began to desert. So-called quacks sprang up by the thousands in my time and continue to flourish in yours. How easy it is to so dismiss them, for they are often half-literate, without any academic credentials; charlatans full of dramatic improvisation and mystic mumblings. Yet often they charge far less than the doctors while offering the patient personal attention, hope, and often treatment that works by utilizing suggestion to turn aside symptoms and give the patient some breathing time. In many cases, physicians themselves can do no more. I am not condoning the more mischievous of such practitioners, but some certainly would rival in successful treatment the record of more conventional medical men.

Nor are a good many physicians above building up their own authority at the expense of the patient, increasing the patient's suggestibility to the most innocuous of the doctor's statements. The medical profession shows a remarkable lack of insight into the nature of its own blend of "mysticism" and drama, for its surroundings themselves confound the patient with instruments foreign to his knowledge, with the vast mysticism of science, evoking the doctor's authority and emphasizing the patient's helplessness.

Strangely enough, the discovery of X-ray equipment did much to build up such an aura. Earlier, the doctor had to rely upon the patient's feelings about the inside of his body. Here, at least, doctor and patient were united in their ignorance: neither of them could see through the patient's skin. With X-rays, however, the physician could view the individual's most intimate inside parts, allowing him a knowledge of a kind that the patient could not possess. The patient had to rely upon the doctor to interpret such pictures and translate them in understandable terms. Feelings became less important. Some doctors even shove them aside as beside the point, but physicians forget that their instruments themselves are highly important also as tools of suggestion and symbolic statements. Certainly on many occasions the tools' physical use may be undermined by their negative suggestive effect.

Later in this book I will elaborate considerably upon the mind's relationship to the body and its health from the larger framework of knowledge now available to me. Thus far, I have purposely held back from making certain statements about my own situation and the conditions of my existence, so as not to pull seniority. I am in fact deliberately speaking in contemporary terms so as to narrow the gap between us rather than widen it, at this point in any case, by emphasizing elements of my own experience with which you must be unfamiliar.

Those peculiarities of my existence do bring me definite advantages, however, and additional information, which I would feel lax in not revealing. These include "facts," certain to me, that still remain in the realm of the hypothetical to the living. These will be clearly stated later on. I will not take advantage of them, however, to fatten my own arguments at your expense. Otherwise I am confining my remarks to areas that are quite apparent in life once they are pointed out, and to comments concerning abilities and tendencies of the soul that show themselves through the agency of the living personality.

# 6. The Nature of Perception, Consciousness, and the Gifted Amateur

Friday morning
February 25, 1977

Man can put his consciousness together in numberless ways and therefore perceive himself and his world in different fashions. Most likely the subjective nature of reality was perceived far differently in previous civilizations. There is no need to call one way superior to another. Each represents a particular focus and psychological mixture, and expresses a unique relationship between man and nature and mind and matter. There are countless casts that consciousness can take. Each civilization, indeed each generation, latches upon one and holds it as its official psychological stance.

It is not just that man perceives an objective reality through the tints of such casts of consciousness, so much as that these tints stain reality in a given manner; so that certain effects splash out from the mind to fall upon the objective landscape, as if half-formed shadow images of the mind hit a certain "window" that invisibly exists between mind and matter. And as the sun is reflected from the outside into a winter parlor, so in the opposite direction the images of the mind, hitting this invisible window, suddenly turn alive and brilliant, casting *their* reflections brightly out upon the objective world.

That is, these casts of consciousness work upon the world in their own peculiar way, so that objective experience is a mixture of images within the mind and objective material without. Much of our perceptual view of the world is learned, and in a flash we can switch alliances, seeing blades of grass in one instance—eyes feasting upon sweet separate tips—or seeing, instead, a glossy, smooth lawn

104

which is only incidentally composed of grass. The individual blades become almost invisible in the larger perceptive framework. The reader can think of many such examples.

The musician's and the artist's worlds are doubtlessly different, for each projects outward those particular nuances of desire and interest that program perception; and though they both share the same physical universe, the differences represent those unique characteristics that make consciousness particular, specific, and personally meaningful. Each person possesses his or her own cast of consciousness, then, which serves as an inner blueprint existing within the mind, and then, at a certain point, becoming fleshed-in through objective experience.

Certainly there must be "something out there" to be worked upon, molded, and experienced, but that "something" is far more plastic, manipulatable, and giving than conventional practical psychology would lead you to believe. It is as if the private cast of consciousness works upon the objective world landscape by giving it its final, private, definite form; as if before the individual perceives objects, there is instead a field of pliable, malleable, pseudoshapes. The perceptions themselves bring these into focus and form, adding all the dimensions of actuality, depth, color, and so forth—these being projected outward upon that landscape according to each man's particular cast of consciousness.

The inner blueprints are themselves tuned in to that malleable "substance," connected with it through the brain so that any changes in the blueprints appear "outside" and vice versa. Thus would imagination and thought work upon the world. The processes are so smooth and automatic, so beautifully executed, that man rarely catches himself in the act of this multiple creativity, as the mind forms the world pattern of objects and events. Yet the creative act can give hints of the processes involved, for here man purposefully forms an intent—an act in the imagination—focuses it through the will, and waits in the faith that a work of art will result. He is equipped with the methods of production, objectively speaking, for he has learned his craft, whether it be writing, painting, sculpture, or whatever. But he often does not know where his ideas come from, or understand how an initial inspiration lasting perhaps only a few moments will explode into a sustained work of art. More than other men, the artist lives and works on faith. Man's continual perception of the world also represents creative abilities that he uses, unknowingly in this case.

Friday afternoon
February 25, 1977

I bring up casts of consciousness because while each one is like a screen, it is a screen of twofold function. On the mental or psychological side it projects ideas and beliefs outward where, at the point of contact, these work upon or slide over the pliable but incomplete field of objectivity, giving them their final form. The outside of the screen, the brain, perceives the finished product. Here we have inner and outer images transposed one upon the other so cleverly that it is impossible to distinguish between the two.

Many automatic adjustments take place before this final merging or stiffening of events, for the requirements necessitate certain correlations; so that while each cast of consciousness forms its own picture, that picture is composed of the same physical propensities or physical field from which others also form their realities.

In this view, the objective universe would be a bank of physical potentials; not an already rigid objective field but more of a gelatinous propensity with leanings toward a number of probable shapes—which are formed to their preciseness as consciousness, through its casts, works upon it.

The brain, being the "outside" of that screen, is physical, a part of that objective field, and must conform to its characteristics, while the mind or soul would be the inner, mental side. *That* side projects its images outward—including the brain, which is perhaps the mind's first projection—but it is not dependent upon the characteristics of the objective field basically. It must, however, use such a field to experience physical existence.

Consciousness is never stationary. The quicksilver nature of your own thoughts should make this instantly apparent. The mind itself is restless and curious. Concentrating upon one subject alone for only a few moments shows the tension that results as you try to leash or confine your thoughts. Considering this propensity for motion, it may be quite astonishing that consciousness focuses for as long as it does in the physical field, through the body. In life certainly the intensity of that attention fluctuates. In dreams, for example, consciousness allows itself greater freedom, not having to confine its experience to the strict rules of waking perception.

Here the mind or soul is seen as existing basically apart from the objective field of reality. Since the physical field is at least locally continuous, however, it stands to reason that the mind field is also, even while it is focused or experienced through individual minds.

To me at least, it is apparent that all hypothetical points of the universe are conscious at mind level. I do not believe the soul to be simply a point of individual awareness in a vast mind field, however, but a potent activator with its own inviolate "cast" or peculiarities, through which it will experience any reality.

I do know from experience that we move through the mind field as we move through the physical one and that, at one point, we move out of the range of regular accepted physical objectivity.

My presence in your world would be of hallucinatory status in your terms, for the dead are "out of tune" with the "station" shown on your screen of reality. We still have mental images, however these no longer coincide with your space-time coordinates, but go off vertically, so to speak, at the point of death, forming angles of experience in some ways adjacent to yours but no longer connecting. We can experience events that are quite physical to us, but they do not appear in your continuum and are not imprinted there.

On the other hand, it is impossible to say where my "here" is, using usual world references. First of all, the strict orientation of physical consciousness, again, is largely learned—consciousness being infinitely adaptable—so the infant learns to focus its awareness through the nervous system, pinpointing events in time and space. These are initially inner events, however, that affect the objective field in a certain way, forming space-time references. Those times and places require the physical nervous system for objective placement through projection outward onto that exterior medium.

The dead cannot *physically* intrude again without another birth into that system.

. . .

(The last passages dealing with James's remarks about the experience of the dead certainly triggered a vivid experience for me. That night as I lay in bed, between sleeping and waking, I realized that I was seeing brilliant mental images; I was looking at a "slice of life" or a strip like a film. It went up vertically from my eyes, or rather from my vision. The effect was as if a long movie film was held vertically above me. On the film was a sidewalk with people walking along normally, except that they were all walking in the same direction, and perpendicular to my vision. The whole strip was illuminated within itself. I realized that the people were normally positioned to themselves. It was the odd angle of the strip to my vision that gave the curious effect. Colors were very vivid, but there was absolutely no sound at all. I forgot what followed, and couldn't hold my consciousness clear enough. I only remember that after this I was shown a special kind of camera that took the film.

(At the time I also knew that the vision illustrated the passages in James's script. "We still have mental images, however these no longer coincide with your space-time coordinates but go off vertically, so to speak, at the point of death, forming angles of experience in some ways adjacent to yours.")

Tuesday morning
March 1, 1977

The dreams of the living make an equally imperfect connection with space-time, for example, also going off at a vertical angle, though in a gentler slope, so that the mental events only cause ripples in space-time, indicating or suggesting shapes in that medium while impressing it too lightly to affect the day's practical reality. The "angle" of dream events is "off," not as precise, so that dream events hit the space-time continuum in a slantwise fashion.

Yet this medium—the objective field—can be considered passive, in that it is willing to be impressed by mental stimuli, susceptible to them, while lacking within itself the stimulation of action. I am making this distinction for your convenience since you think of the objective field as separate, and as a matter apart from mind, while matter is actually a manifestation of mind. In those terms, however, each stimulus forms a separate habit, or induces space-time to be more susceptible to another similar stimulus.

Dream images therefore impress space-time too lightly for your waking neurological perception, and the objective field is filled with shapes impressed upon it by thought; but not strongly enough to be actualized. Such dream impressions do serve, however, as initial imprints, which incline the objective medium to take certain patterns over others, and serve to "prepare the ground" for later physical manifestation. Dream images and imaginative acts then prepare the way for physical ones, impressing large areas in general preshapes which are later "filled in."

It's as if the mind makes preliminary test patterns that are projections in space-time, but in a ghostly fashion. These dream images, however, are laid upon initial fields of probabilities which are characteristics of the physical medium itself. Thusly, certain images will "take" better than others fitting within probability boundaries more easily, and possessing more of the many prerequisite conditions necessary for a fully materialized object or experienced event. Other such images will make scarcely any impression at all.

An event fits more precisely into time and an object into space; that is, an event clicks first into its time slot, and an object first into its space slot. Yet there is considerable give and take, and the building blocks of matter are all "mental intensities"—nonphysical intensities—whose impressions must finally be sharp and powerful enough to form "knots of energy" which are interpreted as objects and events. The mosaics of events necessitate the finest tuning and interweaving of intensities, one with the other, so that these to some extent are inner correlates of the structure of cells and animate matter.

Tuesday afternoon
March 1, 1977

The objective field, then, is a medium with the propensity for leaning toward objectivity; it accepts mental stimuli which imprint it—stamp it—and form it into the habitual grooves of nature's shapes. It is manipulatable, gelatinlike, and composed of inclinations toward probable patterns upon which specifics ride.

All of this sounds quite dry, yet the intensity of emotions, desires, and intents everywhere rules, and is the primary consideration in the stiffening of probabilities into perceived events. Emotional states are characteristic of all consciousness. "States of feeling," perhaps, explains better what I mean, for I am not presuming that a rock loves or hates, but that each physical object is "alive," filled with consciousness, and having states of feeling. These states attract certain impressions or imprints and repel others.

Wednesday morning
March 2, 1977

I can project my own mental images onto your objective field, for example, but they do not "take." Instead, they will make the same kind of impression as your dream images do; they register but do not impress the medium enough to form a fully expressed physical actuality.

For one thing, at my death my habitual "stamp" or mark (made by my nervous system) became inoperable, and I could no longer impress physical reality in the same way. On the other hand, my own experience went off at a tangent, so to speak, so that in relationship to your world my focus is at a different angle that does not allow direct intersection with your field of objectivity. That field is on the periphery of my focus. My experience there remains as, say, background memory, important to me as your childhood is to you, but not my present concern.

I am the William James that was, but I am no longer William James in the same way that the adult is not the child. Furthermore, I have learned much more about consciousness in general, and my own in particular. Perhaps more important, I recognize the limitations of definitions regarding identity and selfhood, for they are bound to be based upon impossibly confusing misconceptions and misunderstandings that appear as a result of earth experience itself.

Existence in the space-time continuum programs memory and, of course, experience itself. Alive, we are only aware of our time selves. We see ourselves live and grow old in time. We experience the moments and identify our subjective reality with continuity in time. But even in life we are sometimes almost aware of thoughts and images whirling past us at a rate too fast to follow, and on other occasions of events so ponderous and slow that we seem only to waken to them once or twice in a lifetime.

Such experiences hint of the true nature of identity, indicating that part of ourselves that cannot squeeze into the coordinates of recognized space-time. In life we are aware of only certain pulses of our consciousness, and we form our identity by organizing memory and experience along the line of these pulses. We are quite unconscious of anything happening between them, or of anything happening at the "other end of the pole" of our own greater identity. There are experiences so far apart in time that we cannot follow. So, in life, our sense of ourselves must be limited.

"Intimations of immortality" do reach us, but through dreams, inspiration, and creativity—by means of the mind field mentioned earlier and through images that impress us but do not directly intersect with practical physical experience.

Thusly, again my appearance in your world (once mine!) would be only of hallucinatory status. But let me clearly explain my meaning here. I would have to impress a mind and nervous system with a picture of my image, and rely upon that living person's intent and desire to project the image outward clearly enough, whereupon the person would perceive it as an apparition.

Had I known in life what I know now, I would have looked for other elements in my investigations, seeking proof for the soul's survival through following other, more promising directions. I would have sought more ambitiously for proof of the soul's existence in life rather than seeking for evidence of its afterdeath existence through communications from the dead.

The soul's abilities in life, clearly defined, would *in life* show themselves to be independent of the body's physical confinements. Therefore I would have looked even more vigorously for accelerations and extensions of the creative abilities as they appear in telepathy, clairvoyance, healings, and out of body travel, and I would have examined those characteristics of mind (or soul) that display mind's control of matter, for that control is like the artist's unconscious control of his technique. While the artist must learn his craft, however, we are born instinctively knowing how to create matter, as instinctively we know how to breathe.

Thursday morning
March 3, 1977

Now, granting the confusion of definitions, I would use Myers's "subliminal self" as analogous to the soul, representing that part of man that forms and cushions his living, simultaneously orders the intricate involuntary systems of the body, and brings him information of extra-ordinary origin. I will have more to say about such information later, but it includes, I believe, the unconscious knowledge of events being formed in the medium of probabilities, and also data concerning events happening apart from the body's location. This subliminal self is the self which forms the twofold screen of mind and brain and, personified, it probably is the source of religion's guardian angels. Its abilities, once you look for them, are everywhere apparent in life, along with its extra-natural characteristics.

This subliminal self is the benign, well-intentioned, creative inner self that searches for the species' finest fulfillments, not through survival of the fittest but through the cooperative development of individual abilities which ever add to man's versatility. It reacts not to the blind events of chance and environment but in response to inner patterns of development projected onto the probable field of objectivity—patterns that act as stimulators of the most ideal nature.

The human species and all species react "in time" to the all-pervading patterns of probabilities that coax them toward their best, most advantageous developments—development not set, however, but rich in choices. This presents a world in which all species are interrelated, not one thriving at the expense of the others but each contributing to the world picture at any given time in a cooperative venture to which man has become relatively blind.

For one thing, science has so objectified the animals that it has closed its eyes to the animals' reality of feeling and, yes, sentiment. Stressing the theories of conventional evolution and its objective considerations, science has completely overlooked the greatest factor in creature life: the very sensations of creaturehood and the vast communications that exist among all species.

I do not mean to overromanticize, yet overromanticization is a far lesser error than an overobjectification that dismisses life's sentiment quality as beside the point, and justifies cruelty to animals by citing distorted evolutionary concepts. While on the one hand denying emotional reality to the animals, science blithely assigns the worst human tendencies to the animal world when it suits science's fancy, and without blinking an educated eyelid. It scoffs at "humanizing" the animals or assigning qualities of love or compassion to them, while projecting upon them and their world adjectives such as selfish, aggressive, competitive, and so forth.

For science since my time has compromised itself, and while it was once the harbor of the truth seeker who escaped religion's dictates and dogmas, now the truth seeker must steadfastly stand apart from science and religion alike. He is therefore likely to be more of an outcast in your time than mine, and he is also for that reason less informed, generally speaking, since he has less access to the learned journals and less say in recognized foundations.


Friday morning
March 4, 1977

Yet the gifted amateur often initiates developments in many fields, since his knowledge is not overstructured. He is not stifled by an overprofusion of facts that in the sciences now spring up like weeds, tomorrow to be trampled underfoot, few surviving to maturity—spindly crops often, barely living through a season before falling beneath a new group of equally valid facts, which in their turn fall by the wayside before the latest variety. Not knowing of this rich harvest of facts, near-facts, and temporary truths, our gifted amateur need not tread as cautious a path as the academic specialist, who must respectfully treat each succeeding crop of facts as the only accepted ones, so that even his most imaginative of theories must serve as a mental basket holding a respectable bed of old facts as well.

The gifted amateur goes blithely by, it seems, ignoring such considerations, determined to search for something he cannot define or categorize, but something that he will intuitively recognize when he finds it. An odd individual certainly, often without scientific credentials, cantankerous and eccentric. Yet he possesses certain assets that go unnoticed: he need not pretend to preserve one set of facts that are already partially superseded by another; he need not worry about losing face with his colleagues, for more usually than not, the poor fellow has none; and because he must rely upon his intuitions and intents more than most people, he refines and develops these so that they compensate in part for the official knowledge that he does not possess.

His nose for truth, then, often lets him follow theoretical scents unperceived by others, and he can often discover a new species of truth since he is tuned in to the unusual. The good academic, however, is still searching through known categories and is not as apt to stray beyond those boundaries.

I do not mean to deride the professional in any field, but rather to point out the many difficulties that lie in his path; psychological, sociological, and economic. Many of these impediments are caused by the characteristics of any organization devoted to a specific field of inquiry. Sooner or later such a field accumulates its own body of facts, to which it can become slavishly devoted. These facts are usually isolated; that is, taken out of context to some extent, considered only as they relate to a given discipline, not as they connect with other fields. Such organizations maintain their identity thusly, so that biology, psychology, physics, and other disciplines each have their own facts, even though the facts of one field may contradict the facts of another in important instances.

By the time our hypothetical young truth seeker finishes his schooling in the area of his specialty, he is already somewhat compromised and prejudiced in favor of his discipline's accumulated body of facts. His education has cost him a good deal of time and money. The very authority of his academic degree and its social and economic implications is dependent upon the truths of those facts that he has mastered. Any evidence to the contrary, any suspicions of the facts' wobbly integrity, brings our new professional feelings of the deepest dismay—and naturally enough, since by now his financial status and perhaps the welfare of a growing family are at stake, to say nothing of his own self-respect and position in the community.

If our truth seeker is true to himself, he continues his search under the most difficult of circumstances: he hopes to discover some new invention, theory, or unifying picture while hoping against hope that any such discovery will not contradict his peers or the dignified body of facts that form the basis of his discipline. He must look ahead and behind at the same time, check his results and, most of all, train his intuitions to follow known facts so that they do not lead him astray and break the rosy bubble.

The gifted amateur has no rosy bubble to break and is often regarded as a fool to begin with: he can afford to dally. His livelihood is not dependent upon his success or failure and, lacking credentials, he does not fear losing what he does not possess. He can cast a curious eye over the various fields of knowledge, nibbling at what pleases him, following where his intuitions lead, discarding what offends his nature.

That nature, with its own idiosyncrasies and individual intents, possesses its own innate direction and focus—its own original cast that has its own methods of organization. So, unwittingly, the gifted amateur is often led to follow a very precise direction. As an ill animal seeks out the proper herb for its own cure, so the gifted amateur can be led to cure his own dissatisfaction with known knowledge. His nature coaxes him to travel through new territories of thought to discover the exact theory or idea that will bring him release, and may solve a cultural or philosophical problem at the same time.

Often also the professional in one field is the gifted amateur in another, contributing precisely where the world least expects it, and astonishing himself by making discoveries in a field in which he dabbles for pleasure. In such instances, the creative abilities are allowed freedom and are not stifled.

In its infant stages, modern science, of course, was quite correct in turning directly to nature away from church dogmas concerning the natural world. Science began with its own Achilles' heel, however. It determined to limit its investigations of nature to objective issues and provable hypotheses, relying upon the physical senses and, later, their extensions through instruments.

What is a flower? No longer would science rely upon old catalogues and classifications, but actively count the kinds, examine the flowers themselves, rip them apart, tear petal from petal so that nothing escaped examination and scrutiny. But since nature's true significance could not be proven, since aesthetics cannot be diagramed, since the poets' sentimental identification with nature cannot yield provable facts, science settled upon studying the details, the particulars, and ended up with a very limited investigation of nature.

Science lost sight of the "fact" that some knowledge forever escapes fact's categories, existing in a different order entirely, one just as valid and just as demonstrable, but in a kind of emotional or psychological equation upon which the validity of facts themselves must ultimately ride. Facts are necessary, useful, and pertinent, but there are also ways of organizing reality that do not rely upon facts *exclusively;* that unify rather than specify, and that honor variances while also perceiving them as a part of a larger field from which those variances emerge.

As far as psychic organization is concerned, facts are "manufactured." They are classifications of information about direct knowledge, very useful but secondhanded. It's obvious, of course, that all the accumulated facts about roses do not and cannot add up to the direct sense encounter of one person with one rose, or approach the intersection of person with flower that happens when we see, smell, touch, and feel a rose. That experience itself cannot be translated directly into the data we "know" about the factual rose. I am not here denying the facts-about-the-rose, only saying that direct knowledge must come first and that the facts will have little meaning without the encounter.

That direct encounter happens when the personality intersects with something not itself through sense data that the personality and the something-else produce creatively together. For something about the rose itself, something native to it and not to us, does set it apart—a variance in a generalized field—and we must partially accept that encounter and merge psychically with that sensed variance. Hence, knowledge can use facts but not be bound by them, since facts can set up barriers between us and our own experience by programming us to perceive in the light of known facts so that, looking, we see the generalized rose and not the individual unique flower before our eyes.

# 7. Afterdeath Environment, "Possession," Apparitions, and States of Mind

Tuesday afternoon
March 8, 1977

Your world is like the negative of a photograph to me now, unfleshed, showing outlines and definitions, but of a transparent nature. I have to "read in" the perspectives that appear so realistically and colorfully to you, for my senses are not tuned in to those neurological keys that cause the world to spring alive.

Now and then, memory and imagination cause a sudden connection and I perceive a particular scene, knowing however that it is in ways a replica of a given space-time picture but not the picture itself, and I cannot enter into it. That is, even though I creatively hallucinate an earth environment of limited extent, it does not meet directly with your world at all, despite its reality to me. Perception of your world is possible, but in a dim overview fashion, for now that reality is the ghostly one to me, its edges unclear, its motions blurry, and its most solid masses having a transparent cast.

I view it as you might an unclear movie in which time sequences jumble, the speed is uncertain, there are bleed-throughs from one picture to another, and the sound is dubbed in, sometimes before or sometimes after the actors speak.

I am more aware of general developments since my time than of specifics. The physical world in which I once played my part still interests me, however, in that my ideas are still alive there; and though their vitality has weakened since my death, they still meet responses in the living and stimulate my own reactions. The ideas I expressed in life continue to move, without me, and rouse my interest. They form a

118

pattern of energy, concern, and inquiry still connected to the part of me that gave them birth. To that extent, even now my interest in that world is lively.

A strange word for the dead to use, perhaps, yet my thoughts in that respect are freer than they were in life, no longer restrained by life's daily experiences. If sharpness of detail is lost, I am quite able to follow large patterns of thought and emotions with ease, perceiving them somewhat above the hard-bed reality of the world, rising from it like multicolored clouds of different shapes, colors, and varieties. All in all, then, I can follow the world's ideas and emotional climate very well. Realities connected with your own experience, but invisible to you, are quite clear from my viewpoint, then, while ordinary events of a physical nature are unclear and shadowy.

I can follow thought's masses as they form above the world, mixing with others, flowing in patterns sometimes light, sometimes dark or dimming, and I can perceive the intensity of emotion that drives them. As a rain cloud will surely bring a shower, from my standpoint it is obvious that certain thought patterns will bring about physical events suiting their nature, so it is with considerable interest that I watch those emotional and mental patterns that surround the world.

Dawn has a glow that I no longer perceive, for I waken each morning from no bed to see the sun rising outside window curtains, yet I do perceive the dawn of new ideas, the glow of peace or faith or contentment as these surround the earth, "rising" amidst the darker forms of doubt and fear; and while I rest, I no longer sleep in the old terms, though I *may*, for the experience. Immediately following my death I slept out of habit, but gradually did so less and less as my sensations of time altered.

That alteration must also have come about gradually, but quite honestly I cannot remember exactly how it happened. There were some very pleasant dreamlike periods in which the adjustments may have taken place. Nor is it easy for me to describe exactly how my experience of time is different from yours.

If I asked you how you kept apart your own memories, for example, while living in each separate today, you would not know how to answer, perhaps saying only that this was somehow accomplished without much conscious effort, building upon certain learning processes that must have taken place in infancy and childhood. You distinguish past from present very easily and, having little conscious knowledge of the future, you need not make many deliberate computations in that area except for the formation of future plans of action.

In the same way, it is difficult for me to say how my experience of time has altered. I can "see" the world's thought patterns as I described them and the world's emotional forms "at once," as you might see the clouds if you were high enough above the earth. I can also "see" my own life in the same way, in its entirety as I knew it, but also in ways that were unfamiliar to me then. The events of my own life appear open-ended to me; I see what I did, but also what I might have done, and can perceive the energy I sent out in directions that I did not take consciously. I can track my own influence then, see the thousands—no, millions—of people I affected, as each of you affects the earth and its populace in far greater terms than you realize. Each contact, direct or not, counts and ripples outward so that each person's life sends out lines of contact intersecting with others on a psychic level, but quite practically in psychological terms. So after death, watching the tracks of one's own influence is perhaps the most fascinating of endeavors.

The eyes of the dead are indeed opened through some such experience, and this probably accounts for the reports of private judgments by God, the "final accounting," and so forth. No judgments are implied in those terms, however, though each individual will of course interpret the experience according to his own beliefs and characteristics. Perhaps the events themselves are even perceived in completely different manners.

It is impossible to tell how long this takes in earth terms, but the inner dimensions of the experience are equally beyond description, for there is nothing in life to compare with the depth, breadth, complexity, or intensity of such a psychological multievent.

I could compare it to the tracking of a million lights simultaneously crisscrossing a night sky while a startled observer on earth watches hypnotized, dazzled, feeling each light's distant flicker in the reaches of the universe, while at the same time knowing that each flicker—and each other flicker—originated in his own thoughts and existed within them and in the sky simultaneously.

So are a person's life tracks projected outward and so do they intersect with those of others, forming patterns of energy, causing new relationships, and triggering actions that never appear to earthly perceptions. Now, for example, it seems impossible that I was so minutely aware of the energy and extent, the far-reaching consequences of my own life. I do not believe that I could have understood, much less realized that the lives of all other persons had the same astonishing greater dimension.

Most interesting of all, perhaps, these lifelines begin before birth and continue after it. The traces of my own life still intersect with and affect those living; and through my own knowledge of my contemporaries, their lifelines mix with mine and with the living as well, as their ideas still relate to mine or are used in whatever way by your contemporaries. From your standpoint as a rule, the life tracks of the living are brighter and of greater intensity than those of the dead, but this applies only generally. The lifelines of the dead could be compared, say, with distant galaxies, while those of the living would represent your experienced world. But in actuality often the intensity of certain thoughts and emotions is so strong that they remain highly volatile.

In your terms, after physical death the division between living and nonliving has little meaning. There are gradations of consciousness, rather; divisions, with one blending into another; and psychological combinations both of identity and perception that are possible outside the physical system, but not within it. Some individuals return to physical life many times. Others live a life or two of great intensity and then follow through with ideas from this end, watching as the physical seeds of that creativity sprout, but from a distance.

In my case, through this manuscript I poke my fingers into someone else's pie, but by my invitation, adding certain exotic ingredients that would otherwise be lacking in a confection that must, nevertheless, sit in the windowsill of your time, not mine, and be presented and eaten at the table of a world in which I can only be a shadowy guest at a banquet I partially prepared.

Wednesday afternoon
March 9, 1977

Communications between the living and the dead must always be translations at best; we cannot directly intrude. The knowledge, experience, and insights of the dead are everywhere available, for they are part of the ever-changing lines of consciousness that crisscross the universe. There are, of course, divisions and here I must again use analogies that are familiar to you in that my main lines of communication are "above" your own mental atmosphere—not implying superiority on my part, but suggesting the separation necessary. So there is a "distance" to be crossed in such communications; one that makes direct apparitions most unlikely.

Such appearances are more like projected images, of transitory nature that cannot "take" in space-time for long—mental traces not filled in with consciousness or flesh—but outlining spatial patterns in response to a communicator who naturally exists in a different kind of psychological medium.

That kind of encounter is difficult for the communicator, for he must adopt a smaller personage or identity than the fuller one he accepts after death, and squeeze himself into a personal context now too small, relating to the living in ways familiar to them, but which he has outgrown. Not that love is outgrown, only the small context in which it is experienced, and the details often sought after by the bereaved relatives have lost their sharpness for the dead, while the patterns of the relationships have been experienced in deeper ways than the living can understand.

The dead can grow impatient in such cases, and thus may prefer informal dream encounters in which the living do not clutter the mental air with requests for proofs and details that are, to the dead, beside the point and a waste of opportunity. For certain conditions must occur before even dream encounters can happen, and the dead are usually satisfied with a less direct but also less troublesome communication. This is often accomplished by the maintenance of a general, distant, but lively concern and by mental messages of comfort, support, or inspiration sent anonymously, usually delivered exactly when the recipient expects it least, in sleep or when the mind is otherwise occupied. Otherwise the startling effect of such encounters often blots out the message, overstates it, or distorts it in one way or another.

The dead still love those they loved in life, but they understand the emotion far better than they did before, and in a way again difficult to express, they do not miss the living. They do not feel absent from the living, only present in an entirely different fashion than the living can fathom. In this, of course, they have the advantage and it is to relieve the loneliness of the living that the dead communicate, even while knowing that such communications themselves can make the living only more anxious.

The dead in their way are jealous of their freedom, and sometimes their communications take the form of hasty, "Yes, I'm all right" messages, shouted over a mental shoulder. Some people forget to send letters when they travel, caught up as they are in new experiences. Similarly, the dead are so involved in their own adventures that sometimes they ignore the nagging of the living, whose thoughts rise up like mental kites with reminders, saying, "Why haven't you written?"

And the adventures of the dead can be quite concentrated. After death, for example, I learned tricks of perception that I now take for granted. I can experience any season of my life in an expanded fashion, using a heightened memory that actively recreates events, giving me awareness of an event as I once experienced it—but expanded to include all of those personal details that escaped me at the time, the subconsciously perceived events that couched the physical one. Or I can telescope the same season, experiencing, say, one given autumn which suddenly becomes a point of action in which the actions in all of my other experienced autumns are contained. These perceptive "tricks" apply only to private events, not to world history.

My position, if that word will do to describe my present psychological stance, is the result of my own interests, idiosyncrasies, and tendencies. In your terms I am still scholarly, given to my studies, where others for example are concerned with emotional relationships and would be involved in different kinds of encounters both with their own environment and yours.

Friday morning
March 11, 1977

The fact of death does not turn the coward into a hero or the fool into a wise man, true; yet those judgments are highly limiting to begin with, and death does bring a man into his own estate. That is, he sees his own characteristics and abilities in a clearer light and after the first shock of surprise he usually views himself with a more generous, lively compassion than he did before.

On earth few men are of evil intent. Most crimes are committed by those "out to right a wrong," and are the result of tangled thoughts and emotions that strangle a man's knowledge of himself and others, so that he acts out of ignorance or is driven by a passion that is the only one he allows himself to feel. This passion also contains all of the inhibited power of all those other emotions that clamor inside him for expression, and like a dammed-up river in flood time, the energy finally bursts loose. Few men commit an act called evil for evil's sake, however, unless they confuse evil with good or justify it as the means to a good end. So in death also, there are no "evil" men, and since understanding is clarified, there is no need for mean acts.

Nor do the dead in any way possess the living. The dead are quite aware of their benefits—consciousness in a mental body that does not age or decay—and the misconceptions of the living in regard to possession lie mainly in their parochial belief in the superior advantages of their estate over that of the dead. Living or dead, however, existence takes place initially in mental realms rather than physical ones, and it implies states of mind first of all.

These states of mind are like mental houses built by each person that form the actual environment in which any reality is experienced. As physical houses in a given neighborhood may be similiar in construction, style, and age; and as the people in a given locality may be attracted to it because of characteristics that fit in with their own, so too people form mental neighborhoods, making alliances on psychological and psychic levels, having mental friends and associates, for example, with whom they may never meet physically.

Living, our acquaintanceships are larger than we know. Besides our relatives, friends, work associates, and others with whom we deal more or less directly, we "make friends" with writers we have never met—contemporaries or those from history's past—and our inner life becomes peopled with all of those who have affected us strongly in one way or another, through our reading or other experiences. A chance line written by a favorite author can have a greater effect upon us and cause life-altering transformations far greater in intensity than any statements made by relatives or friends. Yet in life we largely ignore this kind of mental commerce.

This inner neighborhood of mind has its own characteristics and draws to it others of like "mind." Since such inner environments are open to living and dead alike, possessing no time or space boundaries, then under certain conditions the living may find themselves moving into mental neighborhoods that fit them all too well, empha-sizing their own beliefs and feelings to a superlative degree and, it seems, with supernatural force.

In almost all instances, obsession plus strong repression causes such conditions. Because possession in one way or another has been an issue relevant to survival theories, and because of my interest in such matters, I want to discuss this in some depth. First of all there are certain distinctions I would like to make.

Friday afternoon
March 11, 1977

As mentioned earlier, I do not agree with the "normative" schools of psychology, nor do I subscribe to theories that advocate the well-balanced personality as the end-all of individual or social achievement. Since people are demon-strably different in endless varieties of ways—in casts of mind, emotional and intellectual response, bodily habits and constitution—then now, as in life, I maintain the importance of the variances in human behavior. The cultivation of individual differences adds to the resiliency of the species, and in countless ways, to be discussed later, contributes to spiritual and physical well-being.

Many people are one-sided, and in my time as well as yours, literature as well as common discourse speaks of the sportsman, the professor, the seamstress, teacher, the perennial student, the playboy, harlot, and so forth. Each person relates to ideas about the self in an individual way. A fifty-year-old father may see himself primarily as a son, for example, where another man might be The Father in all of his undertakings with others, even though he has no children of his own. A woman might relate primarily as a mother or as a daughter, or in your time particularly she might stress her affiliation in a profession above all other considerations. But it is idiocy to require the introvert to be an extrovert or vice versa; the sportsman to have the scholar's love of books; or the scholar to forsake his study for the sports field.

Each person is possessed of leanings and tendencies that are idiosyncratic, eccentric, his own to be pursued and developed. Such tendencies often lead to the greatest developments in the arts, sciences, and religions, making possible contributions that would not have been made by more "better-balanced" persons. In these cases, common sense, logic, and the emotions are all used with devotion and care in the service of a prime interest or purpose even if that purpose is not clearly perceived but only sensed. It is followed undeviatingly even though its paths may appear tangled or convoluted.

In obsessive behavior, on the other hand, common sense, logic, and the emotions are all to some extent repressed, shut out, strangled by a prime interest; so that the interest becomes a dead-ended road not permitting any side crossings. There are obviously gradations in both cases, but generally the gifted eccentric is expansive and expressive, using his abilities to an end in which he believes. The obsessive person, however, follows a delusion that he must protect against reason, logic, and emotional understanding, so he denies these, following a goal that is closed rather than open-ended.

Any fanatic follows this latter pattern, and such persons possess a rigidity of attitude that makes them frightened of all change. People may be fanatical in small ways also where certain matters are concerned, while being quite open-minded in others.

There are persons driven by desire of one kind or another—for knowledge, fame, achievement, or skill—who use the finest attributes of reason, discrimination, and emotionalism to uphold and couch their purpose; such persons use their abilities, therefore, for their own individual goals while following the natural bent of their natures. There are also those who refuse to use discrimination, reason, or honest emotions but repress sense and intuitional insights alike in the pursuit of a goal not theirs by nature but foisted upon them by others. And of course there are persons in whom a natural purpose is cluttered with subsidiary obsessive ones.

In cases of unreasonable obsession, the person is already "possessed" in a manner of speaking by acquired patterns not his (or her) own natural ones but those adopted through fear. The mental neighborhood is highly charged, volatile, ready to explode, and the person forced to walk a narrow line, a tightrope stretched to the utmost, afraid to look right or left or to deviate from the patterned behavior in the slightest way. All life happening "below" must be steadfastly avoided, all of the personality's other natural leanings and intents forgotten, and the eyes of reason kept tightly closed. So the obsessive person is often spiritually blind, and even when his physical eyes are open they do not respond with a lively gaze to others, but glitter with their own stationary light.

They move to the outskirts of human commerce, and I am not referring here to the child or adult who delights in solitude or to those whose natural ways incline toward contemplation, but to the strongly repressed obsessive personalities who blot out their natural bents, following artificial goals not their own. Their world narrows both within and without, for they read only journals and newspapers that concur with their own views, deny any emotional contradictions, and censor any conflicting evidence from common sense.

Such people may be brilliant and gifted, or they may be

intellectual nincompoops and aesthetically ignorant. Their characteristics and methods of behavior are the important issues. As a result of this behavior, the inner self achieves only a dreary loneliness; the tightrope is raised ever higher to avoid the contamination of daily life; and even if such a person is surrounded by admirers he can allow no real discourse.

Nature works against isolation and loneliness, and even the lowliest of creatures is curious about the business of others. The animals are not recluses, but lively participators in a natural community in which isolation and relatedness each play a part. So such persons are led to search out those who they hope will understand them, while they are prevented from doing so at the same time, fearing that self-disclosure might ruin the elaborate psychological facade so painfully wrought.

So such personalities characteristically have two main behavior patterns, sometimes following one exclusively for long periods of time and sometimes switching from one to the other. They are given to compulsive repetitive actions, mental or physical; and to explosive bursts of violent activity. The repetitive behavior is comforting, and can follow a slavish attention to details or be expressed through compulsive repetition of certain thoughts or words; and the violence can appear as severe explosive activity of an inward or outward nature through the rupture of an appendix, ulcers, heart attacks, or such, as well as through, say, bad temper or pugnacious behavior.

The repetitive nature of some acts, as cracking the knuckles, incessant talking with certain punctuating rhythms, or even loud table tapping, may also mask any violent characteristics. Any such activities carried on in habitual unthinking fashion may combine both the violence and repetitiveness. Such people are those who need most to "break out of themselves." They are lost in and to some extent "possessed by" intents and drives usually adopted out of fear at a young age. Often a parent or other authority figure is responsible in conventional terms. Actually such persons often fear that their own energy will supersede that of the parent, and are also afraid, on the other hand, that the parent will not be superseded.

In any case, their own thought patterns and lines of consciousness are particularly intent, relatively unaffected by others, and in a peculiar fashion unsupported at the same time; rising up without suitable foundation in the person's natural characteristics. As these individuals isolate themselves through censoring their experiences, they gravitate toward certain mental neighborhoods; they dwell in mental states that are like their own, volatile and charged, caught between the repetition of boredom and the release of violence.

They milk their environments dry in that respect. So, also, they pick up and magnify any other such streams of consciousness, whether from the dead or living—hence frightening apparitions, ghosts, poltergeist activity, and so forth often occur in their presence—where the same repetitive yet explosive elements can appear separately or in combined form, and in an isolated (elevated) fashion in relation to ordinary life.

The incessant repetitive behavior of a mental nature causes certain stresses, as if a series of small explosions of minor degree were so constantly occurring in a given area of consciousness that a rupture finally results, such as an earthslide that is accompanied by stones, dust, fallen branches, and debris. Only in this case down the deep walls of the ruptured consciousness fall all those feelings, thoughts, and considerations that the personality had thus far managed to hold back. In self-protection the personality summons all of its resources—its characteristic modes of behavior and its obsession—to cope, since it finds itself, relatively speaking, at the bottom of the ladder instead of on the tightrope above.

This intensification of intent brings about a super-charge of psychic activity that seeks other reinforcement, and if the personality is near a mental neighborhood or mental state of consciousness of corresponding nature, it draws from that reservoir. The result can be the activation of an apparition, a "ghost" of threatening demeanor, who appears whenever the conditions are repeated. In most such instances the ghost is not a person or identity in usual terms, but a played-back version—the lines of consciousness trailing from an identity as smoke may trail a fire—and the obsessive personality magnifies and focuses these through its momentary intensity, then projects them onto space-time; where, however, they will "take" only under certain conditions.

The personality has attracted those lines of consciousness that are in tune with its own in an effort to reinforce its defenses. The behavior of the apparition will often then symbolically state the position of the obsessive person, who unconsciously feels possessed or dead inside. Sometimes such an apparition may also be perceived by others, and there are certain atmospheres where the constant repetitive nature of these activities can be activated under like situations.

On the part of the obsessive personality, this is a therapeutic procedure. Seeing its own predicament so projected (the feeling of being apart from life and dead to the self) can bring about a shocking recognition of the dilemma, even though this may not be consciously recognized as such. The problem becomes the seemingly exteriorized ghost, upon which the person now projects his own situation.

Before this, often no problem was even acknowledged, hence the drastic measures taken. Religious or psychological aid is usually sought at this point. The recognition and attention rendered bring the personality into needed contact with its contemporaries, allow the individual to ask for help—not for himself, of course, so much as for the ghost—and the entire affair serves as a catharsis.

This does not mean that only obsessive people see ghosts, but that the classic cases usually involve such conditions—and particularly when the apparition is not someone known to the perceiver. The appearance of friendly ghosts and apparitions of family members or loved ones can have quite a different basis, but in all cases there must be a coincidence of states of mind.

Poltergeist activity usually involving children follows the same pattern as with the obsessive adult, except that the child is not usually as set in his ways. Often the child's anger is against an adult who is attempting to make the child follow other than his own natural bent. Here there is rage rather than fear, and the child may sometimes be nearly conscious of its behavior; practicing in secret with moving objects or playing sly tricks with its own energy. The repetitive pattern also applies, the child being overly obedient in many such cases and the even behavior erupting spasmodically into violent acts or temper tantrums for which the child has been reprimanded.

Earlier I mentioned states of foreboding or anxiety in connection with the creative processes, my own melancholy fantasies and precognition-disaster dreams. When I was in such depressions, the most unpleasant associations from the past could be triggered by the most innocent stimulus. Not only images of sorrowful events I had actually experienced, but also doleful remembered scenes from novels or plays would rise to my mind, and the most melancholy passages from philosophers or poets. Such fantasies would accumulate, peopled with characters from real life and fiction, deepening in gloom until they often erupted in disastrous forebodings regarding the future—my own death or that of others, the eventual ruin of the world, the demise of the universe, the end of all.

As I mentioned, an artist might paint a series of dark landscapes or otherwise rid himself of his emotional tremors through his canvases. A poet might write a bleak ode to death. Others, in a further creative step, might unconsciously seek out the unknown shape of the future, their anxiety seeking a cause, and hence find it through a dream in which a future disaster is foreseen. Still others with a different cast of mind will seek out from the ever-present fields of consciousness those lines like their own, and "plug in" to fears that were before inactive, but latent as patterns, and seemingly bring to life again events or persons who are actually quite finished with such activities.

# 8. Views of the World From a Balcony Seat

Monday morning
March 21, 1977

In the universal drama, you might say that I am still in the same theater of events, but I have moved from life's stage to the balcony, where as an observer I am removed from the action in which life's participators are involved. My status allows me a better view. I can look down, symbolically speaking, to see the actors coming in at one end of the stage, leaving at the other end, and I can also vaguely perceive other stages, both above and below. Besides this, it is apparent to me—though not to the actors—that on an adjacent level one stage leads to another; and that at death a new curtain rises.

While not presently involved in a physical drama, certain privileges are also allowed me in that I can shout out my comments and suggestions, urge certain actors on, applaud and boo as rambunctiously as I please. Not being personally involved, I follow the plots, characters, and themes, and because of my privileged viewpoint I can see where certain actions are leading, so that sometimes I call out in alarm, "Watch out," or "Don't you see what will happen if you don't do something quickly?" Or, like a passionate theatergoer who impatiently stands up, stomping his feet, I might feel at least like shouting out my irritation at poorly read lines or inept performances.

Perhaps most of all, however, the intricate patterns made by the generations become increasingly clear. The importance of each minute decision by the most minor actor with the smallest bit part will influence all of the other actions both present, past, and future; for at one level all of the actors hear all of the other lines regardless of the time or

132

place in which they are spoken, and all ad-lib in a simultaneous creativity so that the dramas change themselves constantly, all across the boards.

I understand those issues even though my box seat is so far away from the stage that I only see the larger patterns of action, the greater motions that appear to me quite clearly, while I know from experience on the stage myself that there these are unfocused and difficult to perceive. Still using our analogy, only special opera glasses would allow me to see the specifics sharply, and then these would be perceived through the lenses of my particular intent. That is, only a vital emotional yearning, a strong focus of desire, could bring given particulars into my inner range of vision.

I do not mean to carry the analogy too far, yet my role and that of others in the balcony is like that of the drama critic, except that unlike many of that breed who were dilettantes in my time, we at least began at the bottom—being stagehands, prop directors, then actors, writers, producers. Finally we move aside to study the overall productions, add our comments or criticisms and, backed up by considerable experience, to make what pertinent suggestions we feel will help.

In those terms, there are many others in the balconies. And few of them are bored, for all of us here have inserted our lines into the productions long before. We see them pop up time and time again, read differently, reiterated with a thousand various interpretations and used to further other causes, perhaps, than those we espoused. But to us is given the privilege of standing momentarily apart, watching how our life's actions began before our births and continue beyond our deaths; but more, of perceiving the ever-spontaneous yet perfect order of the generations' interactions; seeing, with considerable surprise how each birth and death is flawless in its timing, and how the most parochial of lives is universal in its effects.

Each barest whisper or muffled cry is heard everywhere, such are the amazing acoustics of this giant theater, which by its nature magnifies each sound and projects each thought outward, where it appears also elsewhere, translated into a different medium. It is as if one actor's spoken line were simultaneously transposed into a musical note in some vast ever-continuing composition; into one original line or color or shape that was part of some massive, spectacular painting always in process; into the physical components of nature—trees, rocks, animals—and into a million other transformations which even from my position would be impossible to follow.

Yet it is equally impossible not to attempt such a venture and like the other balcony-watchers I am aware that my balcony has only one box seat, while behind me is a door leading into perhaps even vaster theaters. When I have learned all I can from my present situation, the curtain behind me will open, of that I am certain, for even now symbolically it flutters. Sounds, visions even, come distantly to me from directions other than those immediately perceivable. For now, however, I sit with my back to that rather mysterious door.

There are also stage directions I still want to add, however, corrections I want to "write into" the world's script, and encouragements I still want to shout, hoping that someone will hear. For in my unaccustomed enthusiasm, I would add a heartiness that in life I did not actually possess. I would like to give my staunchest support and express my affection for a world that in life I did not understand; for a life, that in life, largely escaped me.

For then I did not plunge in wholeheartedly, being more morose than, I see now, the conditions warranted. Yet that critical air with which I examined life and sometimes condemned its terms, was also the result of those patterns that are, in life, often hidden. So from my vantage point now, I would like to remove some of the misconceptions about the drama itself that cause so many persons to "misread" their lines, to stutter, or act without the full knowledge available to them.

My own experience is a case in point, from which anyone can benefit. First of all, however, a few comments. These may at first appear so obvious that my readers wonder why I bother mentioning them at all, yet the very simplicity of the following issues is often overlooked in the sometimes murky or ponderous climate of conventional thought. The main point, so easy to forget, is that each person is the hero or heroine in his or her own life. Everything else, all actions, seem to revolve around us personally in life. This is not an illusion, but a fact of metaphysics and psychology as well.

We are each, in life, a center, a focus of unique consciousness; possessing our own quirks, talents, characteristic methods of expression, and our own spiritual or psychic tints through which all experience is perceived. That is, we ourselves each stamp or stain our mark upon the world. We are each so unalike that we might be members of different species entirely, so diverse is the nature of our inner realities, so different is one person's soul from another's, one person's challenges, dreams, and intimate contact with life.

In society we must, of course, also acknowledge our similarities and cooperate in civilization's ventures. I do not mean to minimize the vast uniting qualities of the emotions, for example, but only to stress that each person will experience them in his own way, and that one man's love may hold depths and nuances completely alien to the same emotion felt by another. More, each person's vantage point in the universe is his own, a platform for all of his acts that can be possessed by no other, is inviolate and, in an inexplicable fashion, absolute.


Monday afternoon
March 21, 1977

It is not merely as astrologers say, that we are inserted into life from our own time and space slots when time and space intersect in a way that will never happen again and never did before, though that is part of it. More than that, however, the universe prepares itself for our emergence in a certain manner so that when we are ready, we slip through a slot in existence's framework that is tailored for our birth and no other's; so that the time is always right. Like a child playing skip rope with others, we know when to leap into the rippling patterns. Yet beyond this, existence couples with itself in such multidimensional ways—multiplies within itself—that no mental or physical characteristics are ever the same and those that we possess are changing constantly, rippling outward in probable loops—as if instead of one rope, the child was presented with thousands, yet knew precisely when to jump.

Once the leap is taken, we are on a platform of our own.

It is foolish to try to match one's own step with others, therefore; yet often I spent a good deal of time seeing where my thoughts fitted into the frameworks that glittered around me. Had I paid more attention to my own footwork, I would have done far better. If others had bound feet, I grew suspicious of my own agility and slowed my pace. My melancholy grew to the extent that I mistrusted my own rhythms and tried to place my intuitive knowledge in contexts smaller than need be, so that I could skip in unison with my fellows. How amusing an image that would be to those who knew me—William James skipping rope—for despite all my talk about exuberance and clear expression of emotion, indeed I dragged my feet and found in the dallyings and partying of others the examples of the passionate, emphatic declarations and expression that I so lacked, and envied.

Ribald gossip of adulteries or even murder amazed and intrigued me. I found it difficult to believe that some people could feel deeply enough to be so driven. Even suicide, which I abhorred as a shameful waste, left me with mixed feelings of regret and envy, for such a person surely, I thought, experienced depression to its limits, where it demanded action of the most violent nature. And I, who could feel compassion at the death of a fly, could never treat myself with such utter lack of it.

My depressions left me only weary and indecisive. They seemed to run like black ink beneath the lettered pages of my thoughts, yet I clung to them as one might to old volumes of favorite books, for through them I translated my life's expression. That is, melancholy was often the only emotion I could properly identify in myself. Though I could sound passionate enough in the search for truth, this was in a way a secondhanded emotion since nowhere could I feel the same way when presented with any one aspect of nature's magnificence. The sight of a rose, or of the dawn, made me nostalgically aware of my own lacks and those of my fellows.

I second-guessed myself at every turn. There are those who considered me a freethinker, but only because they were not aware of the true extent of my thoughts which went leashed and unexpressed. I could not accept the responsibility for my own intuitive beliefs, or bear to face the fact that what I believed could not be proven; and if I was out of step with my times, I was fashionably out of step, still looking over my scholarly shoulder, courting however reluctantly the approval of the crowd.

I gloried in explaining the importance of variety, eccentricity, and the value of seemingly contradictory paths leading to emotional truths. Yet all the while I worried lest my own personal beliefs dull my scientific eyes, and to my colleagues and to the world I presented only those ideas that I felt were respectably enough laundered by objectivity to be acceptable.

To my credit I harangued against the narrow-mindedness of many scientists and religionists alike, and pointed out that much of our accepted knowledge was at best hypothesis—and at worst, malarkey. Yet for all of that, the techniques of science and the possibilities of its methods tempted me with the sweetest sirens' song possible. I was impatient at any felt truth that would not fit into science's framework; angry that the soul's properties, it seemed, refused to yield their secrets to sincere scientific inquiry.

Tuesday morning
March 22, 1977

Had I danced more to my own tune than I did, I might have contributed more to man's knowledge and bettered my own emotional state considerably. It is difficult for a man not to mirror his times, for he is so tuned in to them that despite his attempts to disentangle himself, they dye his thoughts and he is everywhere surrounded by their cast, which is shed alike upon all events and endeavors. Yet unfortunately, perhaps, the more a man finds himself acclaimed by his age, the more certain he can be that his insights are foreshortened.

Nor do I mean this necessarily as criticism of others, but in my own case it applies because of my intents, which propelled me beyond my times, yet mired me in them. For the rich and famous and many of the poor alike, and the humble and the sage, are usually quite happily ensconced in their historical periods, following fashions and styles of clothing and thought, applying their talents to the matters at hand, living their days amid families and business or professional affairs, and are well suited to their times. And if their concerns lie in a lively interest in peoples, gossip, and the commerce of nations, then such people contribute immeasurably to the fabric of society and life itself.

They excel in emotional relationships, and often their creativity goes unnoticed since it is not stated in the arts, but acts in a living context of creative interactions. I think of parents who form each day into a homey psychological canvas of living proportions, painted with tender demonstrations of parental love and affection, tempered by the most artistically applied discipline which does not hurt but teaches. So while such people may pass unknown to history, the artistry of their ways endures and their concentration in their times serves them and history well.

But if a person's mind is given to philosophy—if the heart questions the head, and the head the heart—if the person seeks the answers to questions that rise like smoke from the fire of daily life, if mind and heart alike are united in their untiring search for what comes before and what after; then there is no recourse but to stand somewhat apart from the times. There is no recourse but to steadfastly refuse that concentration upon daily details that others find so fascinating. For such persons see alike life's flaming patterns and the ghostly ashes left behind, the hearths of one civilization built upon the cold embers of another; and question incessantly.

The answers must come from another level that gives meaning to life's daily context, so the questioner treads a careful line of attending to life and not attending at the same time. He must be involved and not involved. In that involvement, despite my achievements, I tended too much to the opinions of others, and ignored many hints that appeared in my own personal experience—again, intimations of immortality, if you will—shunning them because of their scientific unrespectability.

My own existence gave me evidence of the soul's existence: I knew it but dismissed this as beside the point since in no way could I produce the scientific proof that—alone, I felt—could demonstrate to others the actuality of such a hypothesis. As scientific technique, that was proper.

But as a man I pretended not to know what I knew but could not prove before my fellows.

A larger science, however, must take into consideration those inner issues of mind and soul that it has summarily dismissed, for it is not true to say that science ignores such matters; it acts as if they do not exist and bases its theories on the supposition that man has no soul and the universe has no meaning. By taking such an attitude, science is neither objective nor scientific. The main foundations and schools of science have never had an open mind in this respect.

Part of the reason for this, of course, lies in science's need for consistency within itself; and again, the human heart is not consistent. The behavior of people is not predictable, and the soul will not stand up to be counted. Serious disadvantages—yet there is no reason why such issues should be ignored completely. Instead, science should and must rise to the challenge and broaden its frontiers, which are too small to contain important elements of human experience.

I tried to remake science and it nearly unmade me, for it undid my enthusiasm until I looked at life's wonders not for themselves, but with an eye out for provable facts. So everywhere the existence of the soul eluded me. Though I myself possessed one, nowhere could I identify it within myself, and when it spoke through inspiration or intuitional insight, it was then that I doubted myself the most, questioned my motives, and lost myself in petty details while often missing the whole shape or direction of my inspiration.

Wednesday morning
March 23, 1977

Now it is one thing to follow a discipline that deals only with provable facts, and quite another to live a life *as if* reality consisted of facts only, supposing that life rises from them instead of the other way around. Now how do you deal with new facts; again, those that undermine the old ones? Do you say that reality has changed? If you limit your personality so that your experience conforms to known facts, you not only severely constrict your life, but you threaten to shrink it out of existence. Those who follow such philosophies cannot live with them for long; inertia overcomes them.

Yet from my box seat I see that facts are the props of the dramas, and they change as the actors do, for they emerge to begin with from the actors' minds and conceptions—as ahead of time, so to speak, the actors choose the props that best suit their purposes, then change them as they go along—so they move from one set of facts to another as ordinary actors in a physical production move from one set or room to another.

The facts simply serve as a structure upon which, say, the plot is hung; as the given assumptions taken for granted by the actors, or as the rules of the game in which action takes place. Sometimes these facts change drastically; sometimes they serve for generations; but the actors are alive and real, while the facts are simply the exterior sets, secondary, shifting, to be used and discarded as they serve their purposes.

Facts are agreed-upon niches in which to place experience, but they have little to do with experience itself, and a person who lives his or her entire life according to facts alone loses a sense of the magnificence of life itself. Moving the props about, juggling the facts, kicking them aside can be a most enlightening endeavor, therefore, for each time such shiftings occur, lo and behold, the facts give! They are seen to be as artificial as the parlor settings of a popular play while behind the set's papered walls lies the vaster area in which the props were constructed. If you go backstage, Victorian living rooms and futuristic settings would appear side by side.

Facts are the same. Behind them lies the unexplored areas of creativity in which they are constructed to begin with. It is futile to protest that facts, "real facts," agree with one another and are consistent, for the furnishings of any good theater set all agree with one another also. It is only when you momentarily look away that you can say, "Yes, such and such is true—in this set," while knowing that in the theater across the street, a different set of equally consistent facts exists.

So the greater reality—the greater theater of existence—

is one in which the facts or the sets are constructed; one extravagant and creative enough to include vast groups of contradictory facts, each "proving true" in its own contexts. The search for God or the validity of the soul must ultimately lead into that realm, and he who tries to prove the soul's existence in the light of the world's accepted facts at any given time is doomed to disappointment. For the facts hide the soul. That is, the facts conform so perfectly to the set of the times and are constructed so cleverly to fit a particular era that they must mask any experience not consistent with them. They must be known for what they are: artificial props, handy and even necessary. They must be gently shifted aside, however, so that the behind-the-scenes activities can be explored.

I am not suggesting that facts be ignored. Indeed due respect must be given them for they are important mental conventions, bringing order into mental and physical endeavors. Without their benefit there could be no punctuality or preciseness in social relationships. Of course, there are those who wonder at the intrinsic value of punctuality and preciseness both, since many societies get along very well by honoring neither. Industrial societies, however, have need of them.

Facts should be valued for their practicality. They are worthy facilitators, serving as recognized signposts for travelers and settled populace alike. They are like mental maps, indicating certain kinds of explored terrain. But they are, to that extent, manufactured. They are not the land they describe. To treat them as such is a grave error, for a man may study facts about life for a lifetime, learning little of real value while ignoring the greater dimensions of living and existence that are so poorly indicated in the fact-maps themselves.

Because man tries to be consistent, often in such limited, unimaginative ways, but is despite himself highly creative, the facts of one discipline will often not agree with those of another, as I mentioned earlier. The wise searcher will study those contradictions, for there the props are weak, the map's flaws show, and there is a chance of seeing through to that more extensive fabric beneath. That fabric lies not only beneath the facts but beneath man's acceptance of them, in his own mind. That mind or soul contains its own prop-making equipment, and once a man finds himself in the process of constructing one set of props, he can experiment with others and realize that he himself is the fact-maker, and not subordinate.

# 9. The "Machine-Man," Survival, and Afterdeath Communications

Wednesday morning
March 23, 1977

It's amusing and educational to see how our worlds differ; that is, how the time of my historical existence compares with your own. First of all, I must in all honesty state that when I make such comparisons, I am identifying with a part I once played, taking once again the cast of William James as I was known and from that standpoint making my statements. To that degree I fit myself into my historical period: William James was my psychologically factual translation of myself into the setting I had chosen.

Generally speaking, in my time the power of organized religion was beginning to wane. Unorthodox religious experiences and schools of thought began to flourish—on the outskirts—but the main thrust and the exhilarating search for truth was transferred largely to science, which borrowed Protestantism's garb. For if heaven was no longer considered a suitable concept for reasonable men, the ideal of a practical, business-oriented, healthy, free-from-poverty society was inserted instead as mankind's goal; or at least for the growing democracy a practical, pragmatic, bustling society was better than the search for an illusive soul and improbable heaven. "Let the search go on, then" was the chant, with better clothes and housing and opportunity now for the living. Science was expected to produce. The search for truth was to be focused toward more practical immediate goals such as better can openers, vehicles, electricity and, later, toward truth in a vacuum tube.

143

Wednesday afternoon
March 23, 1977

It is nearly impossible now to describe the air of optimism, heartiness, and hope that prevailed; or the innocence, and the value placed upon method and technique. If a machine ran amok, something was wrong with it. A good mechanic was called in. Here was no mysticism, no need to require a god's assistance, no spooky dallyings with good and evil. A machine, acting improperly, was not evil, did not have to do penance or hope for better luck in an afterlife.

Freud was more of a mental industrialist than he realized for, using the same attitude, he decided that if a man acted improperly it was because something was wrong with his inner machinery: errors or built-in flaws that, however, any good psychological mechanic with enough training could cure. He was saying, in effect, that the machine stuttered psychologically. It experienced the same poor performance time and time again, but being only a poor machine, it could not know that its early experiences had programmed it wrongly. The psychological mechanic had to be a specialist, however, with long years of training, which meant that there were hardly enough to go around, since few of the machines were unflawed. The idea was the same, however: the soul or heart of man could be reached through certain techniques and if one failed, no matter, because science or psychology would come up with a better solution tomorrow.

So despite all, there was hope. Men such as myself kept trying to insert the concept of the soul into the machinery instead of grappling with the implied inner symbolism; and we were also hopeful, confident that science was latently capable of examining any reality if only the proper methods were utilized.

Even the best of us were tempted to consider the body as a machine animated by an invisible soul. Thusly, in our searches for proof of survival after death, we imagined that the dead might work the body mechanism of the living much as a one-owner auto might sometimes be driven by another, or as a puppet might be operated by a puppet master other than the usual one. Automatisms of speech or writing were often thought to be "spirit writings" or "spirit speech" in the most materialistically understood of terms. Otherwise, the subconscious was the culprit: in other words, the process was blamed on those "mischievous" but equally invisible portions of the self that served little other purpose except to keep the body alive. The much-maligned subconscious, then, was termed good when it "merged into the supra-conscious," which was spiritual but not inclined toward such mundane matters as bodily survival. For the body, as everyone was beginning to understand, belonged to that nefarious realm of Darwinian and biological cutthroatry, the subconscious; to the greedy Freudian machine-self-with-poor-programming—Darwinian "humanism" gone indus-trial. The soul had to be properly disconnected from such improper companions.

So we never saw the person as a whole, soul and body interweaving; and in rebellion we installed the concept of the soul's evolution to combat the savage earthly variety. The further away from the body and earthly life we placed the soul, the safer it seemed to be.

The soul, however, is both inside the body and outside it at the same time. More than this, consciousness knows many alliances. Thoughts exist as surely as apples or rocks, but they are collected differently. No machine can capture the aura of the soul. Only the mind that creates machinery can discover such evidence, and only by examining itself.

In this manuscript, my thoughts merge with those of the physical writer, because the writer's consciousness moves with a kind of motion no machine possesses, to a place no map can indicate. There it explores my situation by "putting my thoughts on," so to speak, as one might another garment; by donning my reality to the extent allowed by perceptive abilities that belong to the living as well as to the dead.

On my part, I am urged to comment, to add some insights available to me now though not taken advantage of in my lifetime. So from my position—in the balcony again—I call out from the sidelines to the writer, who listens and records what I say, turning momentarily aside from her own role; or rather in a kind of double acting as in a play within a play, she takes two roles at once: a major one, her own, and a secondary one in which additional insights are provided that the first actor missed.

To some extent I have the advantage, since from my

standpoint I can perceive the larger patterns of action formed by your world, while the writer—the actor in life's midst—must rely upon the messages sent from my direction, so that her view of my times is secondhanded in that respect. She sees it through my mental eyes rather than her own, while I perceive your world from a distance, but in a more firsthanded fashion.

Those large patterns of action that move in your times often had their inceptions in mine or before it, even as the theories of Freud were not completely new but intensified, focused versions of other thought, primarily European, that had not "come into its own time" until then. Such psychological concepts were latent in Darwinian views, and again, the background given man by Darwin could not help but produce something like the Freudian self.

Yet this was all in the balance when I was vigorous, and to many of us it seemed that Americans in particular were at the dawn of a new age, truth seekers on the march once again, in a free land where literally anything could happen; where people of all nationalities and persuasions could be assured of justice, at the very least. Yet the old virtues of diligence, hard work, and thrift (so beloved of Protestantism) clashed with the demands for competition. For who could blame the social climber or the unscrupulous businessman when the species itself and all of nature was involved in survival's savage battle, with no holds barred?

This machine-man, while spawned by nature, was nature's stepchild, rising to the top of the heap through sheer meanness, stained by "nature's bestial heritage" and yet denied nature's grace. Nor did nature make this machine-man by any design. It had nothing in mind. Instead, by random chance, man's parts were accidently assembled and accidentally grew, denied even the soul of nature; for nature itself came accidentally into being through random workings of which it was itself ignorant—an achievement of no little merit.

Assembly lines were springing up all over the nation, and a good day's work in the factories could have cleared the air of cobwebby scientific minds, mine as well, for there each piece was produced like any other and standardization ruled. Yet no man-machine was like any other. Each was unique.

Each was, therefore, its own accidental production, stamped with its own integrity; an original model.

So where did man's consciousness come from? It was, of course, the result, the accidental result of such accidental assemblage! When the body died, worn out beyond replacement, consciousness first dimmed, circuits went awry, and consciousness went out like a light.

For all of my own intuitive hopes, I finally decided that consciousness at death became fragmented like a string of spilled beads rolling mindlessly without a container through eternity's open spaces. One or two beads might be captured by a medium's receptive mind; a sensitive might pick up a name or two in a séance—a detail that might seem to corroborate the soul's survival—yet this was the only information contained in the bead, stamped within the fragmented consciousness like a design in a small jewel. But the identity, the entire string of beads, was broken, falling apart ever further as the body decayed and thoughts and emotions dispersed. So it seemed to me that mediums were catching one or two of these separate beads of consciousness, but no one would gather them together again, restring them, or place them in a new container.

My investigations yielded such fragmentary information that such a conclusion seemed logical at the time. Even data that was promising could not be verified as coming only from a departed whole consciousness but could have originated with the abilities of the living as manifested in clairvoyance or telepathy.

Now I see that the living have great difficulty in making the necessary connections, so that instead of picking up clear sentences or thoughts, they tune in to a word or phrase here or there, losing everything in between, leaving gaps that have to be filled in either with their own phraseology (to keep "the lines" open), or by constant repetitions of the information already received.

Yet I was correct in some aspects of my theory, for consciousness does exist in strands, or like trails of smoke of varying complexity and design; each thought, memory, and sensation rising up from the main cluster of consciousness, which is of great intensity. There are clusters of consciousness, then, highly organized identities, "leaving behind" them trails of lesser organized psychic material that is quite alive, only at a different order of activity. After death we learn to distinguish such variations, seeing them as clearly as you might see into a moonlit night sky. Your own existence forms such patterns that you do not perceive. These are literally the shapes of your thoughts and experiences in their nonphysical versions.

Thursday morning
March 24, 1977

In any attempts to communicate with the living, the dead use their own patterns of consciousness as ladders, climbing down (to use an analogy) those spiraling thoughts and desires that are still attached to earth, moving in its psychic atmosphere; and the living "climb up" the lines of their own intent, so that you have nonphysical patterns of consciousness merging to some extent. Clouds blowing through clouds fits the situation, rather than anything so crisp as a telegraph wire carrying precise codes.

To various degrees this commingling happens naturally in any case—clouds or clumps of consciousness moving through each other, merging, with a motion always occurring as, say, the winds always blow on earth, mixing air from all over the planet, but in patterns. From the standpoint of the living, the attempt to communicate with the dead is like standing on a high hill, tossing up a kite— the living consciousness—hoping it will sail with one particular gust of wind and no other; and if this happens, then the kite moves with the wind, is propelled and carried, but the kite is still itself.

The thoughts of the living and the dead flow through each other, then, but in a neutral fashion, remaining undecoded as a rule, general shapes affecting psychic atmospheres and forming an inner psychic climate. In much the same way, for example, the sounds of the audience's whisperings and stirrings rise and merge in the depths of a theater, although the members of the audience concentrate on the drama on the stage, ignoring the random chattering that is closer, but not directed or focused as well. The actors block out such sounds as the living, caught up in their own dramas, sift out the whisperings of those whose parts are already played, or who wait in training for new roles.

In my time perhaps more than in yours, we listened for the voices of the dead and hoped for inventions that would "tune in their voices," imagining as a rule that if there were voices, there must be speakers somehow present. But thoughts and voices exist whether or not the thinkers or the speakers are alive or dead. I could, if I wanted, tune in to my own voice as it spoke so many times in my life, for those sounds still linger.

Now I speak, and with sound, for I can hear my words if I choose, but while they *are* sound, they exist in a different realm of sound that cannot be perceived by instruments, but is allied to your own experience with silent "sounded" thoughts. These can sometimes be picked up by the living, as unheard sound; but it is difficult to distinguish such thoughts from ordinary ones, for they are on the periphery and not attended to. The universe is crisscrossed with such "currents" of consciousness; intertwining, mixing, yet each independent, going its own way.

Friday morning
March 25, 1977

Parapsychology, so termed, has become more scientifically attuned since my investigations, and perhaps had I known this in life I would have been pleased, tired as I finally became with table tippers, planchettes, manufactured ectoplasm, and the whims and varieties of human imagination and deception. Yet it is impossible to isolate specific abilities and examine them as you might microbes; and science distrusts the human personality. It has never come to terms with it. Some schools of thought still consider consciousness far too nebulous and difficult to contend with, preferring to examine it in a secondhanded fashion as its abilities are projected onto graphs, and where its actions in ghostly enough fashion appear as scratchy scribbles, perhaps like the shadow images of hand puppets that are projected upon a parlor wall.

People possess abilities that science cannot explain. Worse again, you cannot pull out an isolated ability, say, precognition, from a person's head like the magician a rabbit from a hat, to study it more thoroughly. And if, in science's terms, those who profess to have paranormal abilities are at best unconscious cheaters, magicians playing mental tricks on themselves, then I must state that each living person is a magician of some note, living in a universe which for all scientific knowledge should not exist at all, and never should have come into being at all except for—chance!, acting in a vacuum, against nothing.

The intangibles of experience, the emotional reality and the invisible zest for life: these frame, intensify, and set off paranormal events. The imaginative scientist, overly enthusiastic, perhaps, finds a good subject. The two personalities click. Emotions and hopes are generated, and results appear. Then, in your time particularly, the scientist's colleagues complain; the scientific controls are doubled. The troublesome aspects of personality are dispensed with. The gifted individual is asked to apply those creative abilities to card guessing or to pit them against some mechanical device, and the results go to chance or below. So it appears evident to many such scientists that chicanery happened earlier, or that some kind of emotional contagion colored the previous results.

A man or woman reports a precognitive dream—simple enough to dismiss, particularly if unverified. But when large segments of each generation throughout history report such phenomena, when scientists in their own times come across such reports, we have another situation. These are events that by their nature happen to people in their private moments, often under emotional conditions. To dismiss such a range of experience is sheer nonsense.

It is one thing to state quite properly that such events are most difficult to assess scientifically, but quite another to deny their common recurrence in the behavior of mankind, or to dismiss paranormal events as fabrication, hallucination, or the natural reaction to drugs or shock. It is also close to stupidity to continue using methods directly in conflict with such abilities in an attempt to prove their validity. Science often uses the wrong methods on purpose, knowing well that these by their nature screen out such unpredictable strains of human activity.

It is precisely in the area of such embarrassing subjects that the most challenging and hopeful achievements of science lie, and precisely in those avenues of thought considered too hot to handle that the answers to man's most pressing problems will be found.

Any hypothesis is an assumption, and to that degree any hypothesis is a statement of faith, however qualified. Science is always operating "as if" one hypothesis or another is true or can be proven to be true. <u>Experience constitutes the greatest proof in the framework in which an event is encountered.</u> A scientist who has a precognitive dream is quite right to admit that he has experienced an event that science does not recognize as legitimate, but as a man, he is bound to accept the proof of his own experience.

Time is experienced, so in practical life time is an event, even though scientists realize that time is relative. Precognition and telepathy are experienced events on the parts of millions of persons, events that seem to connect the realities of consecutive time and Einsteinian relative time. It is ridiculous and shortsighted to say that precognition is contradictory to known scientific principles. Precognition simply points out gaps of the most embarrassing kind in scientific thought.

It is the worst kind of arrogance to ignore the existence of paranormal experiences on parts of large portions of the population, and dangerous to operate with hypotheses that do not include such larger versions of reality. Science wants to be free of myth, yet it sets up its own. Only science's myths lack all of those qualities that give men hope, zest, cheer, or faith, by denying not only the meaning of man's universe but of his very being, reducing his world to a spiritual and psychic vacuum, shoving man out of his own experience and diminishing his sense of stature by denying the events of his psyche.

Then let science beware, for the "common man" may overcompensate and overthrow it; for religion and science have each underestimated the ordinary person, the natural creature, who in the long run may be more foresighted, in spite of all his frailties, than is generally supposed.

# 10. Man and His Times, Reincarnation, the Atmospheric Presence and Knowing Light

Friday morning
April 15, 1977

(Strictly speaking, James's March 29 passages should go here, since that is the order in which the material came. I felt that I'd "picked up" this April 15 passage out of place, as it were, for whatever reason, and that it should actually go as the beginning of this chapter. Following this individualistic but quite universal statement of man's plight in dealing with time, James launches into some of the most excellent material I have ever read concerning life after death and the nature of the psychological medium in which existence itself takes place. I feel strongly that James's passages about his times was meant to initiate this material, not interrupt it as it actually did in the order of its reception. When I wrote it, I felt that I'd "missed it" earlier.

(No place else have I made any changes in the manuscript, and in moving this passage up, I feel I am in keeping with James's intent.)

• • •

My own dying was a relief, and I am convinced now that a person fits together with his or her time in a certain fashion. That is, whether people are comfortable or uncomfortable with their time, they fit within it, are automatically attuned to its overall challenges and conditions, and even their talents and abilities are peculiarly suited to their historic period. After a while, the fit is not as comfortable as it once was. The fabric of time rubs. The invisible seams that connect the person with his times begins to fray.

152

For a good portion of his life, a man so identifies his own purposes with the general conditions of his historical period that the two seem one. Instead, a man's purposes slide like a zipper up and down, connected to his times as the zipper to his jacket, with so much mobility and no more. The groove in which the zipper slides will allow only so much leeway, and the teeth of purposes and times must meet perfectly for the zipper to work at all. But the tension between the man's purposes and his historic times causes the tiny teeth to pull apart until finally the man sees that his purposes must be freed from the fashionable jacket of his times.

It becomes apparent that he no longer fits into his time as he once did. He has done all he can within its tailored conditions. His thoughts and intents no longer mesh with his historic period with the ease of the past. His own desires, beliefs, and thoughts are like new buttons sewn onto an old sweater; they do not really fit the buttonholes.

All of this happens very gradually and in various ways. During the period of a lifetime, however, people see themselves in relationship with the great themes of the day and experience their reality through daily details of life—the ways and means of livelihood which, while seemingly permanent, constantly change until the intimate routines of life, once so much a part of it, give way to others. The thoughts and impulses connected with the earlier, familiar ways must stretch more and more to accommodate the new conditions. Again and again the person sees that his purposes, like the zipper, run up and down the same track; and worse, that the new generation wears completely different suits of the times, with which his ideas now make poor accessories. Finally, he stands out as no longer wearing fashionable mental attire. He sees that his very ideas have frayed.

Even the roles with which people clothe themselves wear out. The child, the rebellious adolescent, the radical young adult, the graduate student, the debutante, the young father or mother, the esteemed director of business or foundation, the grandmother and the grandfather—these roles vanish, rip apart at the seams, as the person watches with dismay—until the valued garment of the times has taken all the wear and tear that it can. In most cases, the people have so identified with their roles that in old age, when the roles are gone, they are actually astonished to discover so much self left over. In some societies the aged are honored. There is the role of wise old man or wise old woman. But in American society, the social role stops before the life does.

I chose, therefore, to end my life before my role ended, while I was still fairly well attired mentally for my times, for even my disagreements were tailored to my historic period. The democracy that I had so fostered began to dismay me. My hopes for science had failed, nor could I find any real scientific evidence for the existence of the soul. Moreover, the framework of the times that had so sustained and challenged me changed. A new scenario came into being. New props slid silently before the mental walls of life's psychological drama, people with different psychic costumes and new mental stances, while I stood in my tattered but once fashionable psychological cap and gown, mildly appalled.

I had thought to bring science and religion closer together by showing the objective reality of religious states and their effect upon life and experience. I had thought that telepathy and clairvoyance might be scientifically proven and taken from the superstitious realm, so that they might be admitted into men's concepts in a respectable way and counted in man's scientific hypothesis. I had prided myself that a rigorous study of man's paranormal experiences could produce evidence for the soul's existence, so that psychology must then count man's heroic nature in its plans for humanity. And in all of those ways, I failed.

The times became more raucous. Religion and science, having briefly been introduced with me as intermediary, parted with bad feelings on both sides. The scientists became more aloof, cooler, more academic; the religionists, more emotional and less reasonable. The spiritualists and pseudospiritualists took possession of the soul, often dirtying the entire affair with shady seánces and cotton ectoplasm, while the evolutionists triumphed on the other side, washing their hands in horror of such a trickster's soul, while giving man instead the natural inclinations of a killer.

One speaks the language of his times, no matter what

the meaning of his words or how ahead of times his philosophy seems to be. Gradually, however, the hidden accents, invisible insinuations, rhythms, punctuations, and inflections change until a man realizes that his very language is old-fashioned and no longer speaks to the times. No matter how futuristic his meanings, his words are tinged with mustiness and only later generations can lift up those words once again out of the dusty vowels and syllables that once sounded so brightly.

So though I spoke clearly—to myself—in later years I could tell that it was as if my very tongue were tinged with dust. Others listened, but with a vague puzzlement, as if my words themselves no longer met directly upon the ears of my listeners, but first had to pass through a gap of just the briefest misunderstanding—so that if I spoke one word, they must translate it in their minds to another, newer one, or change the inflection entirely. Even my most spontaneous sentences sounded mannerly or contrived. The words themselves had changed so insidiously that meanings I gave them slid away, while others were assigned to them. So speaking the same English language, I spoke an alien one; and young people listened respectfully, but their faces were puzzled, again, as if my tongue were coated with dust.

This was more noticeable in the works of my brother [Henry], for he was dealing with American vernacular, showing the aliveness of the American nature as opposed to the studied classisms of Europe: yet his Americanisms, so fresh and even sometimes vulgar, turned too soon into archaic niceisms. His characters no longer seemed alive, because the ideas and frameworks in which they had lived changed, as indeed the gayest scenario must fade and each new piece become dated.

Tug and pull as much as you will, in life your ideas and purposes are connected to the threads of your time, woven into it, and to progress after a certain point there is nothing to do but loosen those threads, cut yourself apart from the times, and take off the constricting garment that has become more like a straitjacket.

And so you die.

In the meantime, however, you have been wiggling for many years within your coat-of-the-times and finally ascertained that there *is* a you within it. You realize that you and the garment are indeed coming apart at the seams, where earlier you so identified with this cloak that such an idea would have been most frightening. You become more and more aware of a secret, knowing self that has always existed apart from the times, one that is now rather anxious to leave them; and of an inner voice nudging you, saying, "You've had your place in the sun. Don't stay where you're no longer wanted or needed. And admit it, you're quite bored and in need of a new start. You've outgrown your times and there's nothing you can do about it."

Certainly I became aware of that voice, though I had always been somewhat conscious of it even in my prime and earlier in my childhood: an independent part of me, rather indignant at having to accommodate to history at all; but curious, putting one foot into life experimentally, as it were, and always rather aloof and slightly superior to the entire affair.

To that extent, I never gave myself to life as completely as I perhaps should have, though I tarried long enough, and far longer than many. My curiosity and rather dry wonder were my main characteristics, so that I would not experience my emotions fully, for example, but study them with the faintest mental nose sniffing; and I used my melancholy, I now see, as a churchman uses incense to dazzle the senses of others while setting up a smoke cloud to separate himself from the crowd.

I say this with all good humor toward myself—and the hypothetical churchman—but without my melancholy I feared I might fall all the way into life as it seemed others did, and forget to examine it as I had initially set out to do.

In life, we are curious about what happens afterwards. After death, earth life is such a small arena of activity that we wonder how it can contain such depths and dimensions of action and meaning. I used to wonder at the hidden microscopic life that teemed in a puddle, or imagine the infinite space a pond must have to a tadpole, or strain to understand what busy relationships must go on between even the smallest of insects; all of these were closed off to me. So now earth life seems incredibly small in that respect, yet amazingly active, packed with events as a puddle with drops of water, each seemingly separate yet each connected. I wonder that I ever put myself into that context. At the same time, that experience added immeasurably to my existence, but I do not wish to repeat it.

Tuesday afternoon
March 29, 1977

Memories of other lives lie piled up in my mind like books still to be read though already purchased, and while I am curious, I am as yet too engrossed in the studies that I still identify as my own. I identify myself to myself as William James still, then, knowing that this is somewhat like a psychological convention that simply makes experience more orderly, and since I am intrigued with the tensions and relationships between orderliness and creativity, I enjoy preserving this particular convention while seeing how far I can creatively push its barriers.

Therefore I can say that other lives of mine are waiting to be reviewed, studied, and explored as if they were journeys taken by me in other lands in which I changed my name, occupation, and took on other family obligations and relationships than those I consider my own. I realize, nevertheless, that some of those "other selves" may well consider *my* life as belonging to them and they may well explore the life of William James from their own stand-points as peripheral to their own intents, pursuing it as you might study, perhaps, the life and times of a favorite historical character to whom your family tree says you are related. Only in this case the study would be far more intensive, so that the times would come alive on the invisible parchment of the mind, and not simply appear as illustrations in a book.

So there is much about the organizations, affiliations, and groupings of consciousness that I do not know.

The dead soon learn, however, that the mind itself is a vast threshold, reaching into infinite depths of experience. The experienced self is small as a tremulous gnat by contrast, hovering at the entry, golden in its light, free but uncertain, attracted and tantalized by that illuminated source of greater mind.

Nor is it possible from my present standpoint to

comprehend the constant new manufacture of times, for each life I feel I have lived also waits to be explored, and within its boundaries time constantly opens up—and with new combinations. I suspect, then, that other selves of mine (from my viewpoint) are exploring my life and historical period, yet I am not aware of any invasions of consciousness not my own, and I also suspect that my life as I knew it contributed to those other lives in ways that none of us yet understand, though we were not in life at all familiar with any tamperings with our consciousness by the others.

I do know that some individuals in my position rush back to physical existence and some do not. I myself am more given to action behind the lines, to a study of the behind-the-scene workings than to center place on life's stage. So I have thus far remained in this very favorable situation. Some care little for any study of the theme of life but are engrossed in its plots, leaping from life to life with the greatest agility, taking part in all of history's dramatic events; enamored of action for action's sake. Others like myself weary of direct participation in life's parade, preferring the sidelines, from which we shout encouragement and suggestions, pursue our studies, and try to help behind the scenes by pointing out situations that the paraders themselves might ignore, caught as they are in life's unremitting glare.

So even in my life I was of that kind of temperament. I say this, again realizing that other lives may have found me of a much more volatile emotional character. I like to think that I was a clown in the Middle Ages, for now and then my hands invisibly perform a juggling act with balls and plates in my mind. Looking down I see stockinged shoes, orange and red, and a bag of assorted coals. I seem possessed of a bitter humor, completely lacking in graciousness but filled with an angry fire formed of resentment, so that the exaggerated smiles of my performing face mock those who smile back.

This I believe was in a tiny kingdom where, first in the streets and later in the court, I was a jester whose jests were innocent of love or compassion. Yet the vigor I sense there, the explosive emotions ever shooting forth, blackly, as pyred jests, stirs a remote excitement. So when I feel that the "time is right," that life so different from my own may be my next project, to see where it went wrong—if indeed it did—and to discover what abilities of mind or temperament were shown that I could learn from.

Does that clown explore my own past life now? I wonder. I can imagine him sometimes in my own old study, or walking with my cane down to watch the ships. I see him in my world-that-was, surrounded by a vast land of plenty, without a king or court, and think that his humor would be less deadly, tempered, and that perhaps he might smile honestly with an open face.

So if such is possible, I might place myself in his world, seeing it with my scholar's eyes. Would I develop the same dark humor? I do not think so, and yet my own melancholy and nostalgia were tinged with a strange edge of irony that never in life left me. Again I wonder: was that cheerlessness the legacy of my bitter clown?

The answers lie behind the curtained door that I mentioned earlier, symbolically speaking, leading from my box seat elsewhere. Yet so far my attention is riveted upon the stage where the actors, the paraders, still march, while I compose these commentaries at my leisure; still, you might say, the gentleman of class, holding onto my cherished characteristics as the gentleman does to his favorite waistcoat, gloves, and cane; still wearing the attire of my soul as I have known it. So I am loath to set it aside, and yet certain at the same time that I shall do so. Yet I enjoy this interlude, this intermission, and this journal, like notes written between the acts on a theater program that I shall, later, cast away.

Nevertheless, I feel myself growing out of myself in a certain fashion. My adopted characteristics are becoming too small and cramped to contain my new growth and development, and I will move on most certainly to larger psychological quarters. It is not only the physical body we outlive, but the psychological house we have chosen. First after death we add new rooms and suites to accommodate our greater experience, but it is soon obvious that the entire structure has had its day. We must move out of it completely.

This "journal" will be left behind, found second-handedly in someone else's mind, quite like an antique book discovered in an attic, mixed with cobwebs, but caught in the rays of the afternoon sun that filters across the attic so that the title on the book glitters. For these thoughts are filtered through another's mind, fluttering "downward" from my box seat to the attic of that mind, while the earthly writer has to rush up the dim stairway, waiting in the emptiness, searching for these pages with mental hands wide open.

I do not know when I will finish this composition, but I will suddenly know that I have added my last comments, written my last words as a tenant of my present psychological manse, and will then move into the larger framework of myself which I feel is being constructed; so perhaps the actor might wait for the latest set to be prepared before he can make his entrance.


Wednesday afternoon
March 30, 1977

Two elements in my present state are particularly significant to me, when I compare it to physical life. For one thing, my psychological and "physical" mobility is astonishing, and my sense of freedom feels, at least, unlimited. In the beginning I found this disconcerting, for my reality at any given time followed experience-organizations of my own making and focus. The bounds of creaturehood—morning and evening, time, even pain, birth, and death—impose a certain order from which the living cannot stray. My state of mind was one of confusion for a while. Imagine if you will a mongrel of a dog, quite used to wandering, suddenly given, say, wings, the use of a conceptual mind, vocabulary, and along with these fulfilling but surprising additions, a million new choices where, before, instinct and the demands of practical creaturehood had kept his curiosity quite well within a limited range.

In other words, new capabilities kept sprouting from my mind, each stranger than the other. A vivid desire of the most momentary nature seemingly transported me from one place to another, with no transition or preparation—exhilarating and unsettling. Countering all of this, however, was the most delightful sense of safety, so that after the first orientations, there is no fear at all; and everywhere, being seems to be couched in perfect safety. I simply use my mind to "go" where I want and the rest of me follows. My body, real enough to me, can appear or disappear in any given place, however, and each environment is formed by peoples' belief in it. I say "peoples'" belief because all of us to ourselves appear quite natural, quite like people, only in a different context indeed.

This freedom of which I speak was not entirely new. It can be deduced easily in life by an imaginative extension of the abilities shown by consciousness in dreams, only here those extensions are the "new facts of life," if you will forgive the term, and must be mastered. The conditions after death, while consciously dealt with, are similar to dream states, then, while the additional self-conscious manipulations add the most vivid clearness and preciseness. The knack is to focus consciousness properly in the desired areas. This usually presents little difficulty after a brief preliminary stage.

It may seem that this existence of mine is more solitary than it is, because of my own predispositions. There are schools, colleges, or whatever the dead choose, but these arise in response to the wishes and beliefs of those involved. They exist quite validly in certain areas of focus and consciousness, but they are "invisible" in other areas. They are constructed by the combined focuses and intents of those so involved, and they attain a permanency over long periods because so many are inclined in those directions. I could visit such "institutions" by desiring to do so, changing the state of my mind, and therefore transferring myself to a "location" that exists only to those in the same psychological state.

This may sound complicated, yet to some extent you have similar patterns. A living person utterly uninterested in learning institutions and indeed ignorant of them—a native in the deepest bush country, say—would have no practical knowledge of a university. Even if later he traveled to an area near such a place, it would have no reality for him. He would probably never visit such an institution unless his state of mind changed and desire for that particular kind of knowledge inspired him. Here, the states of mind create the reality in a direct fashion.

Thursday morning
March 31, 1977

(Here begins some of the most fascinating descriptions of
afterdeath reality that I have ever encountered; not only does
James manage difficult material with extraordinary grace,
but as the material continues, he gives invaluable hints as to
how we can glimpse this "atmospheric presence" in life.
From here on, James soars, his curiosity and intuitions
seeking the eternal foundations from which all realities
spring.
(I was very touched by all of this material. I kept trying
to sense in everyday life the magic and wonder of James's
perceptions, hoping that aside from this manuscript, I could
perceive the experiences James was speaking of.)

• • •

Nowhere have I encountered the furnishings of a conventional heaven, or glimpsed the face of God. On the other
hand, certainly I dwell in a psychological heaven by earth's
standards, for everywhere I sense a presence, or atmosphere,
or atmospheric presence that is well-intentioned, gentle yet
powerful, and all-knowing. This seems to be a psychological
presence of such stunning parts, however, that I can point to
no one place and identify it as being there in contrast to
being someplace else. At the risk of understating, this
presence seems more like a loving condition that permeates
existence, and from which all existence springs.
    The feeling of safety mentioned earlier is definitely
connected here, in that I know that no evil or harm can befall
me, that each of my choices will yield benefits, and that this
loving condition upholds me in all of my ways. As in life I
was always aware of an underlying melancholy, I am here
always delightfully conscious of an extraordinary sense of
safety that leads, say, to heroic acts and courage—naturally.
There is the constant feeling that the universe is with me, for
me, and with and for all others at the same time. Not only
does it not conspire against me, but it ever lends its active
support.

This willingness to help is everywhere apparent and promotes, of course, a sense of ease that, at the same time, stimulates the personality's abilities in ways most difficult to describe. While I mention this presence as itself, so thoroughly does it pervade everything that attempts to isolate it are useless. All theological and intellectual theories are beside the point in the reality of this phenomenon. I *know* that this presence or loving condition forms itself into me, and into all other personalities; that it lends itself actively to seek my good in the most particular and individual ways; yet that my good is in no way contrary to the good of anyone else, but beneficial.

Each person living or dead is somehow a unique materialization or actualization, psychologically "perfect," of this basic loving condition or psychological, atmospheric presence. Each person is himself or herself, and an agent for the universe at the same time. The universe leans in each individual's direction, gives, and is compliant, for each person is part of that psychological fabric, coming to life. It is as if the universe were a multidimensional cloth with infinite patterns, and figures which did not remain flat but sprang alive, lived, moved, and died and came alive again, while the fabric of which they were made never wore out but miraculously revitalized itself and rewove its parts.

The patterns and figures are constantly changing, and the very stitches with which they are made are composed of the basic fabric also, so that there is everywhere communication between all of the parts at that level. Each figure changes the quality of the fabric, however, adding immeasurably to it through experience, for each life multiplies the actions possible to all of the others, on this common level.

Yet this is not known to me without evidence. That evidence is a kind of direct, built-in-knowing—self-evident— and I realize that I possessed it as a child and let it go, on purpose, so that I could discover it again from a different angle. This somehow puts me in a new position with regard to the universe than I was in before, adding to what I can only call my psychological "thickness."

Each living person goes through that process to some degree, and what is discovered is not the same truth that was momentarily discarded, but involves a new comprehension of the self from a different angle of reality. Each time we take on a new identity this process is one by which the universe realizes itself anew—as us and as itself—and in which the identity comes upon its invulnerability from a different standpoint. Obviously there is much here that I have not learned, but each new life is begun with the knowledge of basic safety, from a threshold of security large enough to sustain a physical existence.

There are, again, other groupings of consciousness, alliances in which identities group together psychologically, as people do on earth, physically, in nations. These consciousnesses retain individuality while joining together in joint purposes, pooling separate viewpoints into psychic composites that I do not pretend to understand.

The living often equate death with darkness, for how can the dead see? Even if the spirit hovers beside the body, the corpse's eyes are closed. How can the spirit have vision, disconnected from the organs of sight? Yet here I am surrounded by illumination that emanates from every-where—colors more sparkling than any I knew on earth, a light of enchanting varieties, not even or monotonous but seemingly alive in its own fashion. It emanates from what I see, but also seems to be inherent all about me, whether or not there is anything to be perceived otherwise.

In life I saw brilliant lights sometimes with my eyes closed, and on occasion some small objects or shapes. This light is similar except that it is more mobile and possesses qualities not normally associated with light. I would say it was a knowing light, everywhere existing at the same time, at once; transparent in quality when it exists alone or independent of a visible object or shape. While I am tempted to say that it moves in waves because of its mobile nature, this is not true. Instead it appears out of itself, at each and every conceivable point in the universe. Physical perception "sees" only a small hint of this light, and from it spring all of the lights and colors physically visible.

I suspect that there are other forms of this light, or made from it, that I do not perceive myself, and I am sometimes aware of shapes or sounds just out of my range, like a world just out of reach. But all of this, from my standpoint, may be confusing to you. I hear, but since in your terms I have no physical mechanisms, the sounds must be different in nature or range from those I was familiar with on earth.

I think of a similar experience, when I was alive, of mentally hearing a voice, hearing it surely, even while I knew that my physical ears were not involved. So it seems to me that regardless of the physical properties assigned to sound, sound itself has nothing to do with the physical version. The sounds here are distinct, bell-clear, separate, and each tone if it were visible would be like a crystal. Yet in your terms this would be called mental hearing, and I am sure that the body I possess is a kind of mental convention for my own benefit.

I forget it, then remember it again. When I forget my body I am operating without it; my consciousness is in no way hampered but follows my pursuits. Then suddenly, like an absentminded professor, I realize that not my mind but my body has been absent, and without any transition I have it again. So most likely it is created unconsciously, out of habit. Nor am I frightened, only momentarily disconcerted, when I discover its absence; I reattain it automatically, as on earth I might pause at the door, ready to go out, and remember my hat, putting it on without a thought. I no longer identify with my body, and of course it is not flesh and blood, though it seems to be when I want it to.

I understand that some of the dead identify with the body for longer periods than I, and that different personalities vary in the easiness with which they learn the afterlife conditions.

These conditions themselves vary, accounting no doubt for the many misconceptions about death and the dying that are often encountered in life through those communications that do take place.

I connect the knowing light with the well-intentioned atmospheric presence mentioned earlier, since both have been a constant in my afterdeath experience thus far, and I study this phenomenon rather steadily at times, reminding myself of a caveman or other prehistoric man looking up at the sun and trying to understand its properties. Specifically, I have not called this knowing light an entity, in terms of personhood. Yet I am sure that it possesses a psychology far divorced from any with which I have ever been acquainted;

that it knows of my curiosity and examination; and is not annoyed, but invites it.

This presence must be termed atmospheric. Again, I can think of no better word, and it (the presence) cannot be pinpointed as existing in any "here" as separate from there, but coexists in all places. Searches for an analogy do not particularly help either. The closest idea I have is to compare this atmospheric presence with the quality that exists on the most ideal summer day: the delightful, enchanting scent and touch of the air itself seems to be imparted everywhere, so that flowers, trees, grass, people, mountains, valleys—all seem to lie in its enchantment and add to it. So this atmospheric presence with its knowing light has the same effect, both psychologically and in my experience of everything else that exists outside of me.

Surely such a summer day seems benevolent, alive, and has a buoyancy that is added on to the other seasons. That is, an extra-appealing aura seems to be imparted to earth on such a day. No doubt this is the reason that many spiritualists referred to afterdeath as Summerland, but as a psychologist I am fascinated by something else: I know that this atmospheric presence does not have what I refer to as human characteristics, yet it does possess characteristics of an emotional nature, and it is this exuberance, this well-intentioned quality, that psychologically supplies my feeling of complete safety. It is as if I bask in the light of a psychological atmosphere that corresponds to the physical atmosphere of an ideal summer day.

The summer day, however, must end, and dusk fall with a certain sadness upon man and beast alike; the summer's beauty rests in the very impermanence of its existence. I always enjoyed the changing seasons, wondering that others in more even climates did not get bored with the sameness of the weather. Yet this atmospheric presence is ever-changing while in a strange manner remaining the same. I theorize at times that it is the combined consciousness of the entire universe by whatever description, existing within all consciousness, yet apart. At the same time, I am sure that more is involved. Nevertheless, in this light the conditions of existence are the most supportive and encouraging imaginable.

# 11. The Divine Mood

Friday morning
April 1, 1977

I remember the feelings that seemed to permeate some of the days of my childhood. Even without bringing to mind the particular details of any given day that might have given rise to those feelings, they surge back and I can see that for all their exuberance, they lacked, in contrast to my present psychological state. It is as if the universe now has its own mood invisibly imparted everywhere, in which I move and think. Again, the closest analogy is to the moods of childhood, when it seemed that all things were possible and I was filled with an energy, zest, and sense of competence that vanished all too soon. But this atmospheric presence with its knowing light seems possessed of that mood to a superlative degree, radiating it effortlessly out of its own good intent or desire to please.

Now if such a mood, everywhere demonstrable here, is only a portion of other superlative characteristics; if I am basking in vast goodwill of some kind of psychological personage—then I can only say that the ultimate power of such a being is such that its moods sustain worlds. This is conjecture, yet no other explanation that occurs to me is satisfactory.

Yet such a hypothesis presents its own difficulties, suggesting the presence of a god so powerful that its good nature creates and maintains immense realities. But what if the visage of such a god changes? What if its mood turns only a trifle dark? What happens if it is displeased? For conventionally understood hell would be nothing compared with the disastrous effects of such a gigantic goodwill turned into its opposite. That kind of rage and that kind of

167

power would annihilate worlds beyond all hope. This idea
reminds me, of course, of the old Jehovah, with man at the
mercy of a capricious god who in a fit of anger sends down
floods or storms upon the world.

But in a way impossible to explain, the good intent of
this atmospheric presence is such that any ill intent would
dissolve within it, not be annihilated but transformed,
automatically changed into its best expression; and at the
same time I realize that destructiveness is simply the
inadequate, or poorly realized expression of a good intent.

The psychology, if one can use the word in this regard,
of such an atmospheric presence is such that it ever seeks the
most creative, expansive, loving expression, in such gargan-
tuan terms that our usual ideas of motivation utterly fail us.
It is basically nonsensical to give such a presence human
characteristics, and my interpretation of what now I can only
call a divine mood is most likely my translation of
psychological realities as far beyond my understanding as a
man's psychology is to an ant.

There is an immense, I can only term it, loving
permissiveness that imparts exuberance and zest such as I
have never known, and I feel within myself the coming birth
of a new kind of creativity, involving all of my own
characteristics, abilities, and idiosyncrasies as if each nook
and cranny of my known being was preparing its own
delightful surprise, expansion, and further expression; a
challenge of the most extraordinary kind, as if in life you
sensed the approach of a time when each area of your living
was about to expand immeasurably, the smallest talent being
magnified and coming into practical use. I possessed, I
thought, some latent musical ability never used, for example,
and I feel it somehow rousing within me and feel myself
drawn toward expressions that on earth were beyond my
means.

This atmospheric presence seems furthermore, then, to
possess qualities that act as potent psychological stimulants
of the most profound nature. The words "psychological
growing medium" come to mind, as if this atmosphere
promotes psychic growth to the most advantageous degree,
or provides a spiritual and psychological medium arousing
the creative development of even the smallest incipient seeds

of personality. Qualities and characteristics that I never suspected I possessed now surface within me so that I feel to myself like a garden ever coming to growth, containing far more flora and fauna than I ever realized; and as if earlier I had only identified with one crop of abilities that I called my own.

A steady confidence sustains me also, and a stronger sense of balance than I have ever known, so that these euphoric feelings are not unstable or overwhelming, but taken quite as my natural heritage, adding a buoyancy to my subjective steps. To an extraordinary degree I must have changed myself, then, from who or what I was; and surely my own demeanor reflects at least some portion of the spiritual resiliency and good intent that is my lot.

I find myself on occasion also possessed of a new emotion, or one so different in quality from others as to feel like an entirely original emotional sensation. It is a concentrated version of love, compassion, understanding, and creativity, directed on my part to each of my own thoughts as if they are the most precious seeds, psychologically packaged by me, and sent through the universe forming their own species—beloved psychological infants springing from my creative mind—that I free and send forth to grow and develop according to their nature, each to find expression, take hold, and hopefully thrive. Therefore I find myself again, occasionally, bidding good-bye to my thoughts when they leave my mind, much like a parent who sends children out into the world for the first time.

In some way it seems to me that each of us was somehow sent out in the same fashion, and that we repeat the process anew whether we are aware of it or not. I wonder, of course, if it is fruitful to compare this feeling about my thoughts and my good intent toward them—regardless of their nature—with the more persuasive atmospheric presence and its attitude toward the universe; and toward me specifically.

For that magnificent good intent is strangely combined of impersonal and personal elements, of this I am sure. Intellectually this implies a contradiction, though on an emotional level, none exists. This good intent is seemingly directed toward me because I am me; and I sense, at least, a deep understanding on its part of my subjective reality, a comprehension that far exceeds my own understanding of myself. On the other hand, if I were someone else, this intent would be just as powerful and as personally directed. Indeed, everyone with whom I have come into contact feels in the same relationship to that atmospheric presence as I do.

I do not know whether still others, in other states of mind, perceive more or less of this divine mood or experience it differently. But the varieties of perception are so unlimited here that certainly such must be the case. I do know that this same atmospheric presence and knowing light also sustains earth, and now I can understand some experiences that in life I could not explain.

Before I mention these, however, I want to theorize further about the nature of this atmospheric presence, and surely I can think of no more challenging activity than the exploration of what I can only call divine psychology. My present circumstances put me in that most creative and yet ambiguous position of observing a presence in no way like any I have known, in which I sense superb original—and therefore mysterious—characteristics; this presence is more than a little disposed on my behalf, and yet my position is one in which my old methods of exploration and communication are obviously too weak and puny for the task at hand.

The impersonal and yet personal nature of this presence leads me to make certain tentative assumptions of an intellectual and emotional nature, for now at least I can blend intuitions and intellect in ways impossible for me before—using one or the other separately if I choose, or blending them in any mixture, so that in their combined light a more expansive vision is possible than one alone allows. In so doing, I make automatic adjustments, each one presenting a different focus or view of the subject at hand whatever it is, with each alteration bringing further understanding and giving me the keenest delight, as with new surprise I see how mind and intuitions together ever open up fresh views and combinations.

My thoughts do falter, however, when I try to verbalize even to myself the staggering implications of creativity grasped by my intuitions, even though my emotional realizations also lag and cannot follow beyond a certain point. It is as if this atmospheric presence were a psychological repository for all possible subjective beings, of such import that no one could comprehend these at once or in any combination of "times"; and that each of us draws from that repository whatever it is we require, according to our understanding and circumstances, whatever they may be—while simultaneously our own experiences also add to that supportive psychological framework. In it, personal and impersonal meet and blend, forming new combinations and creative versions.

Friday afternoon
April 1, 1977

Much of what I feel and know conflicts drastically with the ideas of good and evil as held by most religions, and with the like beliefs held by many religious mystics. For I see that repression is a denial of creativity; that evil acts are short-circuited well-intentioned ones, or good acts poorly performed or executed in such a distorted fashion that they appear twice as grotesque in the light of their seemingly opposite good intention. Yet to say that evil acts are the result of twisted, malfunctioning good would have sounded sheer Pollyanna to me in my lifetime. A philosopher who avoids dealing with good and evil is no philosopher at all. Yet the profound truth is that there is no evil to contend with, and this profundity requires that most compassionate understanding of humanity and an examination of man's nature in the light of its best rather than worst interpretation.

Only such an explanation satisfies man's innate search for order and meaning, so that evil is not seen as a negative force in itself, or as an absence of good, but as the misdirected or distorted attempt to attain good. Only in the greater dimensions of good's actualities and expressions do evil's lesser qualities and lacks have any meaning. It has been said, for example, and in my works I remarked also, that religion has often served as the banner of ill will. It is certainly obvious that more murderous acts have been committed in religion's or God's name than in the name of hate or revenge. Even wars conducted by nations against each other are fought under the misconception that good will result. Man agonizes over his ill deeds. He does not enjoy feeling guilty, and indeed guilt would make no psychological sense at all were it not for the existence of man's innate good intent, however misdirected or distorted it may become.

The sense of freedom emitted by this atmospheric presence is so energizing and refreshing, so conducive to creativity, that it is impossible not to realize that in life also, repression is a denial of creativity for whatever reason. As long as evolutionary and Freudian concepts based on man's innate psychological duplicity rule, then man will believe that the opposite of repression is license and the release of savage or primitive drives which, left alone, will ruin civilization.

The Darwinian self would have no reason to feel guilty about any of its acts, however murderous, if they served the end of the survival of the fittest; yet no person alive is without feelings of guilt. Nor do Freudian explanations serve as anything but the flimsiest fantasies in explaining guilt, though belief in those fantasies reinforces them and programs experience, further distorting self-revelations under psychoanalysis and, incidentally, producing no real cures. Those theories have been so projected onto human experience that terms like "murderous rages" are misapplied to violent children's behavior, and Darwinian survival theories tacked on to Freudianism presuppose the desire of sons to murder their fathers and possess their mothers sexually.

Children do desire to possess the abilities and powers of adulthood, to emulate their elders in all of their areas of expression including sexual ones, but the energy of that desire is in no way murderous, though that is set up as the normal pattern of desire and unconscious behavior. The Greek dramatists dealt with such themes, for they gloried in contrasts—in the good and evil, the heights of glory and the tragedy of the flawed character—but these were all seen in a greater light, in which reality teemed with gods, humans, demons, and multitudinous species between, with great tensions and creative dilemmas and interactions; while the Freudian self is stripped of all heroic actions or possibilities of greatness, left only with an untrustworthy libidinal self that must be repressed lest it destroy itself and the civilized world which it has, in a way never explained, managed to achieve.

Monday morning
April 4, 1977

By comparing my own and others' psychic reality now with that general state I knew on earth, I'm able to see what errors of interpretation I made. Hopefully the following suggestions made in hindsight can serve others, and stress man's need for a psychological theory that will encourage and not limit his psychic growth.

In life it is not what particular incidents or feelings we repress that cause difficulty but the mental set or habit of repression itself, and our belief in the need for repression to begin with. Repression on a daily basis restrains and restricts us on every side, in thought and action alike, limiting our exuberance and expressions of love.

The belief in a flawed self, the identification with a destructive, condemned, or fallen species leads to a basic distrust of the self, to an oversensitivity to "conscience," and it is precisely such feelings that caused my own almost constant sense of melancholy in life. It pervaded all of my days and lay like a heavy weight upon my heart despite moments of joy. Each happiness, each cheering event, each achievement was then weighed against what I felt to be the greater pragmatic reality—of man's stupidity and evil tendencies—and against such a black mountain of flawed psychological slag no act, however heroic, no achievement, however brilliant, could appear as more than one spindly flower in a gigantic garbage heap, soon to die and vanish, of no help in any way whatsoever; and no act, however well-meaning, could begin to affect the ultimate weight of man's plight.

How could flawed creatures trust themselves privately; and in terms of a democratic government, how could man hope to rule himself? So it seemed that I must watch myself at every turn, double-check my theories and deductions, be triply cautious of my hopes for man or the existence of the soul. The more my heart yearned to find proof of the soul's existence, the more my mind mocked, for nowhere could I find in man's overall acts a justification for his survival.

More than this, I feared that a faith would only lead to deeper disillusionment, that faith in man's good intent would not last a moment in the reality of his practical world. It seemed safer not to believe, for then the besieged heart could be hurt no longer and could cease comparing man to an ideal that was unrealistic. Yet, against this, I looked everywhere for the ideal.

• • •

(As I wrote this for James, I felt his purpose merge with mine or mine with his, so that he and I both seemed to speak with one voice. This identification continued for the entire passage.)

• • •

But judging all man's acts against the ideal and perceiving how short those deeds fell in execution, I lost sight of man's intent. How, then, could I find surcease in the idea of a well-intended universe? For then, all was right with earth and heaven, with the creatures and the stars, and only man stood out in a glaring flawed inadequacy. He alone marred what was otherwise an ordered universe. Yet if there was no order in the universe, then where did the idea of it come from, that my heart and mind alike sought it out and judged all discordance against its implied existence?

For I could not believe in the accidental creation of the universe any more than I could accept the accidental manufacture of a chair that happened to fit the contours of my body so perfectly that it just might have been made to do so. How lovely and convenient that atoms and molecules just happened to fall in such an accidental yet precise fashion, and that I happened to have hindquarters that could take advantage of such a cosmic configuration.

But for all of that, I could not get the feel of a well-intended universe to support me, to couch me as the chair did, and so psychologically I felt without support while my melancholy reminded me constantly of the dilemma.

I grew disenchanted, and my disappointment with life and its conditions grew in proportion to the hopes for it that once possessed me. Even nature lost its magic, for the contemplation of its beauties only led me to a nostalgic wish that man and his works could in some way compare to that orderliness and grace. The inner atmosphere of my existence was then almost opposite to that state I am now enjoying.

Yet in life I did have some sense of this freedom and possessed hints entirely overlooked, for the ease and motion with which I thought and the action of my thoughts themselves had the same swift mobility, safety, and ease. That is, my thoughts flew out from me in such profusion that I could never keep track of them. Their vitality had no bounds and even the most pessimistic ones flew out from my mind with the same optimistic freedom—sure, that is, of expression—and possessed as much agility as those more cheerful ones.

Now, however, I am surrounded by a sense of psychological luxury and supported by that atmospheric presence whose qualities I find at once so curious and so familiar. This presence is responsive. I am sure that it reacts to me, yet while it is everywhere, it is not obtrusive but again, like the summer day, it is more like a delightful medium in which all living is bathed so that it is quite possible to forget it almost, or take it for granted. I say "almost" because its qualities emerge upon you slowly, or did upon me, so that it was some time before I realized its responsiveness, for example. Therefore I suspect that the dimensions of its existence reveal themselves or are revealed according to the attention one accords them.

Again, as far as I can tell, this knowing light and atmospheric presence are the same, which is to say that at every hypothetical point this presence is wholly here and responsive, while still retaining its atmospheric rather than specific nature.

And I know that I am cut from the same cloth, a self formed about me like the finest garment stitched according to an eternal pattern, tailored with multicolored beads of time, figured flesh without seams. And each self is put on, taken off, and worn again like a beloved article of clothing, never discarded or hung limply in a dark closet but renewed, brightened, newer with each wearing; a living garment, lovingly rendered.

I can only compare this atmospheric presence, then, to some kind of creative psychological medium possessing within itself all of the qualities necessary for existence, a repository of individuation and perceptive abilities. As all the required elements for life spring up from the ground of the earth, which also nurtures them, this medium seems to perform the same services, only giving birth to psychological entities and the entire universe that sustains them.

Wednesday morning
April 13, 1977

I am convinced, then, that this atmospheric presence is the creative medium from which all consciousness springs. This same omnipresent light seems to attract the smallest of my psychological seeds, buried or struggling for freedom, sodden from the overwatering of my melancholy, so that each hope rises once again. My heart becomes ever lighter. More, this light is surely the same that in another fashion lit the skies of Boston, dawned over the ocean and splashed upon my study floor. But the quality of this knowing light differs, for it is alive with a loving intent that is instantly felt and experienced in a direct manner. There is no mistaking its intent, and again I am struck by the ambiguity of its vastly personal and impersonal aspects.

Its atmospheric qualities, for example, its unobtrusiveness, may exist only at certain levels of understanding, for in a strange manner I was comforted by the fact that this presence did not seek me out, examine me, or attempt to overwhelm me in any way. Instead it quietly offers—what? Solace, support, a buoyancy in which my existence is everywhere strengthened, refreshed, and yet led to perceive enticing further developments, or rather to feel itself able to expand, even to be transformed, in perfect safety.

This offering of opportunity, however, also invokes my

own peculiar individual tendencies as if these and no other are uniquely vital and important, to be nurtured; as if these are the seeds of some future fruit, exotic plant or special species, to be lovingly cultivated; or as if I can produce psychological seeds of inestimable value to the universe, and this knowing light nurtures them more surely than on earth the sun nurtures the spring seedlings.

Yet I am equally sure that each other person here feels the same way and is nurtured in the same fashion; and with no way to prove any of this, I know that on earth each person is also supported in the same way. There is no demanding quality to the atmospheric presence or its light, yet it seems possessed of what I can only call a divine active passivity. It attracts but does not push, and yet its force is a passive one in that it seems to exist in a state of active waiting or invitation, ever welcoming, with the gigantic tenderness of power held in control, as if it is so aware of its own energy that it knows its most nonchalant caress could carry such strength as to squash the object of its love.

This last statement again comes close to suggesting a super personification of the kind I have tried to avoid, and there are complications here also, most difficult to comprehend.

Words and even my own impressions and limited perceptions may be misleading in this respect, in that I believe that comprehension of this atmospheric presence is automatically meted out according to the needs and conditions and nature of the perceiver. Again I am reduced to analogies, but using the exotic plant simile, it is as if I am "watered," nurtured, and given light in exact proportion to my own needs; not—for example—given too much light or overtended with fertilizer (richer comprehensions than my rooted thoughts can take), but spontaneously receive exactly what I require.

This suggests some cosmic automatic plant-tending device of impersonal nature, leading to the complications I mentioned earlier. For I barely sense that this seemingly automatic relationship rests upon an intimate contact of the most personal nature imaginable, one deeper than any possible in what on earth is considered intimate contact.

That is, this seemingly automatic nurturing, this

meting out of comprehension and light, seems to be based on an intimate, loving knowledge of my own state and being so complete that it spontaneously delivers what is needed before I realize my own needs—in a way more characteristic of a mother, say, than a father. And as a suckling's pressure on a cow's teat brings forth milk, so in some unfathomable psychological nurturing, the pressure of man's needs automatically inclines this presence to bring forth whatever strength, understanding, or support is required. And as a mother gains satisfaction from nursing her child, so this atmospheric presence feels as part of any creature as that creature's mother in the act of nursing, so that the seemingly automatic cultivation is more intimate, based on an impossibly complicated relationship.

These analogies, swinging from one spectrum to the other, serve me poorly; yet I can think of no other way to imply the nature of this atmospheric presence. To grown men and women, the nursing analogy may seem distasteful, reducing the adult to the suckling infant, portraying man's state as one of dependent passivity; and such is not my intent, for returning to the complications just mentioned, to some extent or another this atmospheric presence also actively desires to nurture, support, and bring into being as, say, a woman for years unable to bear a child finally produces one and is overwhelmed with love, wanting to give it all things. At the same time that I reach for these analogies, it is equally difficult to assign either male or female characteristics to this atmospheric presence, and I realize that such gropings of mine imply projections on my part.

Taking that for granted, let me continue. In the light of this presence I do not feel subjectively an infant in the manner described, but sense potentials or psychological outlines that are mine to fill, as perhaps one person might sense within a loved one the full stature of personality that on earth, at least, it is never possible to actualize.

Thursday morning
April 14, 1977

The artist does not think of a sketch as a "baby painting,"

but has respect for it as itself, though it may well develop into a painting and he may have executed the sketch as a first step toward a painting. To that regard, the painting is implied in the sketch and the artist may very well always see the painting's promise whenever he looks at the sketch. This is perhaps closer to the relationship between the atmospheric presence (the artist) and myself (the sketch). But in this case the sketch is endowed with those possibilities of development itself, and in the presence of the knowing light it feels its own existence drawn out of one state toward another, more fulfilling one.

The earlier infant analogy comes easily, however, since in childhood I now see that we accept such help automatically, taking it as our right; and in life it is everywhere apparent except that man has closed his mind for whatever reasons to what is ever available. The earth itself is given, and all the requirements of life. Men and animals come into a world already equipped with fields, plants, water, air—each element fitting so perfectly with each other and each so contributing to the existence of the other—and this miraculous construction is so workable that man takes its existence for granted.

But the earth *is* given. To imagine that such an entire environment is an accident is, I see now, intellectually outrageous as well as emotionally sterile. I also see how the religions partially understood and ignorantly distorted the qualities of this divine mood in which physical life has its being.

Because man has set himself apart from nature it seems that he must manipulate it to his advantage. He does not let it work *for* him as it *wants* to do, for nature also possesses a good intent, flowing as it does from this atmospheric presence. With man's attitudes, however, it follows that other people and institutions also seem to work against the individual, who then feels alienated from God and man, alone in a chaotic universe, a creature accidentally thrown into existence like a live coal from some gigantic furnace, sizzling for an instant with the cracklings and rustlings of desire, but soon reduced to ash.

With such theories it is impossible to hypothesize about creativity, the worth of the individual or the value of his actions, since all effects are ultimately destroyed and even their existence has no meaning. Man's undeniable creativity and the cooperative ventures of nature literally have no place in such an accidental universe, since these are also seen as the happenstance constructions of a system whose creatures have one intent only—the savage competitive intent to survive, each individual pitted against each other member of its species, each species against each other species, each nation against each other nation—providing a picture in which indeed only evil seems to be apparent.

In that construct, not only is the universe accidentally formed but its intent sets each element in it against the other and cooperation takes place only out of self-purpose of the most selfish nature. If such a universe did indeed exist, the creatures within it would have annihilated one another in the dawn of time. In man's mechanistic approach to such questions, he ignores the meaningfulness felt by even the smallest creature and apparent in all animal activities—the joyful, exuberant playfulness of nature that exists side by side with its more "deadly" attributes.

Without that exuberance, that very joy of being, there is no reason for any species to continue existence. Yet man is fast creating the idea of a joyless world, and in so doing, restructuring his emotional life to fit the "facts" as he sees them, facts that nowhere fit the real scheme of nature and seem to fit only because man steadfastly ignores other evidence to the contrary.

This evidence exists in his own private experience, in all of those realms that science deliberately considers outside of its scope, for it now considers unscientific any data that it has decided a priori might upset its official framework. These attitudes, abilities, characteristics, and experiences that might and would show the meaningfulness of nature's good intent remain as unacceptable data.

Here I include the state of dreaming, the vast unexplored areas of altered consciousness, telepathy, clairvoyance, and above all, the creative abilities themselves. For in man's use of creativity, he definitely allies himself with the meaningful universe and with the good, exuberant intent from which it springs.

# 12. A Master Language and a "School" for Philosophers

Monday morning
May 16, 1977

There is constant "telepathic" contact between the living and the dead, though not in the gross terms sometimes imagined. That is, the thoughts and feelings of the dead are as active and vital as those of the living and contribute to the mental atmosphere, though at a different level, for those thoughts "circulate" in the way that higher air currents might, providing more of a generalized stabilizing atmosphere. The ideas and methods of the natural communication of the species depend not only upon built-in biological inclinations and abilities, but also upon the continuing knowledge of each individual who upon death contributes his experience to the species as a whole, or rather makes it available in a new way.

Learning in life takes place during the sleep state even as in the waking one, and in dreams people venture into that more generalized atmosphere, bringing with them the day's problems and information, weighing these against a heritage of experience that belongs to the entire species, and to which the dead have contributed.

Learning throughout the ages is passed down in such a fashion, implementing the more pragmatic waking methods of trial and error. To this extent, the emphasis upon ancestor worship in some cultures has a valid basis. Nor does learning stop at death but takes place in this different context.

It is known, of course, that some cultures pass knowledge orally down the generations through song and myth. Information is also transmitted through this inner

181

mental environment to which living and dead both contribute, and which can be compared to a field of viable information everywhere invisibly surrounding life.

The thoughts of the living and the dead mix as, say, the air of deserts and seashores eventually merge one with the other and contribute to the world climate, even though locally each has its own characteristics that are seemingly opposite. So I am not speaking of psychic invasion, but stating that men's thoughts and feelings, both from the living and the dead, form a mental field of information and interaction.

The species is not wholly dependent upon physical methods of learning alone, but is ever propelled also by inner incentives and provided with additional data, and so knowledge is transmitted from generation to generation through dreams and inner communications. These acquaint whole peoples with their own cultural heritage and greatly enhance the worth of language, which itself acts as a structure to communicate certain symbols while blocking out others.

Different languages of course represent various characteristics of feeling, thought, and belief; and they dignify some of these through expression and emphasis, while ignoring others as verbal frameworks. Languages are verbal frames as well as, say, verbal paintings, giving expression to certain images and sensations and emphasizing these through the framework of verbal structure, which expresses and restricts at the same time.

Basically the thoughts of the dead need follow no such patterns, and the information received from this generalized mental field of information is given in a kind of "master language" which each person translates into his own idiom. Such translations are automatic, in the same way that photosynthesis is an automatic process on the part of plants; so that any communication in whatever language is already an automatic translation of inner information, as water poured into a glass takes the shape of its container.

These are not distortions but various expressions of inner realities, the languages being psychic containers that serve to display information so that it can be "poured" from one container to another most efficiently.

In basic terms, however, languages are born in each moment, and this atmospheric presence of which I've spoken seems to be characterized by a knowledge in which all languages are understood. That is, no matter what language you use to address a question, the answer is given in the same idiom. And with my mental conversations with others here, the same applies. Here, then, the atmosphere itself seems to translate my words from my language to the language of the hearer. This happens automatically, as far as I can tell. The translation is mental, instant, and complete. No misunderstandings occur in that regard.

The usual barriers of language are nonexistent, while I am equally sure that a master language is utilized that remains "invisible," since the translations are so instantaneous.

Information is specific and makes sense only in the midst of a system of facts in which it fits. The emotions' wisdom cannot fit into the system of mathematics, for example, and as mentioned earlier, information *can* provide knowledge or can, under certain conditions, actually detract from it. All of man's intuitive knowledge, his bibles and other sacred books, consist of knowledge automatically translated into the specifics of one language, which is then translated by man into others. The knowledge flows into that verbal or written container, being displayed according to the images, traditions, mental, and cultural shapes characteristic of a given tongue. The knowledge thus becomes specific, but specific in a necessarily prejudiced fashion. The symbols of a language float atop it like multicolored and multishaped fishes, so that it is also necessary to look between the vowels and syllables to the transparent waters beneath, upon which the fishes ride.

Man's versions of God or the gods, of life after death, of the beginning and ending of the world, are therefore translations—as of course this manuscript must be—and translations that fit the experienced reality to some degree while still leading beyond it. Any person knows that private speech only approximates feeling or sensation, and only a fool mistakes his expression of a feeling for the feeling itself.

There is also, then, the same kind of gap—inexpressible—between my experience "out of time" and my attempts to explain it. Myths are more truthful than facts in that regard, but only if you do not take them literally. My nature is not a myth-making one, however, so I seek for connectives that are imaginative and yet tuned to the facts of your experience.

In those terms, it is true to say that here I speak to others who are more or less at the same level of reality or understanding as myself. These levels of understanding, then, form their own environments, providing certain dynamics that structure experience. Instead of continents and other land formations that structure life on earth, here mental states provide the criteria for various kinds of perception which frame experience in the same way that language structures thought in physical terms.

I am now used to communicating with persons who may be nowhere visible to me, for example, the criteria for communication depending more upon the complementary relationships of mental states than upon "physical" availability. Other environments and circumstances are related to me in such cases through mental images transmitted automatically. These are available, however, only to those like myself who exist "at the same frequency" or who are tuned in to certain frequencies of this vast field of viable information. My experience is related in the same way to those "at my level," and we pool our knowledge, breaking it down to information of a more specific personal nature for ourselves, while our personal experience forms part of the generalized field that is perceptually available. Some of us are visible in those terms to others, but our larger communications are not confined to that degree. There are those more characterized by visual expression, or by sound, who instead of verbal or mental language communicate through a cross-sense language of rich complexity.

In a way, your entire perceptual range is a kind of language through which physical reality is spoken, a language acquired so early in life and so effortlessly that it becomes automatic. It *is* acquired, however, with all the nuances, inflections, and assumptions of any language, only this one possesses biological verbs and mental nouns and it organizes the entire perceptual range.

Monday afternoon
May 16, 1977

Since I, too, once spoke this language, though in those terms
I am now bilingual, I can compare my experience now and
then. Obviously I can still organize my thoughts in the old
familiar fashion (as I am doing now), but ultimately I find
this so limiting as to be impractical except for this kind of
manuscript production.

An intelligent traveler will try to learn the language
native to a country he intends to visit in order to understand
and to be understood by others, and quite practically to make
his needs and wishes known. If and when you travel to other
planets beyond your solar system, you will instantly realize
that what I have just said is true: your physical body and its
entire perceptual range is itself a language, spoken
automatically. Not only would a difference in conventional
language separate you from any hypothetical natives on
other planets, but so would the language of your biology—
the utterances of molecules into cells, genetic passages, or
sentences constructed in entirely different biological patterns.

Some visitors to earth have learned to "change their
language" in this more comprehensive manner, appearing
as much like men as possible in order to examine and
understand the physical world.

Bodily structure and form is a language also, then, and
many in my environment can change that structure, taking
different forms that express their mood or experience as you
might, say, sing a song, write a symphony, or whatever. I am
not nearly that proficient, and as of now my direct
experience is with those whose existences rather parallel my
own, either through complementary interests or historical
connotation.

I am still philosophically minded, so I am in direct
contact with many philosophers both famous and unknown,
most from historical periods other than my own, and many
natives of other cultures and civilizations that were unknown
to me with my stance in the Western world.

In our "dialogues," I am astounded by stories of other
civilizations upon earth's planet, worlds once practical and

real, now lost to the world's history yet very much alive—for like fossils their beliefs give new fuel for succeeding systems of thought and schools of knowledge. Their forgotten languages exist in the pauses between words and help compose the rhythms of living languages, even as their philosophies provide inner rhythms upon which more current theories ride so securely.

Now I smile, thinking how often in life I spoke of the ancient Greeks or Mesopotamians, for from my present standpoint their cultures exist almost simultaneously with your own. The Victorian age is but a whisper echoing through corridors of "sound" in which the loftiest of civilizations represent only one note; but a note of infinite variations, echoing and re-echoing, only each time with the most significant meaningful change in rhythm or cadence.

So these philosophers have already taught me more than I could possibly learn in one or a series of lifetimes. For here is a concentrated type of learning experience of a kind I cannot explain, though I will try.

There were far more civilizations on the earth than scientists suppose, and the earth is far older than your records show, or the evidence will support. Some cultures were so different from those I was familiar with that my questions themselves made little sense, even granting the inner telepathic understanding that unites us.

Tuesday morning
May 17, 1977

I ask one philosopher, for example, "Can you explain the social structure that existed in your civilization?" and I meet a mental puzzled silence. The philosopher smiles, wanting to please me with a reply, yet amused by the definite block in his own understanding of my question. I try again. The words "social" and "your" are the culprits. Mentally he sends me images of a world in which there is no word for "your," but only "ours," and in which the concept of "social" has a thousand different connotations; a world in which men and animals alike are considered social creatures, intermixing at many levels; as if, say, in Western civilizations beavers were given equal consideration with human bridge builders and both worked together, their lodgings respected and their needs met.

Mentally I transmit pictures of the world I knew, with "society" referring to human activities only, and the philosopher shakes his head disbelievingly, ready to dismiss what I am "saying" as a philosopher's joke, not after all in the best of taste.

I persist. "When did your civilization begin and end?"

He looks at the other philosophers questioningly: am I serious? In their midst I see a Western world philosopher of, I think, the sixteenth century; but he, too, only smiles at me, as if he has just been through the same experience as this himself and I must be on my own. The answer I think I receive is: "The civilization reaches beforehand and afterward equally."

I say, "But then when did it flower? When did its arts and sciences flourish?"

"Now," is the amused answer.

Again I persist: "But in historic terms? The civilization vanished millions of years ago, if I understand you correctly."

And before my eyes is suddenly spread a living world of obvious industry and achievement: buildings, cities, people walking down the streets, a profusion of animals intermingling. I was used to sharing the avenues with horses, and as I think of that, the philosopher nods: "An acceleration and continuation of that kind of concourse between man and animals, but on a more equal footing." Somewhere he means to make a joking but fond comment I do not quite understand, using the Latin word for horse* and a play upon the English word for equal; I cannot quite follow the interplay.

He shows me brilliant pictures of bees swarming around flowers, insects flying from plant to plant. Then immediately afterward, growing out of that image, I see a spaceship dipping in deep space from planet to planet. "One and the same principle. We learn from the animals, the plants, the insects——"

*Equus.

I begin to protest.

He says, "As bees leave one flower for another, we left one planet for another."

"But I'm speaking about earth's historic past," I say. "Even from my understanding of earth's science since my death, the evidence for the planet's past wouldn't include the amount of time you seem to be implying. Earth isn't that old."

But even as I communicate this thought to him, I know that despite all evidence to the contrary, earth *is* that old. "But it's impossible," I say, and the philosophers laugh together and agree with me! As I stare from face to face, they say almost in unison, "But quite true." A slap in the face to logic, I think, a logic which presently has my own face stamped upon it. I grow stubborn and for a moment I feel an odd role reversal, remembering rebellious students who stood up protesting in audiences now and then while I tried to explain a given issue. Now I feel like one of those students, and uncomfortable in the process.

Before my eyes flash again images of more civilizations than I can count, each flourishing, using what seems to be the same planet in different fashions, each with different relationships between men and the other species, each reflecting these characteristics through their own languages and—oddest of all—interpreting man's state of being in completely different terms.

I almost glimpse millions of shining points that seem to connect those worlds, holding each intact yet providing an unseen but sensed tension in which each world is related to the other, perhaps like a multidimensional cobweb. But again, I cannot follow. "How could any one science or civilization understand all of that?" asks the philosopher who also speaks for the others. He answers himself: "Within physical life, you can examine only the data given you—the rules of your own world—and make deductions based upon that information."

This dialogue is and is not imaginative; that is, it is a reconstruction of an actual event, a learning process that I frequently encounter, but translated by me through my knowledge of Western customs to an imaginative edifice as faithful as possible to the actual events. At this place in each dialogue, when in one way or another I am shown the vastness of reality, the following usually happens. I become rather angry, feeling certainly like a junior member of the assemblage, accustomed as I have been to grant myself not inconsiderable powers of intellect and insight. I cannot pinpoint the psychological, emotional, and intellectual dilemma exactly; or the faculty of my mind that suddenly cracks open just when my own frustration fills me with an almost agonizing feeling of incompetence and ignorance. But suddenly a corner of my mind *does* shudder, shake itself, and become transparent in essence, as if a thousand veils that previously covered it have dissolved.

What happens then I cannot describe, for I scarcely understand it myself. Perhaps a caterpillar turning into a butterfly feels the same way in its fashion: a transforming process starts, and through my mind's new small but cleared window an immense warm, but not blinding light shines. Whether or not this light has anything to do with light as it is understood earthwise I do not know, but I experience it as a living knowledgeable light that is part of the atmospheric presence mentioned earlier; and it imparts knowledge, or rather comprehension, through methods unknown to me. I receive comprehension as, say, a flower receives light from the sun. I am immeasurably strengthened, supported, and my earlier feelings of frustration and groping vanish.

Wednesday morning
May 18, 1977

These dialogues and learning encounters always end in that fashion, and no matter how inconceivably multitudinous the visions of other worlds—with oftentimes a resulting diminution in my own sense of importance, which seems to dwindle alarmingly in contrast to the cosmic outspread before my mental eyes—despite all this, that knowledgeable living light seems to arouse the smallest portions of my being and shine warmly through the ever-enlarging transparent window that opens in my mind.

After each such experience, I feel somewhat like a young psychological plant being tended carefully in the

shade while being exposed gradually to the real daylight,
while it had earlier supposed that the shade represented the
entire light of the world.

It is as though a curtain were drawn aside briefly, so
that afterwards I do not feel dwarfed by the earlier visions
given me, say by the philosophers. Irrational as they may
sound, I sometimes wonder if those visions in some way
represent psychic blueprints of a reality as distant from mine
as a seed to the entire generations of its progeny. Is it
possible, for example, that I am being shown pictures of my
own complete stages?

Of course I hesitate to come to such conclusions even
tentatively. Yet I am also quite certain that there is a
connection between myself as I am and the visions I am
shown. It has occurred to me that perhaps my thoughts form
such shapes and patterns on other levels than mine; that all
of our thoughts actually fit together like massive eternal
jigsaw puzzles, attaining another kind of being than ours,
another type of awareness; that there are civilizations of
"thought people" whose reality appears quite normal and
natural to them, as earth life did to me and still does to you.

In that case I would be viewing thought-universes in
which my own thoughts participate, for surely I have no idea
where thoughts go when I am finished with them.

I perceive these as visions of populated societies and
cultures of endless variety, intents, sciences, and arts; in my
terms, from future and past alike and from parallel times
that seem to go off like shooting stars from any given
moment. I know better in my position than to wonder if
these are physical realities, currently operative. The question
seems to be, In what context are these operative worlds, and
how are they connected with me? They may, again, represent
mental configurations, representationally apparent for my
edification. Sometimes I feel the way I imagine a single cell
might if it were suddenly shown a vision of the entire body of
its complete form; as if an ovum could glimpse the giant-
sized human form that would spring from its own natural
growth.

Am I, then, in some as yet unknown way being shown a
pattern that represents my own future adult form, but on an
entirely different scale; a mental equivalent for what on earth

would be normal growth processes, but occurring in a mental, psychic, or spiritual medium?

I thought that life on earth presented puzzlements, but the challenging concepts I glimpse are dizzying. For example, dimly now and then when such visions are being shown, I sense an identification of myself or parts of myself with the spiraling images I see. When I try to pinpoint the identification, however, I still feel it but without being able to locate it in myself. That is, association does not seem involved, yet there is a tantalizing sense of familiarity of the most intimate nature, coupled with an equally alien awe, for the configurations represent a majesty and complexity impossible to grasp fully.

To make matters more complicated, I also feel that these visions (shown during the learning encounters) also represent valid civilizations known to the various philosophers, so that the images seem to stand for some expansion or growth of thoughts into discrete realities. I mull these experiences over after our sessions end, and my thoughts finally grow hazy, like clouds drifting away from me, changing shape as they vanish from sight.

Clouds *do* change shape, of course, mix with the earth's atmosphere, turn into makers of rain or snow, and though their exterior appearance may be calm, winds of great intensity may be swirling inside; and though they may look solid enough from the ground, their shapes more or less vanish into mist and their apparent solidity gives way. So it also occurs to me that as clouds combine into different patterns, different forms, and cause differing conditions, perhaps thoughts operate in the same way.

Countless thoughts must have passed through my mind, yet I remember only the smallest percentage and identify, of course, with those I keep as retainers about me, for they provide a sense of continuity. But after my learning encounters, I also sense other thoughts, equally mine, buzzing about me, grouped in various ways but not in a time context: they all are equally present or equally nonpresent. They seem to form shapes, so that I wonder whether I am, all unknowingly, the psychological center of many worlds.

The assembly of philosophers may each be going through similar experiences, but I suspect not. I think that they are the professors, so to speak. They are attentive, yet these questions are mine to answer, and the other philosophers simply provide the medium in which comprehension can occur. Although I seem to be the only student present, I have frequently sensed that there are others also, invisible to me as I am to them. It is as if we are each provided with separate psychological learning cubicles—perhaps to focus our attention. I have the idea that there are comparatively simple mental gestures that will let me see my learning comrades—ways of looking over or under the psychological walls dividing us—but so far I have been too engrossed in my own experiences to try.

It should also be understood that I am describing only my own experiences. In an earth environment, I suppose this would be a school for philosophers. Others may care little for the type of challenges I am encountering, and weary quickly of contemplating the complications that arise from such philosophical engagements. There are those who delve into interrelationships instead, stressing the multitudinous emotional interactions possible, weaving these into various kinds of existence and forming multidimensional psychological connections with others. Such endeavors have their own flavor but would find me an impatient student. So of those schools, you must learn from others than myself.

It may well be, also, that the different subject matter and schools of inquiry are merely various slants or focuses in which the same material is presented, couched in terms of the student's main interest and so tailored to get his attention. I can imagine some kindly, crafty superpsychologist fondling a sprightly beard and saying to his associates: "James, here, fancies himself a philosopher, so let's give him a taste of it, shall we?" If so, I may have bitten off more than I can chew.

# 13. Biological Faith and Nature's Source

Thursday morning
May 19, 1977

On earth, I thought I devoted a good deal of attention to the nature of thoughts and concepts, and the connection between them and private and national life. Now I see that all of the earth's natural events—its seasons, the varieties of manifestation and expression—all represent an inner, inexhaustible Nature that is mental as opposed to physical, if we must use such terms. The given planet, with its astounding framework of creativity in which earth's creatures reside, and which supplies them with all their needs and requirements—all of that represents but one facet of this larger Nature's capabilities.

This Nature, initially mental, propels thoughts into actuality, regulates their development and growth, and provides to each being a given mental, psychic, and spiritual world which is, again, naturally expressed and seeks its own development. Here also, the psychic requirements and needs are met, and a state of grace is safely provided in which action can be taken without care; and by this I mean without the anticipation of impediments.

This brings us to faith, of course, which as I now perceive it is a physical, biological condition of growth and a psychic or spiritual condition as well. It is as if faith were the agent that developed a negative into a definite picture in the darkroom of the mind; and without faith, the events will not "take."

My life's work gave me such ideas, and Christianity's brighter beliefs stress faith—but unfortunately in such a shallow manner that often faith and intellect seem to be adversaries at best, or complete strangers fated never to meet to discover their common ground. Here, however, faith is so obvious and ever-present, its principles so clear, that I am given a closeup view in which faith's importance and characteristics are definitely shown to be the agents in which any kind of growth can creatively happen.

I am not referring to the brassy, almost harsh, false optimism that is on earth sometimes flaunted in faith's name, nor even of faith *in* this or that church or theory or school, but of a faith that exists whether or not it knows its object; whether or not it is attached.

To the extent that faith applies *to* anything, then it is trust in one's natural order of being; the feeling that the conditions for existence are largely conducive to it; that needs will be met within the circumstances of that natural order; and that one is couched and supported in one's existence by some larger Nature from which the natural order springs.

In such a medium, bones, frogs, stars—and philosophers—grow.

I am speaking of a pragmatic psychic or spiritual medium that must be present if any cell is to develop, if any atom is to combine with others; in other words, of a medium in which all events and actions happen. The expectation of motion is involved, whether it be physical or mental motion or both, and a freedom of direction in which action can occur. That is, faith is self-moving or promotes motion and dissolves barriers.

The infant's "blind faith" operates faithful to an inner biological and spiritual vision, providing the necessary belief-in-safety to allow for the infant's accelerated growth, so that the child reaches out, explores, and is free enough to exercise its curiosity. For the development of curiosity is dependent upon just such "blind" biological faith, and curiosity is also one of creativity's underpinnings.

Faith easily makes a legitimate biological claim, then. Its lack in any area results in a vacuum of development, a weakness in which, for example, faith's natural immunities break down or disappear. Faith's presence is an active health-promoting agent.

In my present environment—again, like the summer day—faith everywhere surrounds me, so that its support is one of the most outstanding elements of my existence. There is a complete lack of threatening conditions of any kind. I would have imagined such a state to be lacking also in challenge and creativity. Instead, I am filled with a sense of wonder, curiosity, and impetus that is never tiring. So natural do I now find this faith that it is hard to believe it was not a conscious part of my mental constitution during life.

To the contrary, as mentioned earlier, I was often struck by depression and while attracted to faith, I was also concerned lest I become faith's fool, particularly since I found no element to which I could justifiably attach faith. And to me, regardless of my feelings, it seemed that faith must be *in* something.

Democracy came closest to justifying my faith in that regard. It could rouse men to constructive action and best meld the private and public good. Science and religion in my time each vied for men's faith. But faith that is attached to any one element, be it church, government, or science, is always in jeopardy, for at one time or another the object of faith will no longer justify it, and faith itself will become lost. Or certain kinds of men can attach their faith, like their love, to a series of "objects" one after the other, thus making faith continually operative; each time losing it and then finding it anew.

In life, I was much interested in such issues, particularly where faith was connected with belief systems, for it seemed to flourish equally well in the most auspicious and most inauspicious mental environments, and to grow as well around the silliest and the most profound of doctrines.

Thursday afternoon
May 26, 1977

But what, I asked, stood in faith's way? And if faith did possess a biological value, then why was it so lacking in the majority of my fellows? More than this, faith's appearance was not always welcome and often came in quite abhorrent form, for how many people I met professed faith in the most nonsensical or dangerous of doctrines. How many faiths existed by virtue of their exclusions? For example, there were those whose faith denied either the soul or the body, pinning their beliefs on one or the other, but struck with such a smallness of mind that the tenets of their faith showed by contrast only the limited area of its scope.

Thus, "Heaven" was closed to non-Christians, and belief in Christ often brought membership in an exclusive spiritual club as snobbish as any Londoner's. Other frameworks, such as the Eastern ones, included a faith that excluded millions—the untouchables—or displayed a callousness toward life itself in which the purpose of life was to escape it or any repeat performance.

So I found surcease again in my faith in science and democracy, but faith I now see is a more general, omnipresent quality that is best not attached to any particulars, while it may at any time include them in its larger scope.

On the other hand, faith is personal, intimate, and must spring from the individual's innate knowledge of his connections with nature, following the order of existence into which he was born. Each person *is* born with that spiritual and biological optimism, that psychological aura of safety in which existence is meaningful precisely because each individual feels the presence of a personal universe in which he and every other consciousness has meaning, even though that meaning may not be intellectually understood.

But where can faith's justification be found if it does not reside in the object of its attachment, or if the intellect alone cannot discern it? It can be discovered through the exercise of the intuitions and creative abilities, and through the natural inclinations and leanings of the individual. For I now know beyond all doubt that each person is gifted with natural faith and insight, with built-in impetus and guidance in which biological and spiritual faith are equally merged.

Science, religion, and psychology have unfortunately, with the best of intentions, muddled that inner knowledge and separated man from the practical use of inner direction.

Proof for the existence of the soul and its immortality cannot be found, as I once hoped it could be, by any assemblage of facts, but through direct knowing, direct experience, which can yield a comprehension of those psychic events—but in a different order of knowledge entirely. "The proof is in the pudding," and such evidence would result in a far better world, of course. But more important, in the meantime each man or woman who succeeds in rediscovering biological and spiritual faith receives evidence of that ancient heritage through a complete regeneration of body and mind.

When that regeneration falls short of its mark, the comprehensions have not been allowed full sway. A "cosmic consciousness" experience that denies the importance of desire, for example, is tarnished, rejecting the impulse that initially made it possible, for all creativity springs from desire.

That fact is gloriously apparent to me, though spasmodically, when the intelligent light I mentioned earlier sometimes radiates with a depth of desire almost beyond imagining, as if desire is so intense it must break up into a million segments, each forming a life, a consciousness, a being. That desire and its showering segments are eternal. Of this in my own mind I am assured.

To go along with one's desire, to ride the thrust of one's own life, does indeed lift an individual into communion with that far vaster desire and power, not to the annihilation of individual desire but to its activation at other levels of being. And there lies a paradox, for those who speak of the death of desire and the assimilation of the individual into the whole are often the most individualistic of people, the most fanatically fueled, the most eccentric and one-sided. In many such cases their comprehensions, once begun, are side-tracked, it is true. But in its purest version, natural faith seeks the fulfillment of the most individual and original tendencies of a person and accelerates rather than diminishes his desire.

Monday morning
May 30, 1977

Therefore one man's vision need not look like another's, but each person, interpreting the nature of reality through his own experiences and characteristics, will reflect a different segment and shine with a unique cast, so that all of these visions taken together may suggest the larger picture of man's meaning by pointing out, even if in exaggerated form, a peculiar aspect that would otherwise go unnoticed. Therefore must each person trust his own nature, for in the same way it has a purpose, brilliantly focusing within the world a facet of being that within life's framework was meant to be.

The infant takes its first steps in response to that innate biologically and spiritually rooted faith that instills confidence, responds to curiosity, and promotes motion. The child "knows" its faith is in its own capabilities and senses the properties and powers of its limbs, each of which possesses its own motivation toward motion. The legs want to stand, to run, to use themselves; and each cell within the body contains its own impetus and biological faith.

Wednesday morning
June 1, 1977

I am surrounded now by that kind of faith, only here it seems to be applied in a different manner. That is, I feel like exercising my psychological parts as if the self that I've known is an infant in contrast to some sensed further development. I'm motivated to travel out along psychological paths rather than physical ones—each, however, as strange to me as the front walk to the newly creeping infant. At the same time I feel gently coaxed by the psychological medium itself. The intelligent light draws me outward spiritually in the same way that the summer landscape calls earth's populace out for picnics, parades, or simple walks.

My dreams and memories are now being put together in different ways than I once experienced them. They exist in my mind now like childrens' blocks in a playroom, which can be made to form more than just one castle, bridge, or village at a time. It is as if those blocks of memory can fit together not only one on top of the other, or sideways, but each can fit inside the other, and the sizes of the blocks themselves can change, growing or shrinking. So, I am encouraged to play with my own memories in such a fashion, being intrigued at the different patterns they form, but more—being astonished at the various meanings that can be quite legitimately read from any one block. This is something like a psychological alphabet in which images, words, and feelings undergo strange transformations, so that I understand that no memory is ever a finished thing, but an ever-changing and ever-creative element that actually alters the concept of past, present, and future time.

But now some curiosity rouses within me, or rather now I am aware of it, that urges me toward psychological exploration, that stretches inner psychic muscles perhaps; and I am immersed in a kind of delightful security and assurance that such exploration is possible. I know, for example, that in one way or another the most simple of my memories can lead to an incredibly distant intersection point where it opens up to all of the other memories of man's racial future and past.

I'm more than aware of the necessity—and futility—of analogies, yet it is as if I am traveling like a tadpole through my own psychological reality, swimming through the stream of my own memories, which are multicolored and glimmering; and at some point I will come to the open sea, about whose infinite area rise the psychological shorelines, the true inner landscapes—cliffs and mountains of time, memory, and desire. By then perhaps I will have changed my form as the tadpole becomes the frog. But when I reach that open ocean I will be equipped with whatever mental gills are required, and there true psychological mobility will allow me to transform into "living tissue" (in whatever terms) the product of my mind's vast creativity; a creativity innate in each of us, living or dead.

Civilizations may rise up at my beckoning, for my own self once rose in that fashion. I feel, then, that man's heritage is this: that in ways presently far beyond my scope or possible attention, the physical world and all others are the powerful issue of our psychological reality; that we are immersed in this atmospheric presence or intelligent light, gently nudged and coaxed into further areas of growth, insight, and understanding; and that we travel through psychological worlds in which our experiences also automatically form other realities—one swirling through the other, each cooperatively interweaving with the others.

All of this is based on love, but not as it can be anywhere defined; each being is born through love, however, whether or not, say, a given child is born of unloving parents. The child's seed is formed, threaded, and the chromosomes intertwined by the same love that is characteristic of this knowing light. That love on earth may be often translated darkly, yet by its light only does reality come into existence.

Thursday afternoon
June 2, 1977

Man's faith in science burned brightly in my time and is flickering in yours. Yet that faith began earlier and will linger later; and as I knew it, that faith promoted action, zest, and curiosity. It was rousing, and under its auspices nations have banded together in constructive scientific pursuits. Democracy has utilized the banner of science's faith. Huge corporations like miniature nations produce goods undreamed of in past ages—earth, sky, and oceans being explored in the light and through the thrusting drive of faith in science.

Yet if it can rightly be said that religion took a stance of divorcing reason from faith, science divorced emotion from reason—and therein lay its greatest flaw, for techniques of investigation undertaken only by cold reason's light cannot be warmed by compassion or love, and the end will always justify the means. Fanaticism results, scientists as overbalanced on reason's side as any priest on the side of intuitional faith alone.

The scientist must repress his emotions and the priest, his reason—at least in conventional institutional frameworks. Faith will then ultimately find no justification in either religion or science; for each will show its flaws.

So often in my life I wore the tattered garments of a flawed faith.

Thursday afternoon
June 23, 1977

I could nowhere within myself in life pretend that life's

darker casts did not too often hold dominion, even though I had known others for whom those bleaker tints disappeared for all practical purposes in some vaster, more illuminated vision. I wondered what ailed my own temperament that life's tragic aspects appeared so momentous and optimism often seemed at its best only a darker blindness—for if one is blinded by light, such a light indeed is a useless mockery. Therefore a faith that closes down the magnificent fields of mental or intellectual vision, that blinds the faithful to all save one tenet, is equally treacherous.

A faith that turns the follower into a fanatic is surely based upon the deepest doubts, for it must be protected at all costs. Such a faith provides an unwieldy, desperately manned craft, a-sea amid the tumultuous waves of contrary beliefs which must seem to cast dangerous undercurrents beneath each position of safety and everywhere threaten faith's survivors.

Therefore I could not condone for myself a faith that denied reason or tolerance, even though such a faith often seemed practical enough for others at first or second glance. On examination, however, such a craft of concepts overflows with the sloppy and inexhaustible power of unrecognized doubt, which ever rises in triumphant springs from an unconscious that senses too well the deep denied realities of feeling upon which faith's craft rides. Followers of such concepts must be forever bailing out, separating their beliefs from others, and looking out for the heretic in their midst.

When, for example, I placed my faith in democracy as the end-all, the political savior of man's existence; when I extolled its virtues most, I was most alert against what I considered democracy's enemies—in terms of other societies or governments, or in terms of those antidemocratic tendencies that seemed to mitigate against man's equality. It was when I put my faith in science that it seemed she almost betrayed me, for each unscientific attitude came as a threat—to science—but more, it became a slur against my own good judgment. A man may make errors in choosing a mistress, but let him misplace his faith in the world of affairs and he feels himself a fool.

I make such a statement easily enough, but in so doing I resurrect old feelings and shake them out as one might an old garment, for such attitudes and emotions are no longer part of my mental or spiritual attire. They are stored, however, in the spacious closet of my experience, intact. And while I recognize only too well their poor fit, lack of style, and outworn threads, still they were beloved habits of thought. I stroll among them now and then, picking one out for display purposes that once I would have worn as my normal garb.

When I lived in time I could recognize such ideas as the clothing of the mind when I saw others strutting about in the newest ideas or theories, sporting them like a woman her most stylish party gown or a man, his finest waistcoat. There were others who wore poverty of the mind with as much virtue as a monk might wear rags, carrying a mental sign however, reading "Humility" but spelling "Superiority." Yet my own psychological habits remained invisible, nor did I realize that I donned my melancholy each morning as I did my coat, choosing its degree and quality as I did the color of my socks.

It was my protection lest faith make a fool of me; lest in my search for the ecstatic in man I found it in myself and therefore could not speak about it with objective voice. For while I envied it and desired it in my fashion, I distrusted the disorderly garb in which it was often displayed.

I admired the eccentric in man, sought after the uncommon, appreciated the bizarre, and understood the undying integrity of the individual. Yet to merge these ideas with democratic action and to view the masses of the people as separate manifestations of immortal souls—such was the goal I set myself.

In your times, faith is even harder to come by than it was in mine. More than ever, many people find themselves entangled in webs of melancholy, seeing themselves relatively powerless, not as heroic victims of a capricious fate but worse, as accidental outcasts of a universe accidentally formed, in which each creature is pitted against every other in a battle for survival that none can ultimately win.

In such a mental atmosphere, how can faith be found or justified? In partial answer, at least, I am ending my lengthy discourse with three essays in which a hypothetical individual moves from melancholy to faith. May that fictional motion turn to fact for my readers, and may that symbolic journey be transformed into a pragmatic faith practical enough to comprehend the facts of the soul and wise enough to see through the fictions that swirl through the passages of science and religion alike.

# 14. On Melancholy

Wednesday afternoon
July 13, 1977

As man's body serves as his physical residence and each person relates to that residence in his own fashion, in his mind also man's main moods form a psychic shape that seems to fit the contours of his own subjective reality. If these "inner residences," these psychic or spiritual neighborhoods could be viewed, then those persons stricken by melancholy could be pinpointed in a moment, for melancholy separates an individual from his fellows by constructing about him a moat of fears and resentments. No cheerful cottage of a soul here to welcome travelers, but a gray castle of stoned walls with curtained windows drawn against the sun. Inside—frightened, aloof, angry, and alone—the man of melancholy temperament watches from the highest walls the panorama of daily tumultuous life that goes on far below.

Well I understand the proud disdain that characterizes such midnight of the soul, and know how the bleak isolation itself achieves a cold but shining value to one so constituted. Much of my life was spent in just such a fashion when the day's normal sunlight filtering through my fears seemed the most artificial, gaudy, falsely seductive illumination, promising vitality and nature's good graces only to highlight men's greed and nature's overriding insensitivity.

Castles are by their nature grand if dank, damp, and filled with secret passages, monuments to generations long dead or to tragedies too numerous to recount. They represent superior barricades for the cultivated, as in Europe's dark past the nobles in their baronies protected themselves against the peasants and perpetuated their own grand estate.

In such edifices, vestiges of the past line the walls and

204

corridors—knights' armor, swords crossed, ancient portraits —and in forgotten desk drawers lie old parchments describing wars won or lost, alliances made and broken, claims and counterclaims to estates no longer in existence. So the man of melancholy mind painstakingly collects old grudges and from them forms monuments that ever remind him of past bitterness.

Thursday morning
July 14, 1977

These resentments need not be personal ones such as an ill-tempered man might have against his neighbors, for they have often a grand cast of tragic coloration, representing intense grudges against the conditions of life itself. The melancholy man is angry at the universe, but with no way of retaliating against it he is reduced to grumbling and muttering beneath his breath. He collects instances of life's seeming insensitivity, life's cruelty, man's imperfections, and while he is doing so, feels the greatest virtue. At least *he* is keeping score. Someone is taking the universe to task. Idioms such as "God's in His heaven and all's right with the world" set his teeth gritting. In his incensed mind's eye he sees the unclothed poor, the ignorant, the warring world of men set in the drearier, vaster context of a gluttonous natural world that creates individual specimens only to destroy them, preserving the species by annihilating its vulnerable parts.

Life itself seems a mockery, since it is to be taken away—the ravages of age wrinkling the youngest face finally into a prunelike dried oval, and youth's feelings of invulnerability only too quickly crumbling into the quicksands of justified fears. Hence he retreats to his mental castle, watching sorrowfully from the high buttresses while below the peasants go about their daily concerns, jabber at the marketplace and praise God, shouting fool anthems while the priests grow fat at their expense. Or so it seems.

Nor can he see that science offers any hopes, since the scientist is tainted with his own humanity; he has the disease himself from which the world suffers. How can the scientist, then, pretend to have more reason than other men, blighted as he is with humanity's emotional morass?

So thinks our melancholy man in his darkest hours. To prove his point, now and then he visits the castle's dungeon where, from Europe's past, dark doctrines of religion and science merge to do their worst: Frankensteins rise to confront science's proud aspiration, and the scientist tampering with evolution's ways brings forth beasts that are not animals or men.

Yet now and then, more often than he would admit, our lord of the manor is drawn to the companionship of his fellows. He yearns to join the dancing throngs below. He spies flowers growing even in the rock crevices of his retreat. He is touched despite himself by the sun's warmth as it circles the castle as if searching for entry. He even imagines sometimes that the inside walls are warm where outside the sun, even for a moment, pauses in one spot, and alone he tries to warm his hands against the stone.

Yet to give in would be defeat, would mean that he was giving tacit acceptance to life's conditions—so he strides angrily away, where in deeper solitude he can ruminate upon the sins of God against man, the malice of nature, and the futility of his own reasoning.

Though this picture I paint is exaggerated, some men are captured by melancholy to this extraordinary degree, while others allow their lives to be overshadowed by the same dreariness which creeps into their dreams, blots out their aspirations, and turns the most cozy mental cottage into a dark stone edifice set in forbidding woods.

No joy can mitigate his desperation, no relationship comfort his fears as long as our melancholy man sulks within the confines of his barricades. Such a fellow has faith in neither God nor man. To some extent he echoes the doubts in each man's heart. He is a perfectionist, but one who seeks out mars and overlooks those tendencies toward excellence that appear clearly to other less fastidious men who do not compare them so drastically with a rigid ideal to which the universe must conform—or else!

Yet loneliness can drive even the most melancholy of men outward, for within despair's castle the heart and pulses grow faint. The face pales. The hands and limbs tremble until everything natural within a man finally calls out for light, warmth; and he is driven like an animal from its cave out into the world for nourishment and contact with his kind.

With what squeamishness does our friend emerge, with what trepidation does he step across his moat while crocodiles of his worst imaginings snap just beneath his feet. It will most certainly storm; he will end up rushing back to his castle, his coat in tatters, because the townspeople below will undoubtedly congregate to stone him or yell abuse. So his thoughts go as he emerges, covering his unease with a calm, cold, aloof, dignified air, and wrapping his muffler about him whether the air is warm or cold.

At first he is everywhere surrounded by fog, and he grimly compares his position to that of mankind in general—set isolated in an accidental universe, mind askew upon the carcass of animal heritage, steeped in superstitions of gods and demons. For, despite all his seeming independence of thought, our melancholy man is immersed in the very kind of mire he sees so clearly elsewhere.

He has accepted from science and religion both the most nefarious and insidious beliefs, and he has not examined their inconsistencies. Pausing, he looks down at the village, which now appears through a small patch of sky clear of fog, and he sees human beings, accidentally formed, born without reason yet doomed by a vengeful God—or by a vengeful nature—their puny endeavors useless and even their finest attempts at reason only showing by contrast the shallow idiocy of human mentality.

Yet curiosity so long denied jerks him forward with uneven steps. He scrutinizes the scene, which becomes clearer as his intentions to explore form an active, swirling, freshening wind within his mind. The fog disperses. He stands in the foothills, and close by cluster the peasants' huts and the tiny marketplace. But no, as vision clears further he realizes that he has been projecting old romantic concepts and memories upon what is indeed a modern scene.

Melancholy knows no nationality, yet a man's melancholy is tinted by his nationality, for it is the frame in which his mental picturing is set. So it seems to me that German melancholy carries the deepest passivity. The Chinese, from my little knowledge of their affairs, set theirs most prettily and formally restrain it. The French glorify their melancholy, but the American's is the most poignant, sharp, and compelling. For in that country most of all, men's ideals—freshly born after centuries of labor pains—encountered men's deepest fears. Hopes were raised beyond men's ability to achieve, and all the symbolic powers of good and evil as they exist in men's minds met full tilt.

So our melancholy man upon leaving the castle pauses in astonishment. From his windows he had imagined the peasants going about their medieval ways. Here instead is a bustling city: industry, rousing shouts of workingmen, harbors with ships perhaps just in, men and women jostling elbows in the streets. Far from jeering at him, no one pays him any mind at all.

His cheeks burn with humiliation. No one notices. As he walks along further, however, the situation changes. Now and then some man or woman smiles at him or wishes him good morning just as if the world were reasonable, as if the poor creatures didn't know the predicament in which the species was certainly mired. Children play on the sidewalks and in gutters. Our friend finds himself amazed at their boldness, their unconcern. An ant crosses the sidewalk, seemingly certain it will reach the other side though everywhere shoes and boots clump up and down, threatening not only the ant's journey but its very existence.

At first, all of this activity gets on our friend's nerves. He tells himself again that the world is an accidental mechanism set adrift in an uncaring universe, and what he hears and senses now is no more than the busy whirling of the world's motor, which will slow down eventually. Yet for all of this, his heart quickens. He responds. If there is no God or good-natured universe, at least he feels within himself some new determination and impetus.

Since he has left his castle and finds no place his home, he will become a traveler. He will certainly not be a joiner, but he will look at the world firsthand, seeing whether or not it justifies his low opinion of it. And when he makes that decision, melancholy loosens its rigid hold upon him.

He does not suddenly become cheerful or unwrap his muffler, but now and then he does permit himself to smile. Moreover, now he looks out at the world directly, rather than from behind a barricade as before. To one extent or another, the events of the world take his notice, even if they only appall or amuse him.

His discontent no longer feeds upon generalities but he meets concrete incidents to which he can, and does, react. He still collects injustices and shakes his mental fists at the universe. Yet, despite himself, he discovers compensations overlooked earlier, so that now and then forgetting himself, he pauses to watch a child or animal at play, or delights in the warmth of the sun which falls now directly on his cheeks, or marvels at a fine lunch or good cigar. These "weaknesses" alarm him. He doubles his resolution to remain sober and reproving, to let God or the universe get away with nothing. Yet for all of this, his melancholy is already tempered, and his own good nature begins to rouse within him.

# 15. Faith and Coincidence

Friday afternoon
July 15, 1977

Faith is both active and passive. It acts as a stimulant at one time, as a tranquilizer at another. Its action in the body promotes exactly those biological changes necessary to ensure health and vitality so that the pulses may be quickened or slowed, the hormones activated or quieted. Faith elicits the most specific biological responses by inciting a general overall sense of optimism, safety, and freedom. It therefore returns the individual, for whatever time, to that prime condition for growth, curiosity, and adventure in which he was immersed as a child.

That condition is blessedly free in that it does not acknowledge impediments. Woe to any poor infant freshly thrust into the world who was not equipped with natural faith, for it would instantly be stopped before it began, appalled at the infinite manipulations necessary for its locomotion, dismayed and in despair at its chances of growing to full stature were its own small size and vulnerability not superseded by an inner certainty of triumph and the willingness to accept challenge.

In faith's eyes, then, impediments vanish, not because a person is suddenly struck by a fool's stupidity that blinds him to them, but because they disappear in the light of his newfound sense of ease, freedom and certainty. He is simply no longer afraid. His cowardliness is gone. He comes into his true estate. Like a weary traveler after resting, he takes up his knapsack once again and goes cheerfully ahead, his steps lighter, covering twice the ground in the same time that he did before and wondering, perhaps, what imagined terrors had previously made the journey so frightening. Indeed, his

210

earlier psychological reality may now be meaningless to him: how could he have worried so about robbers on the way, or the possibility that he might not find lodging, or grown weak thinking about the approaching hill so that its height grew in multiplied stages?

Yet what is it that our traveler can find to have faith in? He might well feel that science and religion have each betrayed him. He may not for the life of him be able to believe in a conventional personified God, white beard flowing in the clouds above and blessed finger pointing out heavenly directions. In fact, on ever seeing such an apparition, our modern man might fall into an instant faint, certain that the psychologist's demon, schizophrenia, had descended upon him. For the voice that once was considered the utterance of God speaking through mortals has become the most dreadful of self-deluding monologues, and if God spoke to a modern Moses through the branches of a bush and then set fire to it, our prophet would first call a psychologist and then the fire department.

So our traveler cannot call out for God's assistance in the old ways and may furthermore be rather embarrassed about the impulse to do so. If he sneaks side-glances upward at a particularly majestic cloud, he does not let himself know the reasons for his actions. If he cries out—silently—despite himself, "Oh, God," just as he is about to fall, and then does not fall but finds his feet unaccountably steadied, he smiles, shakes his head, and thanks the nature of coincidence.

For psychology has made him afraid of religious feeling. His intellect has allowed him to see through religion's gaudy carnivals and dreary morality plays alike. So he thanks coincidence for his delivery and goes his way. A traveler in an accidental universe needs coincidence on his side indeed, for it is coincidence that dictates which tree lightning will hit and which it will avoid; so it is very important that our traveler, running for shelter in a storm, know which side his coincidence is buttered on.

Religions offer frosted confections of packaged faith sold along the highway by robed vendors. Across the way, white-gowned scientists hand out good plain doctrines—the new bread and butter for the masses—and disdain the faith makers' honeyed stores. But our traveler finds that neither nourishment greatly nourishes, and as he consumes the various offerings, his hunger grows rather than diminishes.

Nor is our hypothetical traveler alone. He is surrounded by parades of his fellows, whether he would have it so or not. There are bandwagons, banners, armies, shimmering floats. The strutting, dancing, limping, laughing, old and young, all find themselves jostling mental elbows, beliefs, faiths, doubts. Many stride in rhythm. Others like our traveler stop, lose pace, spend too much time in one stall or another sampling the wares, gorging themselves on every available packaged theory only again to find themselves hungrier than before.

So faith seems an impossibility, for if religion, science and philosophy all fail, then where will our poor fellow put his faith, if indeed any remnants linger? In despair and desperation the scientist may turn to religion, the priest to science, the emotional man to reason or the intellectual to sentiment. The sportsman may suddenly plunge into learned periodicals, the scholar discover the ball court, the nun turn harlot, and the prostitute lower her skirts decorously and become morality's model. But in the end, such efforts usually bring only a desperate false optimism, a fake faith that must defend itself against implied threats until nothing seems worthy of faith and it seems to have no justification.

What, then, should our traveler do? For it certainly seems that he is on a highway shared with others on a journey with no apparent purpose toward an end that is at best inglorious.

First of all, he can begin to think and feel for himself. He can start with his present position: he is, after all, alive on a highway going somewhere; he is in motion. He can decide to throw away all theories that tell him not to trust his own intuitions, sentiments, or reasonings, and thusly begin to examine himself in a manner not possible earlier.

If indeed existence is accidental, he can see that it has some remarkably orderly characteristics. Each person grows from an infant upward, for example, just as if the entire affair *were* planned. Moreover, our traveler can note that during all of his musings and bewildering mental footwork, his body continues to keep him alive and reasonably comfortable; it sweats when too warm and continues its normal functions as if it had some intimate information denied to him. So he begins to look at his own equipment, which is after all personal, living—not *the* body but *his* body—and it seems to know where it is going whether he does or not.

Besides this, as he sleeps along the roadside our traveler is frequently awakened by strange dreams, like mental campfires blazing with the warmest comfort amid the frozen forest of his fears. He snaps awake, heats himself, and stares into the fire's circle where, lo and behold, dazzling images leap. Then he questions: is he sleeping or awake? For the dream images may speak to him or show with immense clarity scenes from his own past. But when the affair is over, he wonders. The dreams often seem to suggest that he move in certain directions or make alterations in his plans.

Hesitantly he tries following those suggestions, covering his path with appropriate rationalizations. For if the directions are wrong, they at least offer some recommendations not tried before; and they are after all, his own directions. For a while he may assign any correct or positive results to coincidence. But coincidence, it appears, is more dependable than it used to be.

His body, though weary, trudges on and he notices its dependability where before he harrassed it for not going faster, or worried that it would not keep up with the others. A second wind seems to come upon him, and sometimes a third or a fourth. Every once and a while from nowhere he is filled with a new buoyancy, an additional energy, a sudden exhilaration and enthusiasm—so is faith born again in a man, by leaps and bounds as he begins to trust his own nature and the terms of his private existence.

Wednesday morning
July 20, 1977

Our traveler finally notices that when he trusts himself and his nature, he feels strange stirrings pull and tug at his consciousness; urgings to do this or that, to go faster or slower as if, like a fine racehorse, he had been too nervous and sensitive before and now, suddenly, felt upon his back a new rider who knew what he was doing, looked ahead and prepared him for any barriers, nudged him safely aside, and overall considerably bettered his performance.

Further experience reveals, however, that horse and rider are one, or body and soul together. Where before one seemed to pull against the other, now both are smoothly synchronized, and instead of dreading an unknown journey our traveler is now filled with excitement and zest, knowing that nature works with him and not against him.

Furthermore, those odd rustlings of consciousness seem to move him beyond the known track, and sometimes his awareness feels continuous with all of nature itself. His motions become so easy, transparent, and effortless that he begins to understand something else: his consciousness is not riding astride his animal nature as it seemed to for a while, but instead his consciousness is continuous throughout his body and extends into the rest of nature as well.

Our traveler sees that he is not on a journey or in a race, but involved in a course of action, and he may dimly sense a grandstand and hear voices that shout down encouragement and suggestions. He realizes the grandstand is symbolic; yet when he imagines that he senses it, the suggestions and hints become clearer and louder—directed, it seems, to him alone. Nor is this assistance limited to advice.

On occasion, caught in a mood of disappointment or weariness, he shouts out mentally for help. Remarkably enough, he is provided with an otherwise inexplicable boon: sudden energy or health or the solution to a problem. And he is almost certain that this assistance comes from outside of the normal course of events.

Perhaps for an instant his consciousness leaps beyond itself, climbing in quick ascent above the track of the road to that higher dimension. Its superior position allows him dizzy visions of vastness never glimpsed before, and he feels himself on the track and above it at once, in the course of events and outside it at the same time. More than that, however, he senses an extraordinary, super-natural Nature in which his own existence is safely couched, and a course of events of giant-sized proportions out of which ordinary events emerge.

None of this is really that simple, of course, and our

traveler is not always exuberant, but he is overall less fearful
and more daring. For if a man's most private dreams can bear
messages that point him in the right direction, if his hunches
can sometimes prove valuable in the objective world, then
there seems to be something of a saving nature in his own
subjective reality, a power that occasionally at least lifts him
above his mistakes.

He begins to take greater notice of coincidences, and it
dawns upon him that they are isolated instances of a
different kind of order, partially invisible, representing
intersections, perhaps, of that sensed higher dimension and
the physical one. He suspects that, concentrating upon such
instances, he might discover that they represent those vaster
patterns of action that connect him with his symbolic
grandstand and with the audience that sometimes cheers him
on.

And if one dream can be meaningful, illuminated with
good intent, how can the universe—the road, himself, and
the other travelers—be accidental, arising from nothing for
no reason, and advancing into nothing? Testing, he calls out
to the grandstand. Muses, imaginative personages, or
projected images mirroring some magic disorder of the
soul—still, he feels a response, a lessening of anxiety, an
exuberance of heart.

But what strikes him most is his feeling that someone or
something in the universe is cheering him on, that some
kind of power exists outside of his present course of events,
and when he calls upon it, that power can insert itself into
the world, transform his reality to some extent by working
through nature itself.

In his zest to find some answers, our traveler begins to
ignore all of the authorities with whom he has already
wasted so much time. As he does so, he notices things that
before seemed trivial or beside the point of his concerns. A
squirrel might dart through the treetops nearby, for
example, gathering nuts to put away for his winter store.
Our traveler marvels that blind instinct sees the next season's
snow so well in the midst of the day's balmy weather, and if
our traveler has a spark of lively emotion still left within
him, he is struck by a marvelous humor at this and other
such incidents.

For accidentally winter will come once again, following the orange leaves of autumn with perfect progression. Accidentally the birds will begin their migrations with miracle-like timing. The animals will thicken their coats for the cold spell, without reading weather reports. And without needing to take counsel with himself, the traveler knows that his own blood will thicken. The human body, unfurred, will take inner procedures against the approaching cold, conserving its own heat. And despite all he has heard to the contrary, he is in a flash convinced of the universe's good intent, his rightful place in it, and he senses his existence and the world's rising from another source that is both within and outside the natural framework.

How could he earlier have believed in religion's sinful self, tales of a vengeful God, or in science's mechanical and accidental universe? The rift between intuition and intellect is closed; they are united, their attraction one to the other is consummated and their differences forgotten. All the rustlings and stirrings of nature now seem to find response within his own feelings.

He knows that he and the universe are united yet separate, that some extra-natural force is both within the world and apart from it at once, and the wedding of intellect and emotion brings an offspring of greatest consequence: the birth of a faith that is indeed a twin to the first faith with which our traveler was once endowed. *This* faith, however, is faith-with-knowledge, where the infant's faith need not contend with the world's ways in the same manner as the adult indubitably must. This faith, like the second or third or even fourth wind of the runner, is even more exuberant, for it exists despite a knowledge of the world's ordinary course and of the impediments thrown up by ignorance or error.

The same material world surrounds our traveler now as in his previous torments. He is still walking along the road surrounded by his fellows, and on either side stretch the vendors of various doctrines. The street is lined with shops, universities, and churches. Yet what catches his notice are the simple, unauthoritative events that delighted his childhood: the direct enjoyment and experience of his body and mind, his trust in their achievements, the constant liveliness of the animals, and the entire cooperative commerce of the natural world.

That natural world and his own subjective experience within it shout with multitudinous voices that its existence and his cannot be accidental but share in a concern, a good intent, that is everywhere apparent. And that faith promotes in our traveler exactly the conditions needed for his support. Food does not miraculously appear out of the air for him—a table spread with a banquet—but he knows as surely how to provide for himself as the squirrel does, and he realizes this truth and no longer need worry. He simply follows the dictates of his nature, trusting that the same power that set him upon the road—mind and body in one living package— is no less kindly disposed toward him than it is to the world's other living creatures.

In that moment of trust, he and his experience are transformed. Looking around, he can see glimpses of that trust trying to rouse itself in the religions and sciences alike, but he understands that for all of their merits institutions can speak only generally to any given individual, and that each man's life involves him in a direct confrontation with the universe in which he must ultimately trust both his own nature and the unknown source from which it springs. That greater source makes itself known through the living person in his living and his dying, and speaks directly through his own nature. Only that truth can illuminate and make sense of the facts of the known world. It is ultimately impossible to trust God and distrust the self, or vice versa.

Such a faith is not blind, however, for experience will prove it to be more factual than any mathematical formula. It will be demonstrated through the beneficial changes it brings in a person's life, for faith not only promotes health, vitality, and understanding, but a kind of accomplishment that produces a general overall transformation, bringing to flower abilities and characteristics of the most heroic nature that previously had lain latent and unused.

# 16. Faith's Visions

Friday afternoon
July 22, 1977

Men's visions of nature's source may vary. They may be shoddy or sublime, for they will be like snapshots taken by the visionary camera of the intuitions and no camera is like any other, and our travelers vary in their proficiency as photographers. Moreover, these visions of God must appear superimposed on a film already predisposed as if by mental chemicals to take certain kinds of pictures over others.

The sportsman may imagine a winner's God; the soldier, a God of war; the fearful, a God of retribution. Man will interpret this power, then, through his own individual nature and his conceptions will evolve with his own experience and understanding.

Men who travel to foreign countries are often inveterate picture snappers. People who are so amateur as to be ashamed of their own pictures still want some to show on their return home; so they will buy pretty postcards perhaps, taken by a professional photographer under the best of conditions: the sun will be shining, the sky pure blue. All will be picturesque, yet sadly lacking the touch of authenticity apparent in even the traveler's own poorest picture. On the day of his visit, the sky might be clouded or the rain falling, and the particular buildings might be changed in a variety of ways from the time of the photographer's postcard picture.

So while there is a general connection between the traveler's experience and the photographer's picture, our traveler on his return will know the difference, even though he tries to convince himself that what he saw tallies with the postcard image.

218

In the same way, the conventional images of God distributed by the various religions represent posed, formal yet picturesque, generalized and stylized versions for those who do not trust their own abilities in such matters. These serve as handy. guidelines, representing the personifications of nature's source as glimpsed in certain "spiritual or mental or psychic places." But they must remain general and mass-produced.

Beside this, however, conventionalized religious "photographs" were taken long before our traveler's lifetime, as a rule, and are glaringly out of date with his own experience. On seeing them, he hesitates to comment on the sense of strangeness he feels, knowing intuitively that the images are clothed in a spiritual fabric long since frayed, even though they have been retouched in the pictures themselves so as to appear in good repair.

So our traveler finally begins to take his own psychic snapshots or spiritual photographs, knowing full well that he is an amateur. He must learn to operate his visional camera and keep it in readiness for those moments when he suddenly glimpses that extraordinary power, no matter how fleetingly. His private photo album may be limited in size, therefore, yet each picture will represent his own private vision at any given time, and the pictures may not be similar but vastly different one from another.

At first this may confuse him, for unwittingly he may still be comparing his own pictures with the more standardized ones. His visions may make no sense at all at the start, then. Walking along one day, for instance, he may suddenly feel an inner swirl of extraordinary energy. The sky takes on a cast of light he's never noticed before. The cows in a nearby pasture are endowed with a placid majesty and ancient power. He stands transfixed. The cows seem to possess a wisdom he's never seen in even a priest's or monk's face. That wisdom spreads like a summer breeze from the animals to himself, invisibly entering his soul until for a moment he does not know if he is himself watching the cows, or the cows watching him. He knows only that he is feeling an intimacy with some force that moves and forms cows and men, a spirit more ancient than the meadows and as new as the moment of his experience.

Wednesday morning
July 27, 1977

He snaps a simple landscape.

His photograph is innocent of conventional represen-
tations. It shows no statues or church and displays no sign
that it is anything but the most commonplace scene. His
contemporaries might scoff if he told them the picture's
history: "Is God, then, a cow? Or a herd of cows?
Blasphemy!" Yet stubbornly our traveler, our amateur
photographer, knows that his photograph is significant, that
it hints of some truths that do not show anywhere in the
scene itself.

During his journey he snaps many such pictures, each
meaningful to himself, each different from the others, each
containing some indescribable element that seems to touch
his soul while actually appearing no place in the photographs themselves. These spiritual intangibles nevertheless
add immeasurable quality and depth to the photographs, so
that whenever our friend looks at them again, he is filled
with the inspiration, awe, or wonder that he felt originally
when he snapped them.

Little by little that aura of significance seems to spread
out into the physical world itself. To some extent, each
barnyard scene or city street or daily encounter is imbued
with an extra richness, so that the events seem to be what
they are, yet somehow more than what they are. Our friend
feels as if there is another world shimmering within and
around the natural one, invisible merely because he does not
know what to look for. Not only is he an amateur
photographer, but he begins to suspect that he is an amateur
see-er as well. Just beyond his vision he senses that the
natural world fills out, or is somehow more complete than
his present vision allows him to ascertain.

Almost without realizing it, our traveler begins to
change his focus of awareness, tries to spy out those other
sensed dimensions that surround the world. He keeps his
visionary camera ever ready. Now and then he experiences a
very strange event: while he sees nothing in the natural
world that he didn't before, he senses an inner intangible
detail come into focus with a natural one. A leaf, for

example, will suddenly line up with an invisible counterpart of itself and become momentarily filled out, so that it is itself and something else besides. A new completeness shimmers in its veins and stem so that the one leaf stands out in the oddest fashion from all of the others on a given tree. Yet for the life of him, our friend cannot say what it is that he really senses. In frustration, yet filled with challenge, he stands there snapping photographs, hoping to capture this additional vitality.

Or, as he walks along, our traveler unaccountably feels almost off balance for a moment: the road beneath him shimmers or trembles ever so slightly or odd reflections appear for which he sees no cause. The road seems to connect with another, sensed one, so that for an instant he walks both of them at once; or rather both roads become one. The air about him sparkles. He barely glimpses the people who surround him, yet bits and pieces of them are imbued with that additional intensity while other portions, an arm or leg or side of the face, are "normal" and incomplete in the larger vision. Our friend may almost lose his footing for a moment. Quickly, however, he recovers and snaps a photograph. This time he is convinced that he has captured *something*.

Again his photograph shows the physical scene only. While he admits that this is the case, our traveler also sees that his photographs are improving. The details are sharper and clearer, while the entire pictures have attained an atmospheric quality difficult to describe. Furthermore, changes have occurred in himself somewhere along the line, while he was so engrossed in his picture taking. For occasionally, as he walks along, our photographer feels himself click into a new focus, and when the road shifts in that indescribable fashion he shifts inside himself, seeming to become lined up with an invisible part of his own reality that he had barely sensed before. He becomes fuller, more real, filled out. All of his sensations and awareness are tuned to full focus, more detailed and yet surrounded by an atmospheric oneness that serves to unite them.

This is a new experience indeed, and it gives our traveler due pause. Is he, then, a part of this invisible world also? The affair ends as quickly as it began, however. Our friend steps out of this greater sensed self, finding himself simply walking along the road again. But there is a difference. Now he feels this other self before him or around him, and unconsciously he tries to match his steps to these sensed "giant steps." They aren't giant steps, of course, but they seem to be, to our traveler.

Those steps, while his own in some way that he doesn't understand, still seem more assured than his, firmer yet lighter, and he begins to think that they move with all the courage, wisdom and knowledge that he feels within himself only rarely and seems unable, himself, to use. As he still rather unconsciously walks in his own greater footsteps in this fashion, he notices that the way is definitely easier. He feels synchronized with himself.

He realizes that he is also "more" than he thought he was. As he really understands this, something else happens, and a new motion comes into the world. He feels the natural world with all of its splendor and variety forever coming-into-existence from a super-nature or from a Natural source that gives it birth. And he can sense, though dimly, that same motion in himself: energy rushing into his being, washing into him like a tide so that his existence is not confined to the bubbles of thought with which he was familiar, but filled with depths and swirling power beneath.

That energy takes the form of nature! As he understands this, he looks at his photographs with new excitement. What he glimpsed as he snapped them was that super-natural force coming into natural form; super-nature coming into natural focus. He sees that at each point in his life he is present at the birth of the universe. The beginning of the road and his present position and the end all exist now. Only his focus prevented him from seeing this earlier.

Though our traveler understands this, try as he will he sees only the normal road ahead of him, reaching into the future. Even if he turns around, he moves forward into the future, only without seeing where he is going. For a while he is frustrated anew. All of these matters so take his attention, however, that he ignores as trivial impediments that earlier would have seemed momentous, and he notices now and then that his natural vision has expanded somewhat. He sees a bit further than his fellows into the distance ahead, and his peripheral vision also includes more sideways events than earlier.

This happens so easily, however, that our friend accepts the additional sight as quite natural until he happens to compare his view of the world with that of his contemporaries'. Furthermore, he is so used to the changes that have happened within himself that he forgets his own earlier limited vision, which is taken for granted by others as once it seemed natural to himself.

By now, in fact, his fellows may begin to view our friend as a very strange specimen indeed, since little by little he has ceased to follow many of the conventional dogmas of the day and age. This process also happened so gradually that he wonders how he came from his original dependence upon social, religious, and scientific beliefs to his present rather independent thought. He remembers giving lip service to many such conventions long after he ceased believing in them. Now that he resolutely holds his own, however, new dilemmas arise.

Sometimes members of the scientific and religious communities alike come to him with artificial deference, requesting his views on a variety of subjects. His questioners have ready-made answers to which he cannot agree. Yet his intuitive replies sound childish when rationally rendered. He finds himself saying: "Yes, time is, but it is not," or "We are each individuals forever, yet we are forever part of an indefinable whole," or "No, of course my picture of the cow is not a photograph of God, and yet in other terms, of course it is." His learned friends shake their heads or shake their fists, according to their natures, and either leave him alone completely or attack him in their journals. The scientist may call him a fool. The priest may call him blasphemous.

Our friend, if he has really found faith and if he is really paying attention to faith's visions, is able to ignore such querulous interludes. For his faith is open, still forming, and he knows that it is a continuing way or path more than anything else. So he does not need to defend himself. If he has any sense, he will show his visional photograph album to no one with any intent to prove anything. Instead, he will take a good lunch, pick up his camera, and go his way.

# Epilogue

*The Afterdeath Journal* may have depicted conditions after death, but its production was a part of my life. It was written under the varying circumstances of daily living. Portions were scribbled down in my sketchbooks; some passages came while I was washing dishes, or watching television or taking a nap. The book announced itself on January 25, 1977, title and all, and was finished that July except for the final typing. During much of that time our house was anything but quiet.

We had decided to screen in the front porch, and add a writing room for me with its own porch. The construction men came at 7 A.M. and worked until 3:30. They were a great bunch of men, but while I was "getting James," hammers were banging all over the place. The workers wandered in for cold drinks. Trucks looking like prehistoric monsters came grunting up the road, delivering various materials from cement to insulation.

Quite a few strangers found their way to the house, too. Rob was painting in the mornings and working on his notes for Seth's *"Unknown" Reality.* I kept moving my typewriter to the part of the house that was quietest. And unperturbed, James kept on discussing affairs quite separate from these mundane events.

*Mundane* events? I marveled at the construction worker's physical competence, their sense of camaraderie, their nonchalant ease with tools and measurements. There they were, out in the world, bustling along with the rest; and did they wonder what the hell *we* were doing, at our desks or easels from morning to night? Gradually I realized how many of our attitudes were based on the issues James discusses so thoroughly. We're taught that it's healthy to be outgoing, physically focused, competitive, sports-minded, and that it's unhealthy—almost un-American—to be introverted, contemplative, loners. I even wondered how many closet mystics there were; maybe they outnumbered closet alcoholics.

Not that there aren't as many cults around now as in James's time. Probably there are more. But many such groups just utilize the principles of evolution, only applied to the soul. The competition is in another direction: the struggle to be more spiritual and aware than your neighbor. Believers "follow the leader" in their efforts to be superunmaterialistic, just as the "Joneses" follow *their* peers in the frenzied collection of television sets or cars. In an attempt to avoid meaningless work, often the value of work itself is forgotten.

So while all the bustle went on, and James went on discussing American democracy and the soul, I remembered my own past: writing poetry on the sly while I ran an assembly line in a radio factory for a year; hiding in the stockroom, composing odes and trying not to feel guilty for doing it on company time. Then there were pages of poetry written while I was society editor of a newspaper; and more while I was stock picker in a mill; and three apprentice novels while I was selling everything from cosmetics to washing machines by canvassing door to door. My college background wasn't much help in making an ordinary living, yet even then I refused to use it to get any kind of prestige job. I turned down many: because I was afraid that I'd fall for the entire package—the money, the competition, the status— and stop writing.

As a young man, Rob made lots of good hard cash doing comics; before fine art "turned his head." Then he took all kinds of sign-painting jobs and mediocre commercial-art jobs to get by so he could have time enough to paint. We finally decided on a good compromise: we each worked at part-time jobs. Sometimes we thought we were crazy, like the time I turned down a job as head of women's advertising in a radio station—after being told to join the Episcopal church, change my mode of dress to one more dignified, and become a member of just about every community organization you could name. Instead, I took the stock picker's job; and I didn't even know what a stock picker was.

What does all this have to do with James? Plenty. Our
landlords, friends, and families thought there was something
pretty strange about us for a while. Painting and writing
were OK if they brought in some bread, so you and your
parents could hold up your heads with your neighbors. We
always felt that we were somehow going against the stream
then, and going *with* the stream meant following all of the
ideas James speaks of so eloquently—following Darwin and
Freud to a T.

Until *Afterdeath Journal*, though, I really didn't see the
connection between such cultural attitudes and our own
lives. I didn't realize how much we'd taken to heart those
theories we'd thought we'd outgrown. Surely this applies to
many of my readers.

Some, like myself, were brought up in a religion that we
left when "our eyes were opened" to the fallacies and simple
injustices it entailed. Others, like myself, looked with
"opened, intelligent, modern eyes" to science, which became
in religion's stead the new hope—only to discover, of course,
that science was also fallible. I don't know what we expected
or why we thought that any human agency could be
infallible. Yet I insist that our fallibility does not mean that
we are flawed creatures.

For that matter, I have no deep complaints. This
country, whatever its scientific or religious illnesses, still
provides a framework in which people of entirely different
intents and abilities can survive. But people don't survive
by just meeting the practical needs of the body. They really
survive through enthusiasm, desire, love—and faith. But
faith in what? James addressed himself to that question in
ways that made me catch my breath at times.

In his descriptions of the atmospheric presence and
knowing light, I found a picture of God that "took"; that
held and made sense; a God far more miraculous than the
male God of the ancients, a God big enough to contain all
the worlds we can know or imagine. So, faith becomes a
biological heritage, replacing a tainted earth or accidental
world with a well-intentioned universe, yet with a God who
is reachable, a part of our very structure.

Those ideas are in direct opposition to what has been
the mainstream of American thought, because just after
James's time Freudian psychology, Darwinism, and Prot-

estantism all clicked together. Not that some religions didn't protest against evolution's dogma—on the wrong grounds—but all over America, organized Protestantism went along. Psychology's "norm" just happened to fit the white Protestant male who became the Darwinian model of the fittest. Other nationalities, women, artists, homosexuals, lesbians, and anyone not the right color felt only too well the psychological and social poor fit.

But we all suffered, and we all fell for it, and to that degree we all contributed. It's easy enough to say that we're alert to such issues now, but the fact is that our entire Western world is fashioned according to those theories that effectively deny the heroic in the species, and distrust greatness. It's possible that man may not care to survive in an accidental universe, one without meaning, in which all his psychological values seemingly come to nothing.

As this book was being produced, for example, my own moods followed their usual ebb and flow, and I began to realize that many of my "lows" were connected one way or another to Freudian or Darwinian concepts that still lingered and affected my behavior.

And I chafed at James's automatic use of "man" for human personality, even though his concept of God avoided such prejudices. Yet when, as a result of James's manuscript, I had a personal vision of a Mother Goddess (instead of a God, meaning male), I was somewhat taken aback. Our prejudiced beliefs become almost invisible, though their ghostly content is present even in our languages—by default. Not only do we often want God to be a super-human (rather, of course, than a super-animal or—ha!—a super-ape), but the sex and color must be right, too.

My vision came at the end of the day. I'd just finished Chapter 13. The workmen had left. I couldn't use the small room at the back of the house during the day because it was right next to the construction; so with everything quiet I went back there to my desk. It was twilight; I had my usual coffee and cigarettes, and I could hear Rob typing in his studio. James's biological faith intrigued me. I wanted to experience it myself, in my own way. That, or the atmospheric presence, I said mentally.

Then through the window I saw a light, distant in the

evening sky. It was turned toward me in spotlight fashion. My eyes were open but I realized that the light was a mental vision; that Rob wouldn't see it if he came into the room— nor would anyone else for that matter. The light played over my body, then mentally I traveled up through it, to its origin. Here the light was a shimmering flower and I emerged from its petals as an infant.

I don't actually remember first being picked up by anyone, but suddenly I was being held as an infant in a woman's arms. She didn't look particularly young in terms of our ideas of youth, yet her face was smooth and unwrinkled: I never really saw it clearly; and her head was covered by a veil so I didn't see her hair at all. She was real and unreal, because her head reached far into space and her figure extended down through the earth, the folds in her gown becoming the continents, oceans, and other features of our planet. I felt myself as the infant being held in her arms, while from my chair I watched the vision as a pageant in the distant sky. From my earthly viewpoint, the woman's figure became transparent, transposed over the landscape.

My time sense was distorted because there seemed to be a fairly long period when the woman alternated between picking me up as the infant, holding me, then gently setting me down and picking me up again, as if to show that I wasn't being abandoned. Then I heard the woman speak to me mentally, saying: "If you need me, I'll be there." Everything vanished. I opened my eyes, realizing for the first time that I'd actually closed them.

It was over too soon. There were so many things I could have asked, I thought. Quickly I wrote down what had happened, then I said mentally, "Well, if you really mean it, I need you now." Instantly the woman appeared again, shimmering in the night sky, way beyond and above the horizon. She said mentally: "I'm your mother-father or father-mother, your divine parent, the parent of your being, always present." With these words I was shown a variety of glowing images which I saw from the chair and participated in also. That is, I saw myself as a young child from my viewpoint in the chair, and I also perceived the events as the child.

The woman set me down. Around us were groups of

stars. She directed me to run and play, to explore the stars, much as a mother might tell a child to play in a field of flowers. I have a lapse of memory at this point, retaining only feelings of freedom, ease, and anticipation. I do remember thinking that her instructions must be symbolic, and as I sat there in my chair a bit of irritation flashed through me: what *was* she asking me to do? Mentally I said something to the effect that it wasn't all *that* easy. I had hassles just like everyone else.

Instantly the images changed as she said, "Any problems you have are only growing pains. You've just had a bad day and picked up a few bruises. Everything will be all right." Her tones were so reassuring that on the one hand I wanted to cry; but I also thought: "She's treating me as if I were a young child, coming home in tears to be comforted by the grownups." Upset, I started to say, "Now look——"

Instantly in the sky I saw myself at various ages: learning to walk, falling and getting up again, skating, playing jump rope. There were other images I've forgotten, all showing various learning processes that I'd mastered. Again I had the feeling that all of this involved depths of time, that it had been going on for centuries—while I sat in my chair. Other episodes followed, which I forgot almost at once. I came out of my memory lapse to find myself walking hand in hand with the woman through space. She smiled and said, "See, even the sky holds." The most delicious sense of security and safety filled my consciousness, and the knowledge that the woman did indeed represent my version of the loving atmosphere in which I personally had my being and that formed my life and flesh.

That sense of security lasted strongly for perhaps a month, and now lingers, though I forget it often. I wrote down the entire experience, remembering James's comparison of the attributes of the atmospheric presence with those of a caring mother, and understood the inner mechanics of the vision. It was *my* vision, my picture or snapshot of nature's source, just as James's traveler in his last essay has *his* personal vision. It was also a woman's vision, and I wondered how many women structured their mystical experience according to the male's concept of God. I also remembered that male or female, animal or human, vegetable or mineral—each will find its own reflection in that greater source from which nature springs.

. . .

I remember something else. For a few moments in my vision I was plucking stars as easily as a child plucks flowers, as at home in a sky field as I've ever been in a physical one. I thought: symbolic, of course. Yet suppose the stars *are* flowers in some other reality, alive for only a season while from our viewpoint they seem relatively permanent features of the heavens? Idiotic thought? No more idiotic than imagining that the entire universe—you and I and all our ancestors, animals, oceans, and mountains—was produced through some accidental process in which the emotions and sentiment are offshoots of chemical reactions.

In any case, my vision led me back to James's manuscript, and I really understood the implications of some passages that I'd just passed over before. These issues are vital: God being in nature and apart from it at the same time; super-nature being a source of extra saving experience and therefore a source of transformations perhaps nearly impossible otherwise; super-nature working upon or through nature, altering the rules or adjusting nature when through our own beliefs we've made errors. I really understood James's assertion that the atmospheric presence gives fresh insights, energy, or whatever is needed. James goes into all of this thoroughly, but it takes a second reading. James is actually saying that since the atmospheric presence *doesn't* intrude, we have to ask, to state our needs or intents and they will be met, because super-nature or the atmospheric presence (or the universe) is responsive and actively *wants* to give support. This is a far cry from our usual belief that life must be tooth and claw.

Now I understand James's insistence that faith is action-promoting and transforming; that trust in the good intent of our own being can bring about vital insights that can save us from our own negative beliefs—insights that can emerge in the dream state or in any other state of consciousness. Yet for many of us, faith is hard to come by.

Like James in life, we are afraid of being "faith's fool."
We've taught ourselves to question constantly, determined
not to be led astray again. And like James in *his* time, we see
about us people who profess to just about every conceivable
faith: belief in reason at the expense of feeling, or in feeling
at the expense of reason; belief in the body but not in the
soul, or vice versa.

I've always kept what I consider a healthy skepticism
about my own intuitive and psychic products. So while I
identified with James's feelings time and time again
throughout the manuscript, thinking "Yes, James, yes!" and
following the sweep of his vision, I'd also be wondering,
"Now, is this James? Really James? Or is it, as Seth says, the
combination of my consciousness and a James consciousness. Or——"

Faith's fool. Anything but that, we cry. During the
months involved with the manuscript, I had to take time out
to correct galleys for *The World View of Paul Cézanne,* and
for Volume 1 of Seth's *"Unknown" Reality.* Seth finished
dictating his *Nature of the Psyche* in April 1977, and
immediately began another book. All of those books emerged
from the unknown reality, or course. For all of my own
wonderings and questionings, they give evidence of my faith
in the ultimate good intent of our natures, my feeling that
the individual consciousness has access to knowledge and
sources far exceeding any available according to Freudian or
Darwinian theories; and bear witness to my belief that,
despite our fallibility, we are not flawed creatures.

Not flawed creatures? How can I write that, with the
evidence of our imperfections all about us? With religion
shouting that we are stained by original sin and science
insisting that our very existence is meaningless? I can only
answer that some part of me knows; some part of each of us
in our private moments leaps above the seeming evidence
into a realm of knowledge in which man is blessed, and in
which his good intents outweigh his ignorance.

James says that our private consciousnesses are continuous with nature's source. One evening in June, when
this manuscript was nearly finished, I sat in my studio and
mentally addressed the "parent of my being," asking about
my work with Seth because I was struck by the differences in

perspective between James's viewpoint and Seth's even more comprehensive one. Almost immediately I received the following passage:

"Some [individuals] give the ancient rustlings of Nature speech. There is a multitudinous constant communication between all cells, those in men and women, those rousing within animals and plants and all things within your world; eternal yet living rustlings of knowledge, love, and desire—the inner murmurings of the mind and body of Nature made living. These, through you and in accord with your essence, are given voice; distinctive, reflected, and amplified by the order of your own being, translated through your living into terms that you can understand.

"Yet more than a voice, a personality mounts the echoings of nature. The cells' own wisdom forms an entity touched yet untouched by time; a knowing mind that is the spirit of understanding, merged yet separate: it is the part of yourself that goes forth from the pathway of your present being, outward, boisterously and confidently toward the arena of eternity.

"Can a tree stop its own leaves from rustling in the wind? Its own leaves from growing? Shall it deny squirrels their shelter? Seth is the spirit of the tree of your being, roots and treetops reaching through past and present. His personality represents the fulsomeness of your soul as it comes before and after the time that you know.

"The fruits of your tree are alphabets, more natural than apples or pears. Seth represents the Self toward which each person seeks, the wisdom that is within each, and his words rouse within each person the echoing voice of the oversoul in which earth and spirit are counterparted."

If this is the case, then each of us can to some extent follow the strands of our consciousness outward (or inward), into those psychological and quite valid realities glimpsed by James in the later chapters of this book. Each person's experience will vary, but in one way or another each individual can sense that opening of consciousness into other realities; that intersection of the known self with its source.

# Index

**Don't miss these other Seth/Jane Roberts books from Prentice Hall Press. You'll find them at your local bookstore. Or use the handy order blank below for home delivery.**

☐ Please send me the following titles:

| ORDER # | TITLE | PRICE | QUANTITY |
|---|---|---|---|
| 21945-1 | Dreams, "Evolution," and Value Fulfillment, Volume I (cloth) | 15.95 | _____ |
| 21946-9 | Dreams, "Evolution," and Value Fulfillment, Volume II (cloth) | 15.95 | _____ |
| 45724-2 | Individual and the Nature of Mass Events | 7.95 | _____ |
| 61056-8 | Nature of Personal Reality | 10.95 | _____ |
| 61045-1 | Nature of the Psyche | 4.50 | _____ |
| 80718-0 | Seth Material | 7.95 | _____ |
| 80722-2 | Seth Speaks | 7.95 | _____ |
| 93877-9 | "Unknown" Reality, Volume I | 8.95 | _____ |
| 93885-2 | "Unknown" Reality, Volume II | 10.95 | _____ |
| 01856-4 | Afterdeath Journal of an American Philosopher | 7.95 | _____ |
| 35749-1 | God of Jane | 7.95 | _____ |
| 73174-5 | Psychic Politics | 9.95 | _____ |
| 23899-8 | Education of Oversoul Seven | 6.95 | _____ |
| 34529-8 | Further Education of Oversoul Seven | 7.95 | _____ |
| 64744-6 | Oversoul Seven and the Museum of Time | 7.95 | _____ |
| 18912-6 | Create Your Own Reality: A Seth Workbook (Ashley) | 7.95 | _____ |
| 17206-4 | Conversations with Seth, Volume I (Watkins) | 8.95 | _____ |
| 17208-0 | Conversations with Seth, Volume II (Watkins) | 7.95 | _____ |

Prices subject to change without notice.

| MERCHANDISE TOTAL | | $ | |
|---|---|---|---|
| ADD | SALES TAX | | |
| | POSTAGE & HANDLING | 1. | 50 |
| TOTAL: CHECK ENCLOSED | | $ | |

SHIP TO:
NAME_____
ADDRESS_____APT. NO._____
CITY_____
STATE_____ZIP CODE_____

Send your order to:
**Prentice Hall Press**
**Route 59 at Brook Hill Drive**
**West Nyack, NY    10994**

Important: Enclose check with your order, price plus applicable sales tax for your state and $1.50 postage and handling. Please allow four weeks for delivery.